Almost Complete Poems

Almost Complete Poems

Stanley Moss

SEVEN STORIES PRESS
140 Watts Street
New York, NY 10013
www.sevenstories.com

College professors may order examination copies of Seven Stories Press titles for a free six-month trial period. To order, visit www.sevenstories.com/textbook or send a fax on school letterhead to (212) 226-1411.

Cover photograph by Cheung Ching-Ming

Library of Congress Cataloging-in-Publication Data

Names: Moss, Stanley, author.
Title: Almost complete poems / Stanley Moss.
Description: Seven Stories Press first edition. | New York : Seven Stories
    Press, [2016]
Identifiers: LCCN 2016039997 (print) | LCCN 2016047378 (ebook) | ISBN
    9781609807276 (hardcover) | ISBN 9781609807283 (E-book)
Classification: LCC PS3563.O885 A6 2016 (print) | LCC PS3563.O885 (ebook) |
    DDC 811/.54--dc23
LC record available at https://lccn.loc.gov/2016039997

Printed in the United States.

9 8 7 6 5 4 3 2 1

To departed friends: human, canine, arboreal, avian

Acknowledgments:

American Poetry Review, The New Yorker, PN Review, Times Literary Supplement, Poetry (Chicago), *The New Republic, The Guardian, The Nation, Slate, Poem, Poetry Daily, Poetry London, The New York Times, Dissent, Partisan Review, The London Magazine, The Observer, TriQuatererly, Pequod, Parnassus, Encounter, Tikkun, Best American Poems of 2003, Virginia Quarterly Review, The Los Angeles Times, The Atlantic Monthly, The East Hampton Star, The Drunken Boat, Shirim, Shabdaguchha, The Forward, Exile, Open City, Tiger's Eye, The Kentucky Review, Verse, Exquisite Corpse, The Listener, Poetry Northwest, Poetry International, Transatlantic Review, Quarterly Review, Graham House Review, Wake, Halcyon, Angry Penguin, Hemispheres, Botteghe Oscure, New American Review, New Directions 12, New Directions 13, Antaeus, Book Week, The Sewanee Review, Princeton University Library Chronicle, Vanderbilt Review, The Yale Review, Yale Theater Review, Michigan Quarterly Review, Poetry International, The High Window, The New York Review of Books, Huffington Post*

Much thanks to Peter Jay and Anvil Press, UK and Michael Schmidt and Carcanet Press, UK for many years of literary encouragement.

With exceptions for reasons of entertainment and matter, these poems are arranged in reverse chronological order. Included are early poems not previously published anywhere, as well as some never before collected in books.

S.M.

Contents

IT'S ABOUT TIME (2015) & NO TEAR IS COMMONPLACE (2013)

SUNRISE—MORNING

Noon

Sunset—Night

Eclipse

A History of Color (2003)

ASLEEP IN THE GARDEN (1998) & THE INTELLIGENCE OF CLOUDS (1989)

Skipped-Over Early Poems

Index of Titles and First Lines

Mostly New Poems
(2016)

GRATITUDE

1. AFTER NIGHT FELL DOWN THE ABYSS

After Night fell down the Abyss,
ages after Eros mated with Chaos,
the gods were cut up and scattered.
After Forty-Two Names, the creation, the flood,
after nights and days were everyday,
the laws, the land promised,
centuries before an English word there was the Word,
Jesus alone chose to be born.
First day of spring,
flocks of birds break out of darkness,
hatch without choice
into the universe with the rest of us,
join the elements we know and don't know,
protons and neutrons that live privately,
never chose to be born,
dark holes that did not and do not
choose to be gravitational.
Pushing with closed wings,
soon to fly to its first flower
a butterfly looks out of its chrysalis,
through a torn silk web.
Spring is coming in. A milk-fed race,
that has no choice but nipples,
four-footed and two-footed,
is coming into society.
There are gatherings in vineyards.
In that beautiful, noisy company
I would not choose to be a grape.
I hear a buzzing, a splashing, a *God bless.*
Most will live a day or two without choice
then become feed.

Some frogs, after a three-day orgasm,
may be devoured by a loveless bass or heron.

I pity flies.
I cannot conceive of insect pleasures.
                    After a while
philosophers and farmers are feed,
which we all become sooner or later
unless we choose to go up in smoke
that has no choice where to go
any more than mountains do.

2. Second Choice

A cup of tea, a shot of old whiskey,
comfort for the moment,
I do not choose to play chess,
I play there-is-Heaven-and-Hell.
I choose to sing, *Depuis le jour*, then silence . . .
silence gets me used to silence,
I will hear it for a long while.
No silence in my trees—
I say "my trees," I planted hundreds,
some assassinated in their own beds.
On May afternoons, it is my opinion
the survivors recognize me,
but birds and squirrels living in the branches
don't know me from Adam. Barefoot,
lonely as a cloud I've walked beaches,
I've gathered cubist driftwood, discovered a trunk,
the chapel of a Chinese temple bridge,
I've climbed mountains, found rocks
with fossils of seashells and fish spines carved in.

3. RIDICULOUS

We are made to look ridiculous.
Our bodies are stuck with fingers,
usually ten, knuckles and hair.
We have ridiculous noses
with nostrils that pull air in and out
with the help of ridiculous lungs,
God-made feet with toenails,
a navel that connects us to holes of ill repute
that are made to do outlandish things
with mouths and tongues on pilgrimage or hajj
or going to Jerusalem "next year"
with our pagan ridiculous teeth.
After an outlandish past and present,
we die ridiculously, go to dirty hell.

I hunt for sensible things
in rock without feelings,
both of us loaded with ludicrous bacteria.
I know some people and gardens
that are beautiful, clearly sensible,
are reasons for, but they die
ridiculous deaths like the rest of us.

I'm soon to have my ridiculous salad,
everything is ridiculous
but a good cup of coffee in the morning.
The rising and setting sun is iffy,
clouds are not ridiculous,
winds certainly are ridiculous,
are political but don't vote,
they are left-wing, right-wing, east or west.
I am registered to vote in a cosmological election.
The sun is president.
What is the state of the universe?
Time and space are certainly undemocratic.

Still, in the sensible by-and-by, dark holes
will hold an election, the candidates
real-lifers against supernaturalists.
What ridiculously new
relative pronoun will come of cosmic jousting?
In the distant future tense:
I will will cry over spilled milk.
It is ridiculous as gravity to wait
to pull a string theory on anyone.
Still I am prepared to stay here and wait.
I wait and wait, wait and wait.

4. JUST LIKE THAT

Some of us choose to disappear,
which is not the same as burial.
After wonderful everyday routines,
breakfast and suppers,
Shakespeare and the singing laudy goddamn others
with their lending hands, still part of the forest
in darkness, "for the birds," as they say in Queens.
I delight in my broken circle because
I can say "birds of prey"
and "I pray that you observe the Sabbath."
Praying pays attention, reminds me
Jesus alone chose to be born.
Wishing, I make noise,
"noise for the Lord" as David suggested.
I could write a history of choice and necessity.
I do not choose my dreams.
Time and space, those grown-ups, are choiceless.
If I had a choice, I'd choose to be human,
a farmer or poet, a farmer-poet.
No farm ever chose to be a farm.
Not having chosen my beginnings,
my language, my century, I choose English now.
Some say the poem writes itself.

5. December 21st

I do not think a child
is born simply because
you do it or did it.
Birth is a miracle,
like December 21st,
shortest day of the year.
Death is everyday
like waking up.
Death is hardhearted.
I know flying birds
carry a heart with them
as do sandpipers
and cormorants that dive
and seem to disappear.
Trees' hearts are difficult to find
when they are cut down—
so many leaves, branches, and roots.
A tree has its own soul,
often houses a god,
should be offered a gift.

Mothering is rare,
not like fish eggs or pollen,
but thanks to four holy letters
a miracle happens.
Stars fall in love
at first sight,
have illegitimate stars,
commonplace and steadfast.
Miracles don't have to be holy,
can be profane.
Okay with me if you tell me
you grew up unmiraculously.
"Every living thing is part-miracle,"

I don't know why.
The miracle gets tired,
needs a good night's sleep
we call death.
Death is not a defeat
it is a triumph, the permanent
over the temporary.

6. NUMBER ONE

There are diminishing unshakeable effects,
love, fathering, friendship,
first love, chance encounters.
I may simply stay home.
Life's not a menu, but I can choose a song,
my final resting place for a while.
In the end I'll simply say:
the universe did not choose
Big Bang or Mom and Pop.

Speechless bastard orphan
abandoned on the doorstep of language,
to stay alive I will accept any tongue,
inarticulate as the wheels of a locomotive—
after a month listening I will learn, I think,
first useful words, names of things, foods and drink,
salt, how to nod *thank you* and *good night*,
personal pronouns, if any, some understood.
I think I will learn the possessive quickly.
My new tongue has an untranslatable word
for *gratitude* that also seems to mean
the sun is shining and number *one*.

DAWN

The goddess Dawn seized me as a boy,
clouded me to a secret place on the horizon
where she taught me lessons about her body
I will not share. Now, in old age, I wake
when it is still dark, hoping she will see me
in half-darkness, that remembering when I was young,
she, in error, *in media luz*, will carry me off again,
and share me with the golden goddess Day.

I see time passing erotically:
the rivers of time, the seas of time passing,
on which men, women, everything living
sails, floats, paddles, rows by hand,
enters, kisses, gives birth.
Clockwise and counterclockwise,
passing time is declared profanely like war
against a City filled with Greek whores wearing sandals,
"follow me" written on backs of heels.

I hope, in half-darkness,
Peloponnesean Dawn
will see me, straight and tall,
a timeless waterfall, a crash of water
never frozen, never drying up in summer.
I hollow the rocks I fall upon,
I deepen the river.
I am Dawn's waterfall.

WINTER FLOWERS

In fresh snow that fell on old snow
I see wild roses in bloom, springtime,
an orchard of apple and peach trees in bloom,
lovers of different preferences
walking naked in new snow, not shivering,
no illusion, no delusion, no bluebells.
Why should I live by reality that murders?
I wear a coat of hope and desire.
I follow fallen maple leaves abducted by the wind.
I declare I am a Not Quite, almost a nonentity.
I fought for that "almost."
I lift up and button my collar of hope.
I simply refuse to leave the universe.
I'm all the aunts in my father's house and all my uncles too.
I had fifty great-great-grand-grandmothers
who got to Paradise, like Enoch, without dying.
Once my friends and I went out in deep paradise snow
with Saint Bernards and Great Pyrenees
to find those lost in the blizzard God made for Himself
because He prefers not seeing what happens on earth.
With touch He can hear, taste, smell, see,
and He has fourteen other senses there are no words for.
Memory, He said, is a sense, not a power.
Who am I to disagree with Him?

There are some vegetarians among you,
so I will tell you what He eats.
It's green, and cows and sheep eat it too.
He picks His teeth. I think I heard Him say,
"Gentlemen don't void in swimming pools or the ocean.
I like your dirty jokes, I prefer them in meter."
He told me to carry on.
I thought "On" was a Norse god. He said, "No,
it's just a burden that gets heavier,

the burden makes you stronger."
"Isn't *on* the Japanese debt to ancestors?" I countered.
He resents hearing the prayers and praise of sycophants.

"How come you are speaking to me?" I asked.
He speaks Silence, languages I call "Night" and "Day."
His politics? "Nations" to Him are "a form of masturbation."
Original blasphemy amuses Him, describes
His coitus with living creatures,
mothers, His self,
a whale, a male praying mantis dying to mate.
He likes to hear, "do unto others
what you would not want others to do unto you."
Instead of a prayer rug,
I stitch Him a pillow of false proverbs:
"In the house of the hangman talk of rope."
I asked Him if I ever did anything he liked.
"You planted eggplant too close to the cucumbers
and they married. I blessed that wedding,
sent roses by another name."
"How come you speak to me?" I asked.
He said He was not speaking to me,
"Consult Coleridge on the Imagination."
He waved, He did not say goodbye.

THE THING WRITTEN

The thing written is a sexual thing,
may bite, tell a truth some have died for,
even the most casual initialing
is a touch of love and what love goes for.
A sometime thing, it smiles or has an ugly grin,
on the page or wall may be holy and a sin.
Writing wants, must have, must know,
is flesh, blood, and bone,
proof we are not made to be alone.
Beneath a dove and rainbow
some bank their fire,
wrap their erogenous zones in barbed wire.

Writing may dance in ink flamenco,
kneel before the cross, right
wrongs, fall in love at first sight,
honor the naked languages it holds tight,
kidnap, suck or be sucked for hire,
may look and look or sneak a look,
it has eyes, can read, is remarkable.
From the tower of sexual babble,
when dreams were the beginning of writing,
the angel of dreams descended, stair by stair,
the stone watchtower became the first stone book.

Writing never speaks word, may ache to talk,
and yet each letter of any alphabet
is a fragment of desire,
like half and quarter notes on a staff, or a hawk,
may swoop down, fly higher and higher
to catch a word, and then another word.
The sexual thing may be all love or malice,
eunuchs writing in the Forbidden Palace
where poets dressed in rags, or silk and lace.

The thing written touches, kisses, cuddles,
may be democratic, autocratic, medieval
in the 21st century, feudal, imperial, animal,
sexually digital, a Serf, a King, a Queen,
la chose écrite est une chose sexuelle.
I had a woman beautiful as the letter *L* .
There is the passion of letters, each may mean
another thing, be defaced, after a while.
Writing leans forward,
there is a certain optimism in the written word,
a sexual sunrise that is not daybreak.
Words, words, a carnival of wordplay
on St. Nobody's Day.
Reader, look, there is an *S*, a snake
on the cross of the letter *T.*
The letter of love is still the open-legged *V.*
How can I dot the *i* with humanity?

GOD'S BROTHER

I am prepared to believe Yahweh has a younger brother.
God's brother wears his hand-me-down clothes.
It's pretty tough on the kid. Everywhere he goes,
he basks in the light of family resemblance.
Many use him to get a little closer.
Mortal, he eats, sleeps, falls in love,
he looks in the mirror, sees something of God in his own face.
He knows God never gets tired, never sleeps.
No one ever prays to the brother, the runt of the litter.
God will kill him, see he is buried with a cloud or two,
put stones on his grave, nothing obscure,
nothing ordinary like a sparrow.

DELMORE SCHWARTZ

He heard God coughing in the next apartment,
his life a hospital, he moved from bed to bed
with us and Baudelaire, except he always had
Finnegans Wake tucked in his pajamas,
which must mean, sure as chance,
the human race is God's Phlegm. Penitent,
I say a prayer in God's throat:
"Mister, whose larynx we congest,
spit us into the Atlantic or Hudson . . .
let us be dropped into the mouth of the first fish
that survived by eating its young—
drink hot tea and honey Your mother brings You
till You are rid of Your catarrh, well again.
Let us swim back to our handiwork."

Far from the world of Howth Castle, Delmore died
in a bedbugged hotel, unclaimed for three days.
A week before, by chance, I saw him
at a drugstore counter, doubled over a coffee,
he moaned, "Faithful are the wounds of a friend,
deceitful enemy kisses."
He held my hand too tight, too long.
Melancholy Eros flew to my shoulder,
spoke in Greek, Yiddish, and English:
"Wear his sandals, his dirty underwear,
his coat of many colors that did not keep him warm."

A VISIT TO THE PRADO

I was startled, not like a lion or a fawn,
more like a teacup breaking on a marble floor—
a guide tells schoolchildren after they've passed
the Greco *Fable*, a man blowing on a flame,
a monkey on his shoulder chained to heaven,
that Goya's dog is drowning, not
that the dog is humanity looking up
at a possible Christ in the sky.
No, *señora*, we are God's dog.

I looked for a washroom sign
and for a marble Dionysus,
God of theater, religious ecstasy,
the grape, ritual madness.
I found him in an amphitheater
more Sicilian than Delphic.
The world is more like a paintbrush than a cloud.
I see a changing color, a cloud, a form,
the form two olive-trees high, the cloud
fixed in the corner vault of the ceiling.
I've come to life and death,
wandering in Spain for sixty-five years,
asking for offerings.
I sit on a bench near *La maja desnuda*,
exhausted American
now in the Gallery of Philosophy.
Let me consider how I ought to speak,
then speak, dreaming of reason.

PLAYING SOLDIER

I played soldier as a child.
I took a purple blanket
and made my terrain, mountains
on a fine evening, my universe,
an autumn battlefield.
Out of a tin candy-box burial ground,
not by nation or religion,
enemies made of lead, my soldiers and sailors,
all murderers, good and bad on each side.
I knew and remember their faces.
Troops fought in my bed, for islands,
for mothers and chocolate.
I pulled the chain on the toilet
that overflowed with the big ones of history.
Death was a birthday present
but in my game they all rose again.
At 17, *Harmonium* in my duffel bag,
I enlisted in the US Navy
my service number 7661612.
I was decorated face and chest
by the red and white ribbons
of my boyhood friend Gerry's brains.
Arthur lost a leg. Danny the pianist
who played Chopin sonatas
had his spine made into an accordion.

WOODHAVEN

I was shocked the other day to discover
that I was born near here, swaddled
in lace turning brown like the pinwheels
on the back of pinochle decks. How convenient
my place of birth gives my mind a footing
between the old and new on this island
with its dunes, factories, and state highways.
My birth brought the rage of my parents and a tongue
that choked me. I bit my tongue in half,
my first impossible effort to double my forces.
Trains, not triads, heard all night . . .

The first gift I could accept from my father
was a branch he broke off a sugar maple
that served as a fishing rod,
a bow, and a sign to the world I was
a bender of trees and breaker of branches.
But this was not my truck-farming Long Island
near Whitman's boyhood home, now prosy,
miracle floors, windows face the same sun,
fictitious plumping, no lilac bush, brotherly trees.
A crow walks across the grass
with human steps, sparrows hop.
Mine was the world of David and Absalom,
and I was both. I worshipped the word,
it was graven, and worshipped the presence
of the word, the old prayers, the old revenge,
the old laws of obligation, although
I didn't know them, and never prayed.
I wanted an idol of ~~gold~~ lead.
Life was that mysterious, so I sang all day
comforting myself like a Spanish housemaid scrubbing floors
till they were just about ready to lock me up.
I was fascinated by cracked sidewalks,

four feet by four feet,
thought them ancient links to the past,
I watched the dust and soot
where grass grew mysteriously like me.

BATTLE

Age three, I cried "help."
My head smashed on the cement
like a bundle of newspapers
thrown from a truck.
It was my first battle
near Liberty Avenue
against Jerry O'Brian.
I do not know
why we were fighting.
It was a fight to the death
and I lost.

EPITAPH FOR A COOK

Again the same old stew,
neither potato nor carrot,
I thicken the gravy,
may the good Lord
soak me up with bread.

MY OLD CAR

I.

Lost summers and winters ago
I gave my dog Sancho the gift of my old car
with its 15 years of smells.
I took off the license plate.
When the battery died he could no longer
blow the horn summoning a holy spirit.
I kept open the passenger side window
so he could jump in and out,
closed it when it rained or snowed.
Field animals came to call.
He sat behind the wheel, did not pretend
to be me. He did not know he was behaving
like a temple dog, but to him and me
his car was a holy place, the goodness
of my dog sanctified his dead Chevy.
We fished together. He'd see the line moving upstream,
jump after a rainbow trout breaking water.
If I let him he'd pull the fish in,
to see the joy on his face made me a happy dog,
Sancho dunked his head in the stream, picked up
a round rock, a present for me and the suffering world.

II.

Before I willed him the car, I'd step on the gas,
the headlights showed the road.
You could see the car, with its battery
instead of a heart, coming a mile off
until, like a deer, the lights blinded you.
Once Sancho disappeared from the back seat,
leapt out an open window, chased a deer
across a field, up a mountainside.
A very long hour after, I spotted him
waiting under an oak for me to find him.
How did Sancho die?

What happened to the car? It's a long story.
I guess I had the car, the dog synagogue,
hauled off for scrap. I'm sure I would not take
fifty bucks for what was not for sale.
When someone else was walking him,
Sancho ate some rat poison around a waste bin
in Central Park—he died very slowly
in a hospital cage, his insides crucified.
My dog who loved wilderness
as much as any good wolf looked at me
for weeks when I visited each day, asking
what have I done wrong?
I had a telephone call he was dead.
I swore to myself I'd never let a friend
die alone like that again.

AN AMERICAN HERO

It wasn't all smell of Adirondack lilac
and flowering chestnut trees along Broadway
in the spring of 1824.
Human sewers, mostly Negroes, carried waste in tubs
at night to the Hudson and East Rivers. James Hewlett,
said to be ex-slave, ex-tubman, self-purchaser,
ex-houseboy to English actors, leapt up like a wildcat,
then like a witch he joined a Shakespeare theater of ex-slaves,
billed himself: "Vocalist and Shakespeare's Proud Representative."
I pick his pocket.
He played Richard the Third and Othello,
sang *Il Barbiere, La Marseillaise,* and "O!
say not that woman's love is bought" in one evening.
Humped in silk, Mr. Hewlett called out:
"Now is the winter of our discontent
made glorious summer by this son of New York,"
to black applause. Whatever the beauty of the season,
his actors and actresses were beaten up, his theater
finally burned to the ground with the pleasures of lynching
and cutting out a tongue.

I pick his pocket.

He let the winds of eloquence take him where they would:
often, late at night, he recited
speeches from Shakespeare in the street,
sometimes in the snow.
In disgrace for marrying a pretty-as-a-picture white woman,
he served six months for stealing wine, then three years
for stealing a silver watch from the vest pocket
of a dead man, a show-off laid out in tails.
What good is a watch in the grave?
He answered the sentencing with
"I have done the state some service, and they know it."

While he was away playing with himself,
better people attended the fashionable theater
and minstrel shows, danced the cotillion. The industrious poor—
slaves who bought their freedom, or whose fathers or mothers
had bought their freedom, a few simply freed—
dressed up as no one had dressed before, hired ballrooms,
cotillioned, and held a benefit dance and supper
to support Greek freedom. Late in the evening,
sweating and full of whiskey, their loins sweetened,
they fell to what whites called "crazy dancing
and senseless music" that "frightened the horses."

Out, Hewlett gave one last performance, a newspaper reported:
"to great applause he made a fine speech before the curtain,
which ended up—he could not help himself—
in some kind of talk you had to be a nigger to understand."
I pick his pocket.

Signed up on a crew of freemen and slaves
he made his way to Trinidad,
"Shakespeare's Proud Representative" found a stage,
portrayed Mr. Keene playing nine tragic roles.
Sometimes he gave himself laughing gas to please the crowd
or pretended to. A one-man band,
Othello sang *La Marseillaise*.
He disappeared in New York in the Forties,
the streets slave-free after 1827,
full of Negroes and Irish; older, there is no reason to think
he was kidnapped and shipped south for sale.
What had it come to beyond the gaslights
and wood fires? History as entertainment,
a stained purse I grab. I sit in the dark, listening
to a call and response, a call and response.
For no reason, beauty reports, disappears
not like early-morning birdsong in the city

but like the report of a rifle. I pick his pocket
in the third balcony of my life; segregated from myself,
I am barely a ghost in my own poem.

UBUNTU

I salute a word, I stand up and give it my chair,
because this one Zulu word, *ubuntu,*
holds what English takes seven to say:
"the essential dignity of every human being."
I give my hand to *ubuntu*—
the simple, everyday South African word
for the English mouthful.
I do not know the black Jerusalems of Africa,
or how to dance its sacred dances.
I cannot play Christ's two commandments on the drums:
"Love God" and "Love thy neighbor as thyself."
I do not believe the spirits of the dead
are closer to God than the living,
nor do I take to my heart
the Christ-like word *ubuntu*
that teaches reconciliation
of murderers, torturers, accomplices,
with victims still living.
Jefferson was wrong:
it is not blood but *ubuntu*
that is the manure of freedom.

SM

With spray can paint,
I illuminate my name
on the subway cars and handball courts,
in the public school yards of New York,
S M
written in sky-above-the-ocean-blue,
surrounded by a valentine splash
of red and white, not for Spiritus Mundi,
but for a life and death, part al fresco
part catacomb,
against the city fathers
who have made a crime of signaling
with paint to passengers and pedestrians.
For the ghetto population of my city
I spray my name
with those who stand for a public art.
In secret if I must
and wearing sneakers, I sign with those
who have signed for me.

THE LORD IS MISTAKEN

Death, take a Mediterranean cruise,
drop Murder off at Cadiz
where you were mocked at your labor
in many noble *corridas*.... Let Death's
heart fail in Venice, good news on the Rialto.
Let absentminded Death, always present,
float Cancer up the Nile past Luxor
where they're reading the Book of the Dead,
sail the Meander to Troy.
Let Death drag Death like Hector around its walls
where Helen is sometimes seen walking in the evening.
So far Death has paid me scant attention
despite my war on that *hijo de puta*.
But God with His big heart feels sorry for Death,
lets Death live, play at His feet like a puppy.
God thinks the puppy just bites us a little.
The Lord is mistaken, so we must want
till every living thing is dead as a doornail,
the universe covered with doornails.
Death will not drown, does not starve
long as anything lives. Toward the end, starving,
Death devours the last trees like salad.
Finally when fire and darkness are celebrating
with nothing living, Death falls in God's arms,
looks Him in the face, and says, "I'm your heir."
For His reasons, God says,
"Nein, nein. Auf wiedersehen."

EVENING SONG

In beautiful Russian, Mandelstam wrote
"the soul's a woman."
I remember dead men, their mouths wide open:
no doubt different women,
some naked flew out,
some in transparent nightgowns,
no souls dressed in street clothes
or country clothes, boots, no wedding gowns.
I feel a woman dancing in me,
I speak of her carefully.
When she is angry, anyone can see it in my eyes.
She speaks to me like an orchestra tuning up.
Her mortal opposite is not body, is time
with its dirty timely words.
Every day the soul does woman's work.
It's as if she's trying to unscramble eggs.
There is the question of immortality.
Does the soul get lost?
Is the woman given or do we fashion her?
To hell with public opinion. She is mortal.
To change the subject I like to turn around
like a migrating bird, head south then north
then south again. I inhale my soul
and the souls of passersby, that, who,
sleep in me only for the night.
I am a country inn. I'd rather be a country inn
than Claridge's or the Savoy.
What do I really believe?
The soul must be good for something.

SLIP OF THE PEN

Dr. Abrams, your last name ends in "S,"
that does not mean you're plural
but when I addressed an envelope
with a check inside I left off the S
which means I had the hope
against hope to cut off your penis
with a rural pen, not cause your funeral.
I'm earnest, is your S
more housefly than eagle,
do you use it to jump rope?
I bet
it does not genuflect.
It is more sinful than pious,
more dybbuk than elf,
more Pope Francis than Pius
the Twelfth.
I have no doubt
your S straightens out—
never disguised,
it is more cabbage than Brussels sprout,
hugely prized.
Your S smiles—is not just erotic
but patriotic,
free,
ready to serve its country.

NIGHT FLIGHT

Sleepless,
I smell the 1940 bombings
surrounded by English affection.
Arrived mostly in Manchester, UK,
I call the operator
to hello me later.
I've already run into an honored citizen,
bleeding Nameless Corporal War.
I want to take the measure of pleasure,
and I do, in feet, notes, and handbreadths,
in the sky, not in light years, foot by foot.
I know "men have died and worms
have eaten them, but not for love."
Dressed in green corduroy,
I fall on the bed, I measure worms.

THE AUCTION

Finally it comes down to this,
the buying and selling of Christ's
foreskin and robes,
the bidding on Moses' tablet,
Samson's hair, David's sling and harp,
all come to the block.
The last lot is happiness.
"It is against you, Sir.
Sold to a telephone bidder!"
There is nothing without a price.
Kindness is passed, may be sold
"by private treaty."
There is nothing without a price
except what's loved,
the God's honest truth.

IDLING

There's wondering, idle thoughts,
thinking over what was last said,
some poetry in my head
like traffic outside the window.
In my forgetful marrow, I consider
often lying words, like *everything* and *all*.
Nothing is another matter.
Nothing comes of everything and all.
Something comes of nothing.
I know the word *no* means no,
yes, yes, except when they mean each other.
There's *water*, which means water,
dishwater, that may mean worthless.
It's often better
to say *worthless* when you mean it.
I've come to *meaning*, that can mean
reason for or *reason to live*,
words I might say outright
without first saying *meaning*.
Then there is a mean man.
How did *mean* come to have two meanings?
Take a dictionary of homonyms
and tell me how words got to sound alike
with different meanings and spellings,
a Sea of Words
which is a Chinese dictionary.
Language has its ways,
its altitude and latitude . . .
Stanley, baby, quit jerking on and off.
I'm simply talking to myself.

I am more familiar with the dark night
and bright day of the body
than the dark night of the soul.

Light has an exaggerated reputation.
Goethe's last words were, *"Mehr Licht!"*
Faust was dragged off to hell
when he was content.
Goethe preferred discontent, which needed light.
The seed is contained discontent.

READING HALF-AWAKE

Early morning, what poems I read don't make sense,
are blurred unless I read aloud. It's as if
there were a wall or fence taken down
by speaking out, a cliff I had to climb to see.
I am awake, my mind's eye, my mind's nose and mouth,
stuffed closed,
my eyelids lead, silent poetry a lie—
uncomposed,
Eurydice not found, Orfeo's flute
fingered but not blown, the other woodwinds
playing octets, the choirs gone mute.
The mind attends a thought as a mother attends
her child, and so I write to make sense
when reading silently is not recompense
for bad dreams or a night's silent sleep
into which I fall, but never leap to sleep.

LETTER TO THE BUTTERFLIES

1

Dear Monarchs, fellow Americans,
friends have seen you and that's proof,
I've heard the news:
since summer you traveled 5,000 miles
from our potato fields to the Yucatan.
Some butterflies can bear what the lizard would never endure.
Few of us can flutter away from the design:
I've seen butterflies weather a storm
in the shell of a snail, come out of nowhere
twenty stories up in Manhattan.
I've seen them struggling on the ground.
I and others may die anonymously,
when all exceptionalism is over,
but not like snowflakes falling.
This week in Long Island
before the first snowfall, there is nothing left
but flies, bees, aphids, the usual.

2

In Mexico
I saw the Monarchs of North America gather,
a valley of butterflies surrounded
by living mountains of butterflies—
the last day for many.
I saw a river of butterflies flooding
through the valley, on a bright day black clouds
of butterflies thundering overhead,
yet every one remained a fragile thing.
A winged colossus wearing billowing silk
over a sensual woman's body
waded across the valley,
wagons and armies rested at her feet.
A village lit fires,
and the valley was a single black butterfly.

3

Butterflies,
what are you to me
that I should worry about your silks and powders,
your damnation or apotheosis,
insecticides and long-tongued lizards.
Some women I loved are no longer human.
I have a quarrel with myself for leaving my purpose,
for the likes of you, beauties I could name.
Sooner or later
I hope you alight on my headstone
above my name and dates, questioning
my bewilderment.
Where is your Chinese God of walls and ditches?
Wrapped in black silk I did not spin,
do I hold a butterfly within?
What is this nothingness they have done to me?

A PURGE WITHOUT PITY

to Theodore Roethke

A poet friend was caught in the john
during a Seattle earthquake, rushed out to find
the walls cracked and the chandelier swaying,
convinced that his dumping had caused it all.
Often he broke wind, called it "music"—
on one famous occasion, having eaten
too much cabbage over brandy and clams,
caught on a local train, he had to go bad
but didn't want to get off
to wait an hour for the next commuter
when there was a sudden jolt, a dead stop—
he soiled himself, kept reading John Clare,
thought he was undetected, sat unfrowning,
until a small boy said, "Mister, please—
the next car is empty, can you go there?"
He noticed the Douglas firs the train was passing,
obeyed the boy, asked himself why
it is our fate, that with all the possibilities,
what passes through us is live dead matter,
somewhere always an afterlife
somewhere beyond the treatment plant or gutter?
Three stops, deep in philosophy, at last
at the depot, the poet waltzed into the washroom
to make the best of things.
Tales of poets catching or missing trains
are seldom very funny,
always with a little "afterlife" in them.
Goethe waiting to catch a coach to Italy
heard Mendelssohn playing Beethoven,
"enough," he said, "to knock the planets off their axes."

AN OLD MARRIAGE

I see summer where the winter was,
time, a fish breaking water.
You say time is never surprising.
I say it is like an idea come out of nowhere.
You say, "in the beginning was . . ."
I don't listen. Nowhere is a lie.
Winter is where summer was,
they remember each other.
Look, a cardinal just flew past my frosty window.
I am wrong talking like this, I say
summer resembles winter,
a hellish, icy-cold memory.
If they could speak
and we could hear them, they might just
be comedians (spring and autumn tragedians):
"You're too hot." "You're too cold."
"A little more respect," winter says,
"because I am older than you.
Summer, you play me
in Australia and Argentina."
Reader, I am content with all seasons,
truest words first spoken
"Mama, Papa."
Although summer and winter
may wear each other's clothes,
only the mostly blind
confuse the sun and the moon.
There are summer prayers and winter prayers.
There will always be, as long as the weather changes.
There are the lawless luxuries of love poems,
and there are poems of disagreement
that get down in the gutter and fight.

LETTER TO LAREN

You wrote I appeared in your dream last night in Granada.
Some dreamers have the gift to dream
the fate of others before it happens.
Any good or bad news?
The towns in Andalusia were filled
with such dreaming women dressed in black.
Women mourned for five years,
so most were dressed in black.
Some held part of the collar of their dress
in their mouths, veiling their face.
In the arms of your lover you dreamed of me.
Two's company, three's a crowd;
I know dreams bring unwelcome friends,
strangers, enemies to bed,
and Mom and Pop are always there.

Outside your window, a gypsy girl
was chased by the wind and naked St. Christopher
who wanted to lift her dress and finger her blue rose.
She ran to the house of the English consul
who gave her warm milk and gin.
The Granada gardens are full of remembering
olive and flowering trees that weep sometimes
for the moonlight Taj Mahal gardens
with their night-blooming flowers and sleepless bees
serving queens who fill their hives with laughter
at human folly before they are betimes murdered.
You sleep where blind musicians played
in the bedrooms of lovers.

Nightingales police the fields of paradise
on Sabbath nights while flamenco dancers sit and drink
Anís de Chinchón, listening to jazz.
Your dream made me unforget

I spent seven days and nights
on my first honeymoon in Granada
in March 1953, the month Stalin died,
but that is another story.

BEYOND

Without ambition, I've stolen the world.
Who among you is poor enough to understand
if I had not I'd have no place to sleep tonight?
For what I need belongs to mankind,
yet I stole because I could not bear the human condition.

The world, as far as my eye can see, notices no change,
according to my nature I practice my craft,
hammer out the rose in the spine of a fish.
The ocean is bread, an old gypsy without a guitar
sings in cante jondo, *¿Dónde vas media judía?*
The ocean is bread.

I consider, common to all uses, love.
The only thing more popular than war, orgasm.
I'll make use of death, that it might serve me.
I'll capture war, make it a frightened, hungry boy.
I had the gall for that—spell it G-A-U-L, if you like.

Now my donkey, my lad, my good world,
the meek, the humble, and innocent
I spur with murdered Caesar's boot,
my praetors, generals, kings and subjects
I command to do all things beyond my imagination!

POEM

Teacher of reading, of "you will not" and "you shall,"
almighty Grammarian author of Genesis,
whether language holds three forms of the future
as Hebrew does or no future tense at all
like Chinese, may it perform a public service,
offer the protection of the Great Wall,
the hope and sorrow of the Western Wall.

WEDDING POEM, ALAS

My dear friends
you did not marry as doves cooing
under a bird feeder,
after your combined 152 years
of mischance and luck. It was fate.
Eros at a Bacchanal whispered:
"What is yours is hers, what is hers is yours,
you may keep each other's 'sweet company,'
kiss away yesterday's kisses,
wear each other's nightgowns and pajamas!"
Then Eros flew off, a hopeful God.
Old vows broken were repaired,
all vows to ex-husbands
and ex-wives broken, repaired,
as were the vows of your children
broken and repaired.
God blesses a just cause.
I send love. Beware the wrath of the dead.

ROTHKO

My best customer was Mark Rothko,
who bought six copies of *The Wrong Angel.*
I note I write this with blue ink,
but I pay little attention to the color.
He would make Biblical without a word
different shades of blue,
Deuteronomy black, Genesis serpent-green.
He could obey or break the commandments
with a brush or palette knife, paint the colors of time.
He lives in the sigh of the past,
his heart and soul hang themselves on walls.
At night, when no one's around,
his paintings sing Hebrew, Greek, and Yiddish songs.
If the play's the thing, Oedipus tore out his eyes,
Mark killed himself thinking
he painted psalms and proverbs,
"tragedy, ecstasy, doom"—
then he saw what he'd really painted on a wall,
his sweetheart sucking off her naked lover
in a mirrored chapel, so he bathed them
with blood poured from his well-cut wrist.

THANKSGIVING

1

Because I've lived beyond my years, I'm in the soup.
I don't spit in the soup from which I've eaten.
Because I am in the soup
amuses a satyr sunning himself on Greek rocks
where Eros masturbates
with a fantasy he is Mars making war, not love.
I read poetry and write garlic lines.
I swim in a *zuppa di pesce*, my company,
my wife the catch of the day.
Young, there was the question of civilizations,
borscht, wonton, chowders, gazpacho,
an antediluvian primordial soup—
sorry, but I went from soup to soup to nuts.
I loved obscene Andalusian lullabies
sung by abused nannies and wet nurses.
Older than a crabapple tree,
I sing unaccompanied songs,
ghost songs with my mother and father's voices
on Liberty Avenue.
A <u>riff</u> on a ram's horn,
I am a short repeated phrase, frequently played over,
changing chords and harmony
used as background to a solo improvisation.
Eros daydreams beneath my window.
I don't spit in the soup from which I've eaten.

2

The satyr believes, because of one song I wrote,
my "Satyr Song," he is my heir.
He says, "I'm broke, extravagant.
Since you will be dead before five years pass
you should turn over your interests to me now."

40

He's not an honest murderer.
No songbird, my satyr has appetite for my liver,
but I've stolen more kindness than fire.

Reader, keep out of mind my transparency.
The dead never block the view from my window,
or from a mountaintop, or from poetry
that may take the place of a mountain.

You can see I'm in the soup.
I offer you a spoon. Taste how it happens:
the satyr repeats, "I want my golden future now."
Eros, I leave you a checkbook of unsigned checks, my love.
This is not the first time I've talked only in metaphors.
It's Thanksgiving, I give thanks.
I can still carry a tune.

PISS

Just out of diapers, I am a giant
standing in a harbor, pissing ships
to shipwreck against the cliffs.
I have some memory how proud I was,
my first standing-up-like-a-man piss,
later pissing into the Grand Canyon,
proof I could piss half-a-mile.
I was beaten by Old Faithful,
the steaming, pissing earth
at Yellowstone, where buffalo and moose,
when the sun is right, piss rainbows.

A POEM FOR ALL OCCASIONS

The mind is a family, dreams are father and mother.
They head the family:
the children are wishes, thoughts, inclinations,
and there are orphans.
If a dream, forgetting nothing, mothers or fathers
a notion, he, she, or it may grow up to be an idea.
We all can remember dinners
when our family of the mind sat at table,
hope and despair opposite,
loneliness dressed like an ocean
in blue, green and white.
Or is the dream simply an uninvited guest
who rules the mind night and day?

The mind's family is never far apart.
The triplets of love tell lonely jokes—
there's the one about Miss, Mrs., Missing You.
They go to celebrations, secular and devout.
Today is Buddha's birthday.
I say happy birthday to the World
that has nothing to do with first or last,
because they are twins, as are good and evil.
I grant you they are fraternal, not identical twins.
They fight for their cause, honor is at stake.
"How stand I then?"

A HOOT FOR WILLIS BARNSTONE

On the Bible you translated I solemnly swear
I read a poem to you on your dentist's chair:
I could hear the drill, the dust of your jaw bone,
impacted wisdom tooth on the telephone.
I know you have more teeth than languages—
truth is, you have Latin, Greek, Chinese teeth,
French, Spanish and German molars, English front teeth
in one mouth—gives you advantages.
A Sanskrit incisor would not be missed.
I don't think Alcibiades is your dentist.
A little laughing gas makes you silly,
you say, "Crown my tooth with the shield of Achilles,"
while a phalanx charges your root canal.
You tell me my Delphic oracle
wears sunglasses—"You had better sing for Argos,
leave Willis Telemachus."

I say Eros, the builder, is always near us,
consider how many cathedrals were built by Jesus,
but Notre Dame
is not worth all those murdered in His Name.
He saved His wrath for the moneychangers
but left us with greater dangers,
racism and war. What are little miracles good for?
We walk in brothers' blood, He walked on water.
We seldom see a bird with a broken wing,
He gave us the first garden, flocks of birds flying.
The donkey and cow did not kiss in the stable,
love between the species must become comfortable.
We are God's dogs, may He feed us under the table.

I don't know the year, I don't know the century.
John the Baptist was dried with a towel—for a fee,
I'll sell you his sacred towel *prix d'ami*,

but not for paper money.
I hope to love every stranger that I meet
but I do not offer God a prayer, milk and meat.
I'm a broken CD, so I repeat:
I really prefer the curs whose breath reeks o' the rotten fens
to immaculate heaven.
There are American questions, and the question
of death that has a worldwide reputation.
I've told you this before:
we have lots of darkness and light, later just death,
or, if you prefer, we do not enter life by the front door,
but the door that leads to the basement beneath.
When I'm having my colonoscopy I won't think it silly
if you call me and say, "I want to read you a poem, it's Willy."

DUET

You are a viola
and I am a bow in your hand,
or am I your bass and you my bow?
We play,
pluck strings, pluck
and pluck the night away.
You wake me in the morning,
call me your "bow" again.

PILGRIM QUESTIONS

What if you don't have money in your hand,
a novel, her breast, or your day.
On the brow of the hill,
do you finish draining the radiator, do butchers
continue sawing through bone? What if your knife
is slicing a round bread in Spain
where bread is called the face of Christ—
if the bread falls on the floor
do you pick it up and kiss it?
His body was never a shaft of wheat or rye
although His body is bread.
I do not believe He will receive me,
barefoot, with shoes or sandals,
I do not really believe He will be there,
He does not care if we are deodorized,
strawberry, not garlic breath.
What if you face an idol you do not believe in,
do you turn supplicant with the smooth talkers?
Does He want us to join the stammerers?
What of political hacks? Surely He knows
their speeches, in fact He has heard it all before,
seen it all before.
I will not run to greet Him at all.
He is amused by my ventriloquy.
I shall not put it over on Him—
I will not walk to Jerusalem. I will not con Him.
Better my live dog words than my dead lion voices.

TRUMP

to the worthless poor

I see America sitting at Trump's table,
to speak of anything but money is taboo.
His pals think the wrong side won the Civil War,
slavery was worth fighting for.
They say he's suing Louis Armstrong
for playing the trumpet, he damns King Kong
for climbing the Empire State because the sinless
real estate monkey business is *his* business.
His barber has made a fortune selling his cut golden hair
with the gold dust dandruff of a billionaire.
Trump's Spray, his broken wind, rare fragrance,
the perfume of love, once the rage in France,
given his plans for Muslim and Mexican immigration
now off the shelves by counter reformation.
One plus nine zeros make a billion
but no number of zeros make number one.
How many lies make a mistake?
Every twinkling star, the moon, the sun,
has Trump's face, every snowflake.

You may want less, but I'll give away the store:
wrapped in the stars and stripes, patriots galore
shout "Trump for president!" want his face
on paper money, pennies, nickels, and dimes.
"End the dirty news in *The New York Times*!"
Monuments to his victories like Samothrace:
Donald's tennis racquet, golf shoe, and sneaker,
anything his, a stain from a love affair,
is worth as much as a Van Gogh ear.
I heard there was sold at auction somewhere
out of the tax zones of the human race
for the price of a Rodin bronze "Thinker"
a Trump toilet seat, a burnisht throne
he called his "little gold mine,"
proof top of the world and bottom meet.

Without sin, he casts the first stone.
History's a sissy, let's bring back the guillotine.
A judge with a Latin name is Pontius Pilate.
Build a wall, Mexicans won't let gringos come in.

Trump's rule: 100-proof love of country
is buy a farm or building in every state.
Money, money, money, money,
is what keeps America great.
USA! USA! USA!
He denies he built the Great Wall in Cathay,
in Mobile, Alabama he forgot three Ks.
Donald is an oak, his foes pussy willows,
his enemies crooked marshmallows.
Trump is proud in a public shower—
between his legs, a twelve-inch root
flowers into a redwood.
Judas was a liberal, made a hell of a deal.

Trump Ocean will cover Trump Tower
when all the holy texts are drowned,
when sharks have devoured the last minnow,
the one good book afloat: *The Art of the Deal.*
Because no is yes, and yes is no,
pray, our Father who art in Trump Tower,
hallowed be thy portfolio,
thy casino come, thy will be done in real estate
as it is in Heaven . . .
Getting old, the earth is black hole jailbait.
Evangelical citizen, with *angel* in your name,
I find a terrible ugliness in TRUMP heaven
along the parkways, his name in saintly skies
twenty-four seven,
longer than the moon or sun,
the Statue of Liberty's evil eyes
and Trump's searchlight on everyone.

FALLOUT

ISIS
and Fidel Castro
give me gastro-
enteritis.
Remember the missile crisis?
Fidel wanted to drop the atom bomb
on us. Asked what would happen
to Cuba then, he said, "Annihilation."
That's the forgotten rap on
Fidel, but there was something finer—
MacArthur's plan to drop thirty atom bombs on
the People's Republic of China.
While bombs are bursting in air,
Nixon urged Ike to bomb Red Square.
Ah, it's better to take the trouble
to remember Chardin's boy blowing a *Soap Bubble,*
David's virtuous slingshot killed a giant,
Teddy Roosevelt told us "be self-reliant."
Auden wrote, "We must love one another or die,"
changed the line to be true, "love one another and die."
As time goes by, I think it shall be seen,
to survive we must do something in between,
respect the golden mean.
More than ever, respect one another.
Even a Nazi has a mother.
We are able not to murder our brother.
Rather than bomb, we can just wish the other dead.
It's not nice, but burn books instead
of dropping bombs. They burned and sacked Rome,
still some manage to read or write a poem.
Long as I can hold a pen, so to speak, I will write fables,
celebrate a good book, wines and vegetables,
greens, epics, and tomatoes.
I celebrate potatoes.

Memorial Day, Washington D.C.

NEW BORN

The first thing I did against my will is see light.
Older, in my mother's belly with a good mind,
I sometimes dreamed different kinds of darkness.
I kicked, had sweet dreams and nightmares
something like death, unborn happiness,
blind hallucinations, memories I can't name
that still push me to act with unborn hands,
all before breathing.

What last thing will cross my mind
after last rights and wrongs?
They say the grand finale is like sleep,
I may feel love's nuts and bolts unscrewing—
it's best to be held tight. A pillow does not kiss.
May I never waver in peaceful unmindfulness.
I've seen passionate suffocation,
I've felt exquisite pain. Far better doggerel:
"Nurse, nurse, I'm getting worse!"
Undone, I'd like my last thoughts to rhyme:
                    I did not lend
              you my love. The end.

THE TABLE

This red oak table has no memory.
Its mother was a tree
who needed earth, water, and sunlight,
a forest's love of sunlight we can envy.
Trees are deaf to birdsong,
dead trees cut into boards join
celebrations beyond their understanding:
Thanksgiving, Christmas, Passover suppers.
A hundred years from now
I'd rather be an antique table
than Yorick's distant cousin.
No living tree is indifferent, casual, or half-hearted.
Never indifferent, Voltaire could not forgive
the Jews for giving France Christianity.
Surely he would rather be a Revolutionary table
in the year of our Lord 2016
than a Louis Quatorze table under a chandelier.
I believe there is a battle between
the kitchen table, bimah, and altar.
The kitchen table
that serves food to hungry strangers wins.

WET PAINT

1

Today, my Italian-American electrician
who's never been to Italy
and doesn't want to go
because it's out of his way,
smells the cinnamon in my oatmeal
from across the room,
that I can't smell
holding the hot bowl in my lap.
It's true, I can't see
what's playing on a marquee
half-a-mile away anymore,
that I say, "What's that you said?" quite often,
English mustard and horseradish are less hot,
but I can touch more than I could touch
a little while ago, and more touches me.
I am not lying when I tell you
I touched Courbet's *Origin of the World*
when the paint was wet, the summer of 1866.

I smell a rat, I am too old.
My nose is Roman partisan.
I remember the smell of different ladies,
Lady Cinnamon, Lady Turmeric, Countess of Cloves,
a Saffron ungrammatical companion
who sang, "Is you is or is you ain't my baby?"
Smelling, whispering and wolf-growling,
young me had a den, paper hills, drafts
of poems and books rugged the dirty floor.
They tripped me, I almost broke a leg.

2

Deaf rivers try to lip-read poetry,
blind rivers read Milton in windy braille.

They do not have diction because they are voiceless.
The riverbanks, I know, are thighs, male and female.
The river tongues, tastes the shallows.
Greetings, my senses, my salutations
are old, not fashionable. I don't kiss hands
as some Italian *signorini* do
wearing a bathing suit at the Lido.
The senses change from season to season.
I love fashionable forests
that change from day to day, season to season.
This is a preamble to my anti-Platonic dialogue
between fashion and Mrs. Death.

UNFALLEN

This morning, the merry-go-round
in my head stopped to let the kids climb
down horses, lions, and swans with backseats.
I'm off to the Boston Post Road,
the traffic moving north bumper-to-bumper,
pushing, not blowing horns.
Best to back up, some drivers and passengers
walk on the shoulders, in ditches—
it is something like turning back the clock
an hour from Daylight Saving to Eastern Standard.
At the same time, I'm crazy as a grandfather clock.
Don't I have hands, toes, two eyes,
don't I need winding? I've learned
something about the wind and winding.
Wasn't there a banging wind that blew time
into the universe? I can't help but go back:
I shift into reverse,
a necklace of June days under my shirt,
on six fingers the rings of May,
last April's earrings, a pearl tie-pin,
in my pocket a crucifix that opens to a knife
that came in a box of candy in Cordova forty years ago.
I've a drawer full of lunar calendar animals.

*

God and the gods wished the rich to live longer.
On the sacred mountain above Granada,
there is ice and snow year round,
unmelted, centuries deep ice and snow,
Iberian, Greek, Carthaginian, Roman,
Jewish, Muslim, Catholic snow and ice.
Most lived short lives
when the chief product of trade was the color purple.

Oh, yes, across the straits
that part the Atlantic and Mediterranean,
waters and winds famously confused,
armies made their way from west to east
and east to west after they were driven
from the Christian north, whatever the weather.

Mr. Speaker, point of disorder:
in the Sinai, where there are hard winters,
on the mountaintop above the rocks and sand,
every spring the ice melts, apple, pear,
and fig trees have bloomed since Moses.

*

The unblue bird flew past
the unred robin redbreast,
flew past the unred-winged blackbird,
past the unbald eagle,
the ungrounded groundhog in the underbrush,
past understanding,
something unreadable became un-
the unknown god I've come to tell you about.
In an untidy way, I re-write uncle.
I've forgotten unhappy, unfaithful, unending,
I've got to be down to earth and up to earth,
to be unnatural, to be true, natural and unnatural
before my timely untimely end.

I am getting out of grammar.
There is a prefix, *be.*
I beget, begat, become, befriended,
because of those bedamned, beguiled,
I did not bequeath or belittle. I recall
I was bejeweled, bewildered years ago.
I am running out of prefixes,
I step out of my coffin, not resurrected,
to begin again, unfallen.

SPRING MORNING

God, how do you dew?
The grass I planted is growing
with the help of you.

TIME'S BONES

You said, "Let time's bones be broken."
Please tell me what time's skeleton looks like.
Any vertebrate, Mrs. Bones?
I wonder what human bones time may have,
something like a nose to smell space
in a sky bed? Time and space are married,
exchanged saturnal rings, and rings of other planets
out of our solar system.
Our planets and stars are something like flies
around time's head. I say "time's head,"
but time has no head, has temperature,
and that's not the end of that.
Time has a language, of course,
speaks sonata, sign, speaks up Volcano.
Time has sung love songs for some thousands of years,
outside of what I'll call space's window.
I would lie if I said, "time has a heart."
But perhaps falling, gravity everywhere is time's heart.
Time is falling, not just falling,
something like the beginnings of falling in love.
Question, Mr. Speaker—if time has bones,
is falling, where is time's marrow and blood?
Darkness is blood. (I've out-metaphored myself.)
I can't break time's bone. Did infant time wet the bed?
Perhaps time sat on the potty, making constellations.

Alas, poor time, I did not figure him,
never having seen him, but I know

when he or she is passing. I am happy to salute time,
because he or she is Admiral, General, and President,
Prime Minister, Dictator, still husband and wife of space.
I am a Seaman Third Class,
which will always be my rank.
But I carry the flag in an honor guard,
the flag of poetry gets the salute.
I must look ahead, and stand up straight.

A POEM CALLED DAY

Day is carved in marble, a man reclining,
a naked giant suffering.
Preoccupied Day faces Night, who is a woman,
huge, naked, Herculean, both pillowed
on their uncarved rough marble bed.
They need light to be seen, neither
has anything to do with the sun or moon.
Art is not astronomy,
but the heavens are useful as gardening to poets,
not useful as love or loneliness.
If I write out of arrogance and ignorance
a poem called Day, my chisel and mallet, words
and pen, paper my marble, I must not confuse
sunlight and Day, petals with hours. I could rhyme,
perhaps by reason and chance describe the nature of Day.
I might discover Nature is surprisingly
sometimes moral, unexpected, a principle
over which the lovers Night and Day quarrel.

In my poem, faithful Night and faithful Day quarreled;
rhyme told me they quarreled because Day is gold
Night hates the thought of celestial money,
rages at the starless differences between cost and price.
Michelangelo did not choose to make a sculpture

Prezzo, or put the finger of God on a coin.
Day and Night saw Danaë's legs spread apart
for Zeus to enter as a shower of gold.
They are not household gods or saints.
Better I write about things nearby,
a chair, a stool, the principle I'm sitting on.

Day is my dictionary. If my Day were animal, he might be
a baby elephant who eats leaves.
My good Day stays close to his mother,
who is murdered for her ivory tusks.
My Day is an endangered specie. I whisper
into elephant ears, *peace, my darling little Day.*
An owl hoots, *your Day has no given name!*
True, I refuse names useful to many others:
Sabbath, Sunday, Friday, Saturday.
My Day is not baptized, circumcised, or blessed.
I pick him up and hold Day in my arms.
I put my head in Day's open mouth.
I tongue Day, and Day tongues me.
Yes, although my Day loves Night,
he tongues me in and out of bed.
My Day knows Night carnally,
lets Night know me.
So I love Day today.
And I love Night tonight.

It's About Time
(2015)

&

No Tear is Commonplace
(2013)

Sunrise—Morning

THE POEM OF SELF

I often write in my diary the obsolete poem of self
with my obsolescent pen and ink.
So I throw a poem for a lark, like my hat,
off the Brooklyn Bridge, where Hart Crane, bless him,
"dumped the ashes of his dad in a condom,"
I was told.
I watch my hat glide toward the Atlantic,
wait for a miraculous rescue—
but my poem-hat alights, drifts, sinks down
among the bottom feeders,
the fluke, crab, catfish in sewage
of the East River, still musical, distantly related
to the North Sea. I hope my drowned hat
shelters blind, half-dead newborns
that lip the taste of my sweatband,
the taste of me their first breakfast
of undigested unleavened waste.
The River Styx has clean water where Elijah
swims with the Angels Gabriel and Raphael.

So the poem of self gone,
poetry must face, may two-face,
must honor the language, point out to readers
the garden of delights, hell to paradise,
almost, but never seen before.
Are the playhouses of God metaphors?
Is God rhyme? The God of everyone obsolete?
Then in the beginning was the Word,
the Word, let's say, Fish, a live-bearer—
the fish grew fins, then feet,
asked questions without answers.
To wish or not to wish that is the question.
Every word is a question.
Put a question mark after each word,

the question mark is a fish breaking water:
poetry? mother? anything? kiss? glory?
So remembering and forgetting are over,
useless boredom is plagiarized,
human beings are spawned,
trees genuflect, there are
Stop! Look! and Listen! prayers
at railroad crossings.
Truth is, *je, yo, ich,*
a Former Obsolete First-Person Pronoun,
stole the word "so" from a friend—
seems a petty theft but is a felony
when the word packs a deadly weapon.

Looking back, God is a verb, adjective,
article, contraction, infinitive, any part of speech,
any language, since every living thing speaks God.
God is a verb—
"He was godded once by the Lord,"
means created or killed, and God is a noun,
adjective, article, infinitive, any part of speech,
birdsong, neigh, hee-haw,
bark, bray, buzz, all God's speech.
Now the poem of *you* is obsolete
and the poem of *he, she, we* obsolete—penis and vagina,
mouth, anus, hands
holding on for dear life to each other,
everything that dreams obsolete,
everything but what in the good old days we called "love."
Now Johann Sebastian Bach
is a verb. Bach you! Bach you!
So help us or don't help us, God,
we have the luxury of tears, others weep
with fluttering wings, falling leaves, so help us
or don't help us, God,
breaking my vow, so help me God.

JULY 4

Thank you for the clover that bloomed today
full of bees after last night's rain. July 4th
seems just as it was under the British,
the day Jefferson, age 33, and the Fathers
signed the Declaration they wrote together,
not the rough draft
that demanded the right to close slave markets
but the soiled version I fly the flag for.
The same apple and pear trees are here.
There is a Continental Congress of birds,
seeds of equality planted by the winds,
insects and fallen fruit,
things living with and without hearts.
Some animals, bless them, are free
despite dry walls, hunters' guns and traps,
everyone a creature of the times, like us,
a few, like John Adams, farmed without slaves.
I read glacial writing, the Hudson River
demanding on granite cliffs
freedom of speech, religion, and assembly.

Often, private property was not theft,
but murder: there were promissory notes
and paper money that "bought and sold Men."
Some died in the earthquake of slavery,
some in today's after tremors,
some were burned alive, crippled, turned to stone
by the filthy-mouthed volcanoes of hate.
On the 4th of July I celebrate the preamble,
the runaways, the everyday decent folks
who do not need revenge, and those who did.

I remember: via the Spanish ambassador
the Infante in '75 sent Benjamin Franklin

his translation of Sallust's *Historiae*.
Franklin sent back by packet boat his views
"the Muses have scarcely visited these remote regions"
so he provided the Continental Congress's
Declaration of Causes and Necessity of Taking Up Arms.
Washington's army was soon to escape from Brooklyn
across New York harbor because the wind
was right and there was fog. My darling Deist thought
rebellion against tyrants is obedience to God.

PARABLE OF THE PORCUPINE

The only animal that cries real tears,
my porcupine weeps in terror of Sancho, my good dog.
A crown of thorns crawls under the lilacs.
With her just-born swaddled in quills,
nursing her child, impossible piglet,
she scrawls in mud, in rodent Aramaic,
something like, "Do not touch me."
Touched by two mouths now and first needles,
bless you for hiding in your sepulcher of leaves
while Sancho, his mouth full of quills,
in faith and hope rests his painful head in my lap.

BRIGHT DAY

Vivo sin vivir en mí,
y de tal manera espero,
que muero porque no muero.
      —Santa Theresa de Ávila

I call out this morning: Hello, hello.
I proclaim the bright day of the soul.
The sun is a good fellow,
the Devil's my kind of guy. No deaths today I know.
I live because I live. I do not die
because I do not die.
In Tuscan sunlight Masaccio
painted his belief that St. Peter's shadow
cured a cripple, gave him back his sight.
My shadow is a speechless asshole, a nether eyebrow.
I walk in morning sunlight,
where trees demonstrate against death.
There's danger, when I die my soul may rise in wrath.
I know the dark night of the soul
does not need God's Eye
as a beggar does not need a hand or a bowl.
In my garden, death questions every root, flowers reply.

PARABLE OF THE BOOK-MAN

Half man, half book, he spent the day
reading himself, the night
half in bed, half on the shelf.
He did not like to turn his own pages
so he went to sea, slept in a hammock. The Northwind
abducting Orithyia turned his pages.
The Atlantic turned him forward, backward, forward.

In a deserted forest, above the beach, a sailor
on shore leave, he sat on an oak stump,
watched a heartless fire ant
peacefully working her way down the bark.
Frightened by the book-man
she let off a God-given scent that warned
slender-waisted subjects
slowly moving a mountain down to an anthill:
Danger! Never surrender!
Their civilization, almost all female,
prospered. Even so, sisters and half sisters
battled other nations, red carpenter ants,
the dead uncountable,
while queens and gallants were safe in bed
or sipping nectar in a gorgeous peony.
Despite so many reasons to be dead,
how many reasons were there to be alive?
Book-man on the beach, his kind outlasted
by continents of ants.
The littles will outlive all tears and laughter—
nothing left with a dangerous heart.
Still, it is and was better to be human
while God plays a game of horseshoes,
throws wreaths of life and death
around our necks, some saintly leaners.

PAX POETICA

The earth needs peace more than it needs the moon,
that beauty without which the oceans lose their intellect.
Peace in bombed gardens where butterflies swoon
into the sun, living one day and dying in the shelling
of that night, where joyous rat and knife inspect
the numerous wares the dead are selling.
The earth needs peace more than it needs the moon.
Sometimes the dead lie hand in hand: six, seven, eight
after a night of minuses and endless decrease,
they do not serve, or stand or wait,
they unpeople themselves flogged in the sun.
No caesura. No rainbow. No peace.
I pity the poets who think that war will be undone
by poetry, the hate-filled world saved by music. I am one . . .
A little more time and poetry will set things straight.
It took time to find the Golden Fleece.
The useless dead hang in markets of the sun,
alone as pork thighs. Every morning comes and goes
more quickly. I know where wild thyme blows,
that naked beauty steals naked to my arms, then goes
to pay a debt to sorrow. No peace.
In a sometime-sometime land, there will be no joy in killing.
We are meant to hold each other but not for keeping;
we kill—just as the toad cannot keep from leaping.
In the grave there is no work or device
nor knowledge nor wisdom, I read in *Ecclesiastes*.
Still, fishermen lift their nets, hoist death weeping,
throw back death twinkling like a small coin into the profitless seas.
Look, the eternal fish swims away leaping.
Moonless, we still have starlight, the aurora borealis,
fires above the Conqueror Worm and beneath
till the sun runs off with the earth in its teeth.

PAPER SWALLOW

Francisco Goya y Lucientes,
I dedicate this paper swallow to you and fly it
from the balcony of San Antonio de la Florida
past the empty chapels of the four doctors of the church.
My praying hands are fish fins again,
one eye a lump of tar, the other hard blood,
my flapping lids sewed down to my cheekbones.
Time, the invisible snake, keeps its head
and fangs deep in the vagina of space.
Reason blinded me, banished me.
I fight the liar in me, selective desire,
my calling nightmares "dreamless sleep."
Blind, *coño*, I made a musical watch,
the image of Don Quixote points the hours,
Sancho the minute hand. I hear the right time
when I listen to my watch play church bells.
Mystery this, mystery that.
I have another watch—wolves howling and dogs barking.
Now the invisible snake swims in the Ebro.
I look out of my window to see time
as if it were not in my mouth
and all my other two-timing orifices.
Don Francisco, I swear at the feet of the dead who maim me
and the living who heal me that the least sound,
a page turning, whips me. I owe my blindness,
this paper swallow, to you, because I lived
most of my life, a *marrano*, in your deaf house.
I pull open one of my eyes like the jaws of a beast.

En Zaragoza à mediados del siglo pasado, me
tieron à un alguacil llamado Lampiños, en el cuer
no de un Rocin muerto, y lo cosieron; toda la noche

FANTASY ON A GOYA DRAWING

Father Goya told me
after the puppets were cut to pieces
you, Franciscan or Jew,
began the year in an ungodly place,
your head collared, protruding
from dead Rocinante's asshole,
the horse's belly lanced open
then laced with cord like a boot.
A commoner, you wrestled
through the stench, through the offal and bowels—
barking dogs around your gray head.

A week before, you did not celebrate
Christ's birthday as your own, as a Russian poet did.
You did not finish your book of unhappy deaths
as Cervantes finished his sacred, funny book,
the master, five years an Algerian slave,
his left arm sacrificed at Lepanto.

Mi papá Goya told me, under the arch
of a bridge not traveled, it was you
who killed the knight's horse
and crawled in, worked your head out
of a stained-ass window. You died living,
these your last words:
I've seen my face and a cloud reflected in a well
but only the sun and moon reflect in a puddle of blood.

SONG OF BARBED WIRE

I've heard the red deer of Eastern Europe
climb with their fawns up rocky hills
to graze on poor patches of grass
rather than go down to green valleys
that once were cut off by barbed wire,
'round national borders and death camps.
They respect, fear, remember
the razor wire no longer there.

I graze on fables:
thou-shalt-nots passed on by deer-talk,
that has the sound of our long wet kisses—
buck to doe to fawn, nose to nose. I hear
commandments sent by antlers scraping trees,
received like the color of eyes.

Nazi and Stalinist barbed wire words
send me up a hill to graze.
I know my red deer-like progenitors
passed on to me a need to suck,
to be afraid of fire.
When I try to kiss my way into green valleys
I am afraid to move beyond the human,
I am not naked, wrapped in barbed razor wire.
There is an original blessing.

DEATH IS A DREAM

Death is a dream. Time,
perhaps the illegitimate sister of silence,
mother of space, is seldom dealt with
as a living thing, male or female,
male and female. Time "worships language,"
does not kneel but is a passionate lover
with respect and disrespect
for what is or ever was.
Again, time lives! "Again" is a word
that tries to cage time in
as does the phrase "ever was,"
but the cage is just a grammatical mirror,
without a right or wrong.

I have a lover's quarrel with the followers
of life is a dream. Time
sits at table with a musical family,
sitting and reading from left to right:
free verse, iamb, spondee, Alexandrian, trimeter,
inflected and uninflected languages,
dear cousins, ancient aunts and uncles.

In a dark repertory theater death is a dream.
Time stands in the pit. She is also an actor.
Like the universe, the theater is empty and a full house.
The play's *The End of Everything*, a light-year's farce.
The action: Rights and Wrongs, each plays the other,
changes costume on stage. Then speechless tragedy:
time measures space inch by inch—
the pity is, in the end she turns back,
unmeasures herself and every other thing.
Death is a dream without measure, no light-years,
no days, no meters, no milestones,

no paces, no walls or fences,
no pints or half-pints, no pounds, no ounces,
no cubits, no handbreadths.

*

Mozart's music prolongs my life,
but his *Requiem* could not prolong his.
I stand on a soapbox in Washington Square,
flying the stars and stripes.
I speak to dog walkers, the homeless,
any passerby:
if death is a dream, it is something else,
without a face, without heaven or hell.
Death is not eternal, will dream and die.
The question is, just before death dies
is there a kind of waking up,
a slapstick *Liebestod*?
Summer dresses as winter,
night and day fall in love,
die in each other's arms.
I am proud time lets me stand here, sit at table
from time to time, so to speak, with the family.
We are communal, like the Jews at the Last Supper.
I had a dream I saw a giant silver sea bass
swimming in sky as if it were ocean.

56,000-YEAR POEM

This morning I'm part me, part anything.
In my notebook I uselessly draw
a leaf, a rat that loves a cat, Fatima's hand.
After anywhere, any place, secondhand,
I set down words on blue lines, like pigeons
flying through the open doors of the British Museum,
or crows on a fence.
I remember . . . a Renaissance painting,
three astrologers, I believe the Magi,
at rest in the desert their faces look inward,
sextant, hourglass, charts beside them—
the intelligence of clouds in the morning sky.
They cross the painted desert without words.
Beyond the reach of their prayers,
they find a Child stabled with His mother,
linger . . . witness the circumcision,
then journey homeward in the dead of winter.
I gnaw a bone of Spanish poetry.
A thousand years of illumination and wars,
the cow becomes a symbol of Christianity,
the donkey is the Jews. In my España,
protected by Maria and Guardia Civil,
at Easter they slaughter a donkey to please the Child.
Reader, come a little closer, have a whiskey.
Before the stars were named, before there was prayer,
some 55,000 years ago when there were
perhaps 10,000 worldly Homo sapiens,
the DNA in my spit shows
my ancestors hunted in what is now Iberia.
Darling, hairy great-grandfather
to the hundredth power, I blow you a kiss.
I point to your nose and my nose and smile.
I point to the sun and say, *the sun, el sol.*
I point to the moon and say, *the moon, la luna.*

A democrat, I look the other way.
I see a thousand years of grandchildren.
My skull blows them a kiss. Margaret
kisses back (I hope my mother's name is still useful).
I hope she's heard of Hamlet, speaks some English.
I say to my distant granddaughter, *Jew,*
tell me what you know about the stars.
A penny for your thoughts.

SEEMS

It doesn't take one day for water
to turn into three feet of ice.
— Chinese Proverb

Changing right to wrong takes time
or never happens. Changing wrong to right
takes longer or never happens. Life to death,
death to life is no walk in the countryside.
Under three feet of ice, an old brook flows
into an ice and snow silenced river
that empties into the understanding ocean.
Who can say, "Seems, seems, I know not seems"—
words never spoken by the Prince of Peace?
All water has a face. Oceans welcome,
do not devour rivers and brooks.
In winter, rivers and brooks
become oceans' beards and eyebrows.
Old to young happens—an old North wind
becomes a summer breeze.

A MISFORTUNE

To idle without direction is best,
forget north, east, south and west.
It's up and down, out and in,
no room at the inn, and, and
I love a Bernini fountain.
My mother still takes my hand,
leads me in and out of my mind.
My footprints are all I leave behind.
Any time of the night or day
waves may wash them away.
The truth: it's better to be a whale
than a snail,
better to be a bard
than a postcard.
I'd rather be this than that,
I'd rather be a shoe than a hat,
I'll take a chance
that sometime I'll dance,
Lord, sitting on the fence
is better than pretense
but there's a lot to be said for nonsense.

TWO ARIAS

In an empty house I'm trying to sing a high F,
you've heard my baritone and bass,
tonight I'm Coloratura, I'm the Queen of the Night
in *The Magic Flute*,
from a mountaintop I reach out my arms,
open my wings, lift a clawed foot and sing:
"O do not tremble, my dear son,"
it is the penis and vagina that hear confession,
nipples are saints, the orgasm gives absolution.

Moonlight is not beyond my authority.
Still, there is a king who mounts my darkness
with lion head and eagle-claw feet—my nation.
After, later,
a certain sadness in my haunches I call dawn,
I return to my night owls, my nest of dry grass and time.
There, there. Everything comes home.

*

Morning, I'm a Hudson Valley baritone.
I live a mile from where, age three, I saw
my first field of wild flowers. I swooned
while my father fixed a flat tire.
Yesterday, twenty-first of June,
I drove through the woods to a concert hall,
roadside wild flowers tuned up, improvised.
I half-forgot music did not come out of
a phonograph, musicians have faces . . .
In good time, the wind blows from all directions.
I tried to live in a house with beauty
constant as gravity.
I tell myself,
you're living in a child's tree house.
I caught myself saying if I die, rather than when.
I pretended death was a supernumerary,

so I found myself weeping over little things
after I saw friends I love had little strokes.
I watched them grow thin
with occasional trouble speaking—
the thinking *prima ballerina*
has trouble going up and down the stairs.

*

Enough! There's something between gravel and semen,
between seamen and seeing men. Fantastical
sons and daughters, now that I've confused you—
I remind you, when they boiled a kid in its mother's milk,
a tribe said, "Stop!" and "Stop!" when they killed the firstborn.
In time of war, all four-year-olds ask,
"Why do they want to kill me?"
I did not tell you I fell down
ancient cobblestone steps in Jerusalem,
broke my wrist that quickly turned blue,
I wandered the streets and found cool waters,
the well of Lady Miriam (Mary) . . .
Pope John Paul flew overhead in a helicopter.
I was simply trying to make a name for myself,
following the ancient, popular belief
that each person is represented by a star
which appears at birth. Firmament of parliamentarians,
I simply want to be worthy of such an honor
when I sing, buried alone in my tomb,
man in two persons, son and holy ghost.

REVENGE COMEDY

Running out of time,
I can keep time with my foot,
with or without a shoe.
Truth is, time keeps me.
When I was seven, my mother gave me
a Mickey Mouse watch I hated.
I purposely overwound it.

China has one time zone.
When it is 5 am in Shanghai
and the sun is rising, it is 5 am in West China,
where it is the middle of the night.
My time differs from street to street,
from one side of the room to the other.

So much happened that is always.
So much never happened that is always,
centuries when truth was painted
as the daughter of time.
Hard to believe God pays attention
to what time it is anywhere.
Running out of time,
years, degrees, minutes are dirty little words.

When I was a child I slept as a child,
the sun used to wake me and my mother.
We had intimate conversations while my father slept.
He awoke and lived with nightmares in his eyes,
perplexed, enlightened, without a Guide—
son and assassin, a boy, I was his disciple.
He and I fished with copper line, a gut leader
and a spoon for landlocked salmon.
He caught one beauty. It was, he said,
the happiest moment of his life.

My father was whipped by time
and he whipped back. I was in the middle.
What was knifing him, cutting out the flesh
under his shell I never understood.

Now I wake at dawn, the sun mothers me.
My father sees to it and I say *okay*,
every day is a school day.
Until I was 50, I never wore a watch,
then like Antonio Machado, I set my watch back
24 hours. My sundial never tells lies
when the sun is down.

BURIAL OF THE GRAVEDIGGER'S DAUGHTER

I'll take her to the hill
Near the olive tree.
Can I do it in the daylight?
I'm afraid what I shall see.

Not all the graves I've dug,
Dry and wide and deep,
Can hold the sweetness
Of my daughter not asleep.

In our village someone
Must dig the graves for all,
Her death has just begun
Under her prayer shawl.

My shovel is my cross.
My shovel cannot bless.
My child, I must soil
Your white lace dress.

WHAT

My first dream came with a gift of *What?*
the infant's first wordless question.
I stand before you a sleepwalker
rubbing out, out the damned spots of yesteryear.
A saint or Zadig invented the words:
"¿qué causa?" *"what?"* so we might ask honest questions.
In a dream of curiosity, I ask—what,
how, who, which, where, why?
The dream of curiosity stages matters out of the question:
dramas about the living and the dead,
where each often plays the other. A little rouge,
a little powder, a change of wigs, who knows what's what?
Night changes to day, and day to night.
You think it's all sun and moon, not trickery?
True I hold the portfolio *chargé d'affaires* of my life,
but I am a corrupt official, easily bribed
by a tree into saying "beauty is the answer."
I sell visas to Anchorwhat and Paradise.
                              *
What is an atheist on the temple mount, and way of the cross.
What says "Rome's Wolf is younger than Manhattan's Mastodon."
Rivers of what, what, what, what,
run into the ocean, flood two thirds of the world,
"The poet is the instrument of language,
not the other way around."
Flocks of where, how, which, who, why—fill the sky,
while over Latin American jungles voiceless *Stringbirds*
sound cello-like purple-feathered love calls with their wings—
now stringed instruments—a dark paradoxical gift,
like John Milton's gift of inner sight after his loss of outer sight.
                              *
There is no proof that reality simply is what is.
What—does not enter the past but is entered by it.
What—protects the truth by offering itself
as prey to the raptor fact.

The *Stringbird* is never caged,
as gods are caged in houses of worship.
Sometimes I hear its wings calling in the woods.
What . . . happens . . . is never quite comprehended.
What is a tree whose roots are a bear's heart;
the blood of *What* flows in mountain streams and rivers,
past spines of ocean life.
Because Proverbs says,
"The leech has two daughters—
Give and Give! . . . and the fire never says enough"—
I remember Kunitz put in a garden for Cal Lowell
and Caroline, in Ireland. When Stanley returned
in June, he found only wildflowers in rubble.
Still, walking with them across their hillside,
hell and love glances in their eyes,
there was reason to hope because of love,
laughter and nightingales, the lovers might find
the golden bough that once allowed a Roman
to pass safely through the underworld—
but dreadful, unwanted guests were coming.
What's to do? Turn the key, it may unlock or lock the door.

                              *

Now death is in fashion but life's not out of style,
whatever the hemline, glove or cuff.
I don't see proof death's worthwhile.
It never says *enough*.
I spit in death's ocean.
Death is time away
from here, from everywhere,
today is here,
anterior.
Life and death are hand and glove:
life's the hand, death's the glove.
What caresses my face with love
smacks it with an empty glove,
heavy as the ocean.

WHY

I know my love of "whys?" is a faithless sin.
I am a worm. You, Lord, are my Robin.
I think the Holy Spirit is a Crow, a Dove, any bird.
Born beyond redemption, I will never repent,
I curl around the serpent,
temptation to temptation, disobedient.
I never swallowed that You made the firmament, Your Word
that in the beginning was the Word.
I swallow my foolish questions—many "whys?"
I pick from between my teeth the letter "y."
I am not wise. Now I am absurd.

Since there is no place in heaven for curiosity
or anyone with my beliefs,
I will take in the long haul earthly simplicity—
I will sleep with Mother Nature, my weak spot,
perhaps dreaming of questions, not in a Greek pot
but in the dirt among the leaves
parked under an apple tree to rot
in a place less pagan than hallowed ground,
never again to fool around in the company
of any living thing that
fools around with me.

One day when I am far from useless,
You will throw me still wriggling in the river of loneliness
while You listen to the praise of gulls, frogs' applause.
"Why? Why? Why?" Your grand answer: "Because."
Old Fool, I have no desire for the afterlife.
I want to stay here with You, to hang around
with Your trees, Your animals and my wife.

Noon

ELEGY FOR OLIVER SACKS

I see pain all over the place, visible as sunshine.
I miss your holding the hand, paw, wing,
standing beside the bed, the den, the hive,
the tunnel of every living thing, doctor.
I wish evil obeyed the law of motion,
that it produced something equal and opposite,
a good breeze for an ill wind.
The crow of truth is eating something dead
on the highway. I can't tell what it was,
but you studied some who came back from the dead,
glorious accidents. Doctor Oliver Sacks,
you simply did not give up on the livingdying.
Because small realizations add up to larger understanding,
75% of Columbia University neurology students say
because of you they chose neurology,
because your empathy, empathy, empathy
taught them not just to study the brain, but the mind.
(You would not be a cardiologist,
because the heart is just a pump.)
You kept the periodic table always in your pocket.
It must have gone up with you in smoke.
I'll place *Oliver* with *Oxygen, Osmium* and *Iridium*
when they let me remake the world.
I try to find you with a microscope, a telescope,
my own two eyes. What I see are books on my desk.
Johann Sebastian Bach does not play musical chairs,
but when I hear the Bach mass, or simply an aire,
I figure you're around.
This afternoon I called at your country house,
nothing around but a fawn in the field,
two spiffy cars in the driveway.
In your well-kept garden, hydrangeas insist
death is an hallucination. What do flowers know?

POLLEN

Still, near Santa Maria in Trastevere,
I saw a painting called *No War* and another, *I Love You,*
by an American woman eating a peach.
I was reborn in old Rome, still remain,
not a marble fragment, not a painting, more like
the Cloaca Maxima, an old, stinking survivor.
Much I had seen I did not recall:
ugliness and beauty, part of me
as music, unfinished work,
the "wrong note" effect,
—what I wanted to forget
and what I wished to remember,
that her lips upon my flesh
said, "You are changing,"
then, "You will never change."
                              *

It is time to uncover the mirrors—
there is no death in the family now.
It is time we wear each other's skin,
fur, scales, feathers, our mouths covered with pollen;
let's sing insect and reptilian songs.
It is time for the carnival of love.
I describe *caprichos,* I narrate beauty I fight for—
its protagonists and antagonists battle within the poem
down in the dirt. Beauty has a tale to tell:
ugliness and terror cut out of skin
and marble—a labor Phidias knew something about.
                              *

I can hear the earthworm's laughter.
Taught to respond to light, cut in half,
each new half responds to light—small stars.
It is time for asterisks, stars that point to human life.
May my liver, kidney and heart severed
recall good times—I was there

and I refuse to get out of here.
My head, severed from my body,
remembers love, perhaps irregular verbs.

*

What happened to pollen? We die without insects and birds.
My friend going blind thinks life is a dream.
I do not know why yet I live to say
I've gone to seed, I'm not sure of my name.
Winds carry pollen to quarreling cornfields,
on the same bush, a rose quarrels with a rose.
This dust produces that mud. I write in mud
with a stick, with my finger or my tooth.
I have found gardeners on their knees,
farm workers bent in the meat-eating sun
no less reverent than nuns. Every man's soul
is an immigrant, enters a new country
without speaking the language, works long hours,
attends night school. Reaching Paradise,
sometimes he longs for the old country, his body.

*

In my ward of ninety-some "casuals"
at St. Albans Naval Hospital
I wrote a love letter for a one-legged marine,
his good leg eaten by rats when he was in the sand under a Jeep.
His last name was Love. On his own,
he dictated the titles of popular songs.
A couple of days later, remaking his bed,
a nurse told me Love died, "surgical shock."
I was entangled, beaten by missing body parts.
Something of my body stays at sea, dismembered.

*

Virgil thought purple was the color of the soul.
Saint Jerome woke from a dream black and blue,
whipped at the judgment seat for reading Latin poets.
My body, bruised, turns purple, is hardly proof
my soul is at home in my body.

I walk knee-deep in a swamp, stinking of heaven.
A two-year-old child says, "How disgusting!"
I am surprised the child knows the word.
Entangled in water lilies and devil's paintbrush,
I'm up to my knees in spirit.
Yes, yes, it pleases me to go into the dark.
These words are body. I try to find something
man-made in the sun that is all over the place.

*

It's no time to die, almost everything's left undone.
Angel of Death, fly off with your black wings
with the first flock of starlings,
out of place among swans with your thick, dirty neck!
I am what others abandoned
that I save. Rather than bury my old Bible,
I leave fragile pages to songbirds
that build, warm their nests and eggs with psalms.

CHRYSALIS

I wonder how my life might twine and untwine
if, like the brontosaurus, I had a second brain
to work my tail from the base of my spine.
Two egos at odds in one bed, two ids
might cause two dreams at once, hybrids,
one sweet, one nightmare: my bottom half in the mouth
of a brontosaurus, long as a railroad train.
She and I do what most would find uncouth.
Same time, I am in bed, young me with a beauty,
dreaming I'm having a birthday party—
I'm spinning, a butterfly breaks free
out of my ear that is a chrysalis,
circles the room, finds an open window, flies south
to join the millions it needs for company.
I wake, it's morning, I read, a good guess,
what I never knew I thought before: poetry—
poets who simply honor the language.
I'm a psalmist with a Miss-directed penis.
Cupid plays at cards with me for kisses.
Venus, who never spanks, spanks me,
whispers to Mars in bed, "It's time you turned the page
on Stanley being Stanley.
I thought he went out of style in the Ice Age."

WINTER

Lunatic solatic,
Mrs., Ms., Mr., Master, Misreader
I sign my name ice-skating
on a frozen pond. I skate
a letter "M," circle an "O,"
gracefully skate "S" twice.
Still when spring comes
my name will be unspelled by the sun,
ripple somewhere, water again, cloudy,
water my houseplants.
I would never skate "David,"
my middle Psalmist name.

LETTER TO A POET

1.

We never made love, but still I believe
we share some intimate knowledge,
something no one else in the world knows—
who were your next door neighbors
when you were a child and teenager,
my parents' friends.
We drove to the Chicago World's Fair
that celebrated "A Century of Progress."
(I sang on experimental television
before television, before you were born.)
I remember the sound of their voices,
Hannah's intimate laundry, her wonderful brassiere
hanging in the bathroom—
I smelled the unimaginable.
I remember decent people, that Max bought
78 turns per minute, "classical"
RCA records every week,
a painting showing a Russian maid scrubbing a cello
hung in his music room,
that Hannah gave me tomato juice,
an extraordinary kindness,
instead of half a grapefruit I hated.
Our remembering might help them out of purgatory
if Dante was right. It helps me out. How about you?

2.

Writing this letter, I was slapped in the face
by a mandrake root.
It slipped my mind
how often you came closer to the truth
by making your reader believe what never happened.
Sometimes, lonely, or never lonely, Fernando Pessoa
accomplished this with five different names.

So your brother was born aged 8 or 10
in the intimacy of your bedroom,
you played, talked and bathed together,
your mother soaped you front and back
in an iron, lion-footed tub.
In those days, the soap was *Ivory*,
99% pure.

I will kidnap your brother,
use him as a sister, so he can help
with a poem about Lilly I can never write.
Still, your brother almost got you killed crossing the street.
You simply had to Stop, Look, and Listen to him first.
He did not cross at corners,
but he read lines to you before you wrote them.
For all I know, your neighbors had lilacs
and wild iris in their garden in Woodmere
that was farther away from the Atlantic than it is now,
but still, you could smell the salt in the air
when the fog came in.

SISTER POEM

My sister was a Unitarian,
she loved life, the God-given gift of the world.
She did not need Paradise to make her a Christian,
thought all religions that promised Paradise
offered a business relationship with a jealous God.
She made a funny face at the mention of early martyrs
who preferred to be fresh meat for lions
to living in the world, likely as slaves,
rather than praying for show to the Gods
Trajan or Emperor Augustus.
Her Lord preferred His followers deny Him
rather than sacrifice their lives,
He wanted the living to live, love strangers,
their neighbors, the Beatitudes.
She certainly thought it wise to hide your Judaism
from the public fires of the Inquisition;
she damned the excommunicators of Spinoza,
believed in doing what you could honorably do
to stay out of cattle cars.

When I was a small child
I thought my sister Lilly
was mysteriously related to water lilies,
daylilies, lilies of the valley.
Imitating her handwriting, I made my first e and l.
I am ashamed, when I was seven, she was four years older,
I wrestled her to the ground to show I was stronger,
proof the state is stronger than language.
Our dog took her side, barked, "get off her."
It was a rare day I did not ask, "Lilly read me a story."
When I stood one foot three inches taller,
she gave me her violin. When all I could play was "Long, Long
Ago,"
she taught me Mozart and Bach,

that all things in the universe showed the hand of God.

Years passed. I thought prosody survives history.
She read Rimbaud to me in French and English,
and Lorca, whose photo I hung next to my bed.
My sister wrote to me, "Please speak at my funeral."
Not long after, I said, "To death there is no consolation . . . ."
I read most of the lines I just wrote.
I insisted the chapel doors and windows were open
to a congregation of birds and insects. Loners
swooped in and out from noon to sunset.
Not a drop of excrement on the mosaic floor.
A hawk dropped a live mouse that prayed to live
on her coffin. She would have liked that.

CODA

My sister Lillian was a Unitarian.
She insisted I not speak at her funeral.
She made necklaces, pressed butterflies.
Her husband invented our famous intercontinental
space rockets, miniaturized atom bombs
so they could be used as tactical weapons.
Her closest friend, who married a Haitian, and Black Americans
were not allowed in his house. She did not protest,
hold her breath, turn blue and faint,
as she did as a child to get what she wanted.
Lillian taught poetry, had four great-grandchildren,
she wanted our mother to have a Unitarian funeral.
Our mother was not a Unitarian.
My sister mailed me my mother's ashes
first class. Later, I collected my dad's, buried both
side by side, Montauk daisies between—
their unmarked rocks not too close.

For a wedding present two years after our wedding,
my sister gave us a folded check, $25 to "buy a tree"
and a rope ladder to keep on the top floor
in case our house caught fire.
I am grateful to the poet who taught me
how to get closer to something like the truth,
which is my understanding,
an unenumerated right, protected
by the 9th Amendment to the Constitution.

A REFRESHMENT

In our new society, all the old religious orders and titles
are ice creams: Rabbis, Priests, Mullahs,
Gurus, Buddhists, Shiites, Sunni, Dominicans,
Franciscans, Capuchins, Carmelites—ice cream,
never before have the kids had such a choice of flavors,
never before have the Ten Commandments
been so cool in summer. I believe
when the holy family rested on their flight to Egypt,
in the desert heat, they had a little mystical lemon or orange ice,
before chocolate and vanilla crossed the unnamed Atlantic.
Let us pray, not for forgiveness, but for our just dessert.

VISITING STAR

I woke at sunrise,
fed my dogs, Honey and Margie—
to the east a wall of books and windows,
a lawn, the trees in my family,
the donkeys and forest behind the hill.
Sunlight showed itself in,
passed the China butterflies on the window
so birds watch out, don't break their necks.
On the back of a green leather chair for guests
facing me in sunlight and shadow, a sunlit Star of David,
two large handspans square.
I call to my wife to see the star
she first thinks I painted on the chair.
Soon she catches on—no falling star.
We searched the room and outside.
How did the star come to be?
Without explanation. None.
The star visited a few minutes, disappeared,
or became invisible. Why?
I wondered if it was *le bel aujourd'hui*
or a holiday some Jews celebrate.
Playing fair, I told myself: watch out for
a crucifix anywhere before which
contrition saves condemned souls—
watch in the forest for portraits of the Virgin,
the wheel of Dharma down the road
that teaches "save all living beings,"
when the moon is full a crescent moon
reflected on a wall or lake.
Watch for flying horses!
I read the news of commandments broken.
Thou shalt not kill.
I write between the lines
Thou shalt not steal

seventy-five years from the life of a child.
Next day, I found my Star of David
was a glass sun and star reflection of
a tinkling shimmering wind chime made in China.
A pleasing, godless today fills my study.

THE CARPENTER

i.

That boy who made the earth and stars had to learn
to make a chair in his earthly father's shop.
Above in the hip and valley of the rafters
held fast by joints his father cut
there is a haloed dove with outspread wings.
To the boy the workbench with its candle seemed
an altar, the tools offerings. That boy
could speak the languages of Babel. "Bevel"
he learned refers to an angle not cut-square.
At first he heard *angle* as *angel*.
He heard "take the angel directly from the work,
the only precaution being that
both stock and tongue be held tight to the work . . .
The boat builder bevel is most venerable."
The person of the dove shook head and halo
from side to side, vented a white splash
that smelled of water lilies on the boy's cheek and shoulder.
Then a whispering Third Voice filled the workshop.
"It's time to make an Ark to hold the Torah.
Learn the try-square, hammers and nails, veneers."
It was Friday afternoon, just before sunset.
The boy went to the steps of the synagogue.
He told the gathered doctors: "God commanded Moses,
'Build the Tabernacle of acacia wood, gave
exact dimensions, in cubits and hand-breadths.'"
The boy's mother called him:
"Carpenter, Yeshua, come to supper."

ii.

At night the boy returned to the workshop.
He shoplifted himself from the Holy Books
and the forbidden Greeks. He grinned:
a god deceived his wife Hera, who threw snakes
in the crib of the misbegotten babe Heracles

who strangled them. The boy giggled at the great
deeds of Heracles and his labors, that he only
became immortal after being burned alive.
In the sawdust Yeshua smelled forests,
he could tell cedar from pine, from oak, eucalyptus.
He saw the valleys of death and life.

With his father's tools he cut dovetails,
male and female angles, lapped dovetails
that show on one face but are concealed
on the other with lap and lip, secret dovetails
where the joint is entirely hidden.
The boy had spent a sad afternoon with the people.
Why were so many ears, eyes, and hearts deaf to him?
He told them it was written in Chronicles:
"The house of the Lord is filled with a cloud . . .
the Lord said he would dwell in the dark cloud."
The boy had never heard the word *kristianos.*
He saw his face in a pail of water, a cloudless sky.
He heard a cock crow, drunken Roman soldiers
laughing in the street. It was morning.

DRINKING SONG

It makes no difference if friends and family
are ashes thrown into the ocean,
or flesh and bone buried in holy ground,
their names barely attached. Awake or dreaming,
I see them as they were young and old, living
some other life, never in rags, never dressed to kill.
I don't trivialize the dead,
put them in a playground on a seesaw
or climbing a maze.
I remember their voices like
warped 78-turns-a-minute records—
stumbling voices.
I drink "to life!"
drinking a little from each glass "to death!"
because everything that is has death in it.

Look, the dead are school teachers,
they remember our names,
they grade us by number or letter;
they teach, "Fools, you don't know
how much more the half is than the whole."
The dead are trees. We are cut from their lumber.
And the dead are stars that no longer exist,
so far away their light is just reaching us.
Death is a doormat that says Welcome,
a good night's sleep, a handful of stones.
To a little death before I die! *La petite mort!*
Because the breast taken from the child
is a first death, I drink "to a nursing mother!"
and a first death the Christ child must have suffered.
I do not sing of phantom paradise
but offer a little phantom pleasure,

justice delayed—a hacksaw
for the phantom pain Ahab felt
after his severed leg was replaced by whalebone.
A hundred years! Bottoms up!

LETTER TO DANNIE ABSE

Doctor, I could have asked but never did
why weren't you a teacher or a drunk?
I could have asked you about your caring for
the wounded Nazi Luftwaffe Offizier.
Poet, you wrote love poems in your old age.

Jew, not by chance your son's name is David—
honors the psalmist and Saint Davy.
We celebrate spring at the same table,
suffer the same wintry fever.
In a pub called The Good Life the landlord serves
with every glass of joy a tankard of sorrow.

Husband, I never asked about your marriage,
it would have been asking why there's morning
and evening. Welshman, we first met at Hay-on-Wye.
You said, "The Welsh are a defeated people,
they identify with victims."

I send you brotherly love.
You don't need a brother, but I do.

A KID IN A "RECORD CROWD"

It was a little like what I feel now
walking around the City
remembering the old buildings
where new construction is going on.
It is a little like getting older.
I remember my fear as a child
being pushed by tens of thousands
at Yankee Stadium Memorial Day,
afraid of falling, being pushed over and squashed,
not being able to find my father,
some shouting, some singing in victory,
then packed in the subway back to Queens,
lucky American, far from the cattle cars,
the ovens, franks and mustard on my lips.

SPRING POEM FOR CHRISTOPHER MIDDLETON

1.

It's Monday, I phone. You answer, coughing, whisper:
"My doctor says two days and I'll be dead.
I'm afraid of falling off the bed into my grave"—
that means to me a couple of twists
of the screwdriver or monkey wrench
and you'll become unintelligibly human.

My mind is a waterbug. I write chatter . . . Life and death
are unhappy lovers. Is there a marriage,
is life the bride or bridegroom?
How many times can a father give the bride away?
Do life and death create a nation, like the marriage
of Fernando and Isabella—death Aragon, life Castille?
No reason, there are always the disasters of war.
Dear friend, *death is part of life* doesn't work for me.
I prefer *the end is part of the play.*

Actors and gentles, there is a change of decorum,
a grave eccentricity performed in an O.
It is winter. The sun is like a slum.
Without a bone, your frightened dog
already shakes at the stench
of your death. Without philosophy,
he licks your face and feet
in hope of resurrection. A winter passion,
your life is disrobed before the public,
you are denied another Sabbath for no reason.
It should displease the Lord—this passing on
we know nothing of. I do not say the beads.
I pray there is a God of love who reads.

2.

Ten winter days have passed. I phone.
I'm certain telephones don't ring

in Heaven, Hell, or Purgatory.
You answer, "Hello . . . the crisis is over.
Now my neurosurgeon says I have some time,
a day or two, a month, you never know,
. . . my handwriting is very shaky." Hurrah,
it's March, there's reason to hope you'll see
Texas summer corn, roses in Westminster in April.
Soon, I'll send you this poem for a laugh.
Metaphor and reality have not come together.
I invented your good dog,
a gift to keep you from loneliness.

3.

(Is it better that the dead are buried
or go up in flames in clean clothes?)
In your poetry, you write under oath
not to treat as a thing of the mind
things that are of the mind only.
After their jealousy and lovemaking,
beauty and truth marry at the local registry,
take the vows of all religions,
or just have a long affair. I toast "To life!"
Christopher, brush away death by failing heart;
better Zeus, on a distant evening,
when you are surrounded by love,
ground you with a thunderbolt.
A hundred years! . . . Christopher died yesterday.
Metaphor and reality have come together.

JERUSALEM WEDDING

to David Amichai

The dead poet,
father of the bridegroom,
invited the guests by printed invitation
that was placed, in love, by the son and his bride
on the father's grave the morning before the wedding.
I brought colored stones from Long Island.
The happy ghost of the father
attended the wedding, cried out
like Hamlet's father, "Remember me"—
but instead of asking for vengeance like the murdered king,
the five hundred guests
heard the poet's voice among the blessings.

SPOON

To Jane Freilicher

I was scribbling, "Goya painted with a spoon" when I heard Jane died,
I knew enough not to be surprised but I was.
Saturn gnawed his sons without a place setting.
I never got over the Berliner Ensemble's *Mother Courage,*
when she screamed, "I bargained too much"
(for her murdered son's life).
The actress wore a wooden spoon as a brooch.
Tongue tied, I kept "spoon." It is not a decoration.

In a daydream, I avow without reason
Jane Freilicher painted with a spoon—
potato fields, Watermill, pink mallow,
her early painting Leda and the Swan,
nothing we see—and with everyday palette knife,
brushes or late-invented forks,
useful for painting hydrangeas and eyelashes,
proof painters work like translators,
English into Chinese, everyday English words:
daylight, flower, woman, moon
are different in Ming, Tang, and Song:
different characters, different calligraphy.

She painted with a silver or oak spoon
ponds or stars, bones were oblongs and triangles,
nothing we see. She painted light,
mastered it, was mastered by it,
moved the world by "tipping the horizon up."
My honor: from a distance she painted
my house on Mecox Bay, my Corinthian columns,
my garden and sandspit
along the old Montauk road, my beach plums,
fireweed, roses of Sharon, day lilies, love
mostly washed out by hurricanes.

I say "my," but I never thought
I had good title to anything or anyone.
Then there was her battle of dreams
versus hallucinations, battles without a heroine,
the colors of fate, breathtaking, inevitable colors.
She would never forgive
those who think painting and poetry
function about the same as wallpaper.
Sometimes she painted small pictures
easily hidden from search parties
as Goya did, hiding from the Inquisition
because he painted nudes,
Protestant fields, Catholic fields, Jewish fields, like her.
She suffered the heresies of the Hamptons
where most painters of roses, whatever their personal faith,
and all poets, as such, are polytheists.
Again, she studied the many moods
of the sun and ocean through a window.
I studied Chinese at the Beijing railroad station,
eight thousand years or so of Chinese faces.
Every Chinese knows five cardinal relations:
ruler subject, father son, husband wife,
elder and younger brother, friend and friend.
I share the undiscovered country that begins
at the Southampton railroad station,
the beauty and color of Long Island
in the mist . . .
I sit shivering with the old-timers, gossiping
about the steam engines
from Penn Station to Montauk
100 years ago, faster than now, the island's
chestnut trees harvested for firewood,
the cemeteries, a little away from the railroad tracks,
cornflowers and poppies,

off Routes 114, 27, Springs Fireplace Road,
overloaded with painters,
I kiss my Yoricks. I knew them well.

*

Jane, we watched the pagan ocean
that holds bottom feeders
that thrive in fiery volcanic waters,
and birds that never come ashore.
Often we met at the beach, half-naked,
barefooted or in sandals.
We knew where fifty-six swans nested,
that Long Island painters seldom painted
the night, or character. We chased whales,
saved wounded seals.
After an Atlantic hurricane, in our trees
with salt-drenched curled leaves,
thousands of fooled monarch butterflies gathered
on their way to Mexico.
We embraced 65 years ago—
not a long time for a redwood,
a long time for an oak or an elm.

The day you died,
I wish *ex cathedra*, Pope Francis said, "dogs go to heaven,"
so fawns, foxes, and rabbits aren't left behind.
You understood shadow.
At first look, you never painted sorrow.
You picked up stemless flowers, homeless
like beauties standing on street corners,
gorgeous juvenile delinquents.

POEM OF THE PILLOW

1.

I believe love saves the world from heartbreak.
I'm learning to play the concrete harp.
I'm tired of traveling by my name only.
It is time for tears held back and washed away,
days that mean "yes" and nights that mean "no."
Look, the moon never disconsonant,
lies down, sleeps under a bridge.
Still, when I am asleep, at breakfast,
reading a book or walking across a street
thinking I am far from eternal sloth, a God
for his comfort will push me out of sight.

2.

Veiled Fortuna, because knowing who you were,
I made you laugh and gave you pleasure
when you opened your mortal dressing gown,
give me proof that has no text—life everlasting
is to be loved at the moment of death.
Now my thoughts drift to a Japanese woodcut:
a sacred lake, a child's sailboat, the shore
a woman's open thighs, her gorgeous vulva.
At a distance, a flowering plum mouths a tall pine.
Deep within her leaves there is a poem of the pillow.

HAPPY 87TH BIRTHDAY

to Willis

Years are numbered, as if they were the same,
some leap, some scythe-carriers are lame.
You know the date you were born
but nothing that happened for a couple of years
when you started remembering—an acorn—
you became an oak—forgot miracles. Your fears:
falling and fires—you knew love
before you knew the word. Mother's milk
holds many secrets, some cruelty and milk
of human kindness. What are you made *of*?
What are you *from*? Words different as silk
from linen and wool. I send a kiss and love
by email, modern love, not Adam's stuff.
We are *of* clay, and *from* porcelain.
Death is a volcano, we must not fall in.
From now on every day is Christmas.
Amor pesetas y tiempo para gastarlas.
I believe in original blessing, not original sin.

LETTER TO A FISH

I caught you and loved you when I was three
before I knew the word death—
it was a little like picking an apple off a tree.
At 20, I caught you, kissed you, and let you go.
You swam off like quicksilver.
The Greeks thought a little like that the world began.
You splashed and smacked your tail, made a rainbow.
Funny what drowns a man gives you breath.
Where are you, in ocean, brook, or river?
You suffer danger, but cannot weep as I can.
They say one God made the Holy books.
I offer Him my flies, spinners, feathered hooks—
not prayers. I swim with you in the great beneath,
to the headwaters of the unknown, in the hours
before dawn when fish and men exchange metaphors.

THE FISH ANSWERS

My school saw the Red Sea parted—you speak
to me only in North Sea everyday English
or Cape Cod American—why not ancient Greek?
I speak the languages of all those who fish
for me, and I speak Frog, Turtle, and Crocodile.
The waters are calm, come swim with me a while.
Look, the little fish will inherit the earth
and seas. Fish as you would have others fish for you!
Swallow the hook of happiness and mirth,
baited with poetry, the miraculous rescue.
I read drowned books. The Lord is many.
I heard this gossip in Long Island Sound:
three days before he died, one Ezra Pound
told a friend, "Go with God, if you can stand the company."

SNOWBOUND

I can't walk far or drive away.
I'm here, deep in snow.
Still, I can follow the heart
better than on a sunny day.
Snow, rain, and stars have a language
I've heard them speak,
beyond understanding, a language
they've written on earth from the start,
older than Chinese, Hebrew, or Greek,
indifferent to human weather
or where we gather.
I'm snowbound,
not sure if snow is prose—
ice, poetry—
or the other way around.
The winds live timelessly,
the weather comes and goes.
I adore a snow goddess
in her white drifting dress.

ROPE

If I held a rope in my mouth,
you pulled and I pulled,
I would not enjoy it for long—proof
I'm not your dog.
If you pull my tongue with your teeth
I might find it fun a little while—
proof of strength, tug of war.
Then there is a tug of peace,
a long kiss when we pull together against death
that is the opposite of everything.

SIGNIFIER

Ill-mannered, it might have been a death,
a sudden inhaling and exhaling, something before,
after, or during speech, not a word,
nothing to do with discourse, not a breath,
yet a blessing to a drowning man. A blessing
to the infant after the mother's breast.
I sing not of the wrath of Achilles
but of thin air and effect, a kind of aftertaste
that may be veiled, suppressed with a finger
to the lips, a sign of a certain changing, as water changes,
not tide, not pulse, not from the heart at all,
but a sign of life, a mumble within the body,
invisible, unintelligible, comic perhaps,
a poor, strutting player, signifying something,
unpersuasive, possessing tone, pitch, distantly
related to the yawn, the ah, without ecstasy,
no more important than this pounding
base bass voice.

PACEMAKER

1.

I take no pleasure in saying
I'm not a pacemaker or stallion on a dead run,
part of my history,
without a halter. When I was 23,
I pulled a wagon
from 10 Quai Voltaire,
desk, books, and pretty dresses,
to 13 bis Rue de Tournon.
I stir the summer dust:
a lady said she heard my heart
beating across the room.

2.

Years past, sometimes on a dead run, a dead walk,
I fainted like a Victorian girl.
Now, I wear a pacemaker connected to my heart
by reins and wires that protect my heart from beating
37 irregular beats per minute.
Yesterday, tomorrow, today
my heart is fixed.
My pulse, andante, seldom allegro,
continues with its versification.
Lady with the sweet countenance of a soup spoon,
lead my heart through enjambment, spondaic,
iambic syllable count, in and out of schemes,
to the last syllable of my heartbeat,
awake and asleep in praise.

GRANITE

When I was five I loved climbing a granite boulder,
almost a mountain. I kissed it and grown-ups laughed.
Standing on top, almost naked,
I could see to the other side of the lake,
the lily pads and forests. I felt immortal.
My father spent that summer
in Venice and Vienna.

I remember an August storm, I was in the clouds
surrounded by my thunder, rain, and lightning.
I loved them, but I lost my footing,
slipped down, tore the skin off my back.
I still have the scars and the granite dust
in the scars under my shirt.

Today I returned to the lake,
paddled along the shore. I had to trespass,
but I found my granite boulder.
I kissed her again.
Who else can I kiss that I kissed when I was five?
I kissed the flowers in her mortal crevices.
Does she dream she is a dancer, alabaster?
I held my boulder close as I could.

Sunset—Night

I SIT MUCH WITH MY DOG

When I write at home my dog is not far off.
When I read poems aloud, mine or others',
I sometimes scare him. If I had a house I would
let him outside on such occasions,
but in my apartment, he's stuck with me.
My dog, alas, is stuck with poetry,
as I am. I read a poem
that is a hearty call in the night.
My dog becomes morbid. I think
I'm getting an inch closer to God.
My dog thinks I'm angry at him,
doesn't know what to do, or what to stop doing.
He just looks up and can't help it.
I call him over in the middle of my reading,
reassure him that I am still my smelly self,
but there is something changed between us.
As soon as I begin to read out loud, he thinks
something's wrong, or something's about to happen.
Sancho, if I knew how, I'd write you a dog poem.
Somehow I know there is something
I can never make up to you,
that sniffing after beauty I terrorize you.

HELL

—thanks to George Herbert's "Heaven"

O who shall show me such suffering?
Echo.   Ring.
You, Echo, immortal clown all men know.
Echo.   No.
Still in the mountains don't you die away?
Echo.   Way.
I wept when the King of Jews came harrowing.
Echo.   Rowing.
Prophets of slavery and war I applaud:
Echo.   Laud.
those who celebrate Christmas
Echo.   Mass.
by first cutting down a tree
Echo.   Tree.
rather than planting an evergreen.
Echo.   Green.
To celebrate peace on earth
Echo.   Earth.
I take gifts to the rich then sing
Echo.   Sing.
Come all ye faithful . . .
Echo.   Full.
Tell me what is the supreme horror?
Echo.   Or.
The truth, God the clown created us
Echo.   Us.
for laughter not for praise that he abhors.
Echo.   Whores.

The business of the soul is live for profits.
Echo.   Fits.
Onward indifference! Starvation! Fiery justice!
Echo.   Ice.
A touch of kindness makes the devil fart.
Echo.   Art.

CAUTIONARY TALE

I said we don't know what your 63-year-old
schizophrenic son may do with his history:
he made fires in hospitals, called 911 "for company,"
cut himself, jumped out windows,
leaving behind feces in dresser drawers,
in and under the bed. Dreadful et ceteras.
Mostly silent, he talks sweetly to dogs
he calls by dead dogs' names.
You said, "It snowed a foot yesterday
doesn't mean it will snow today."
I didn't say, "No snowfall ever played the piano."
We both know John Little played Bach on the piano,
went home on a weekend, killed his mother and father.
I remember, for no reason, when I was sweet and 20,
when the snow was deep in the city,
the streets at night almost empty,
I climbed the snowdrifts and sang arias from *The Magic Flute*,
recited lines from *Hamlet* and Yeats, Hart Crane.
Truth is, a good blizzard with drifts two meters high
gave me the opportunity to speak to a full house.
Snow blind, I wish I could take your hand,
I insist I can find the way through the blizzard of madness
down the road to the mailbox.
I will not crawl into a schizophrenic cage
with you and His Majesty.

SONG OF JERUSALEM NEIGHBORS

What proves I am not your enemy?
Our dogs fight. Your music gets in my hair,
you think my voice has a bad odor.
Your laundry hanging or drying on the ground
looks like mine. My prayer shawl is invisible,
I'll be buried in it—your Islamic robe
covers you with clouds. I look at your wife's red bra,
you look at my wife's black lace panties.
We each have handkerchiefs for weeping.
We are suspicious of cans and pots
of geraniums, blue and pink anemones.
Who brought 613 laws to the Sinai,
red ants? I don't gloat when it rains
only on my side of the barbed wire.
When I broke my arm I thought
something in your eye twisted it.
I thought your baby was beautiful—
I don't want her to kill anybody.
You say, "Unless I get to you first. This is
middle-class donkey shit."
Neither of us curses in his own language.
Jehovah and Allah are lollipops
for the motherfuckers who find war
sexually attractive.

AFFLUENT READER

to Oliver Sacks

I borrowed a basket of grapes, I paid back in wine.
I borrowed a pail of milk, I paid my debt in Gorgonzola.
I borrowed my life, I tried to pay back in poetry:
an autumn breeze blew my poems away—
dry leaves, *insufficient funds.*
I'm still in debt for my life.
God is a lender, has a pawnshop,
hangs out the sun and moon, his sign.
He is in business 'round the clock:
I receive summons after summons
often in the middle of the night
demanding payment dollar for dollar,
for every year every minute and heartbeat
for every penny of my life—my death
plus interest: usurious eternity.

THE AMERICAN DREAM

Stuck in my suburban flesh and marrow,
the static news of mass murder, Blitz, burning ghettos . . .
At fifteen I made love in deep snow
in moonlight. I did not go all the way,
betraying myself, Claire McGill and poetry.
She was seventeen, half naked, used her tongue.
It would have been a miracle, my first time,
not hers. Is she alive, does she remember?
I raved about Lorca and Rimbaud.
It would not be long. I learned to kill before I learned to rhyme.

I limp into her chamber, a goat with old horns.
I think she will recognize my ghost, young,
able to make her laugh, among the coterie
of ghosts she did it with, while I cavorted
with Maria de las Nieves, Eros of the snow,
obeyed the commandment Djuna Barnes
gave me when I was 27, waving goodbye
with her walking stick, "Follow the heart, follow the heart!"

My heart led me to illusion, but it didn't lie.
I was manned, boyed, womaned and girled.
I learned to trust trees, blind trees, lonely trees,
forests. I rely on their wisdom—as I will after I die.
Today a child asked me, "How much love is in a kiss?"
I said: "I don't know." She said, "The whole world."

NO TEAR IS COMMONPLACE

No tear is commonplace.
The prophet said,
"Woman is the pupil of the eye."
All beauty
comes from God,
butterflies
fly from and to God one by one
and to the forests of Michoacán
where Mexicans nearby make
Jesus Christ
from parrot feathers
and wings of hummingbirds.
You can hold such a God
against your cheek,
then you are as if
under a wing,
a firstling,
warm and comforted.

DECEMBER 8

May these words serve as a crescent moon:
in Barcelona 58 years ago today
I saw on the front page of *La Vanguardia*
beside the main altar of the cathedral
two polished cannons blessed by the Archbishop
in the name of Saint Barbara, patron
of Generalissimo Franco's artillery
on this day set aside to celebrate
the Immaculate Conception.

Today in a Greek gallery off 5th Avenue
I saw Aphrodite blinded by a Christian,
a cross chiseled into her eyes and forehead.
Outside in a hard rain, Christmas season,
no taxis. I was chased by the wind
through the open door of Saint Patrick's Cathedral.
Up since 4, I slept in the false Gothic darkness.
A bell announcing the Holy Spirit woke me
to a mass celebrating the Immaculate Conception.
Can a Jew by chance receive a little touch of absolution—
like a touch of a painter's brush
like a little touch of King Harry
visiting his troops in the night before Agincourt?
I have prayers put in my head
like paper prayers in the cracks of the wailing wall.
The heart has reason, reason does not know.

ELEGY FOR THE POET REETIKA VAZIRANI AND HER CHILD

If life were just, for strangling her two-year-old child
before murdering herself, my dear friend
would be sentenced to life at hard labor:
fifty lines a day before she sleeps
in a bare room with a good library and her son's guitar.
When will she have a change of heart,
when will she take pity on those who love her,
when will the terror she caused her child no longer appear in the
sky?
The sun and moon hang around absolutely without conscience.

NOTICES

Once an Irishman in his coffin
had to be wrapped from foot to chin
in English wool, not Irish linen.
I saw this notice: "Some striped scars on his back,
runaway slave stole himself, calls himself Jack."

MOCKING GODS

Lost in the library of Alexandria, proof
Selene the moon goddess mocked Apollo
her sun god twin, each mocking the other
about mortal offsprings—
off-summers, off-autumns, off-winters.
More than "divine," an inadequate human word
for speaking about gods, all words
are mostly useless. A messenger whispered,
"That's why prayers and sacrifice were invented."
Without Apollo, simple daylight, music
and poetry, nothing on earth lives.
Beautiful beyond belief, Selene spent years
in front of her mirrors, the oceans,
so close to the earth, she said the breathing
of humans and animals sometimes kept her awake.
Crashing a feast of the gods, a mortal boy
in rapture surrendered to Selene,
who gave birth to another moonchild.
Apollo and other gods remembered
Selene had fifty daughters with Endymion.

What fools call "twenty years" passed,
the moonchild, male or female,
had a lover—pity the darling who held close
a celestial body, equally at home
on earth or sky—half a night or day,
especially since that moonchild in turn
might have a child, more mortal now
than half moon, but still mooning,
playing in the park among other children
with everyday faces.

Put the case: Apollo and a mortal beauty
could have twins that brighten the darkest room

or forest, who fight as brothers and sisters
to prove who is father or mother's favorite—
neither so naughty to challenge Apollo at music.
At night, the children would weep for their father,
busy with godly affairs.
The poor mortal mother, mostly in the kitchen
preparing meals, finally insisted on her right
to be Jew, Christian, or Muslim
or better still, she said to the sun god, "all three!"

Today I heard the sun laugh, I swear I heard
happy thunder, thunder without anger or lightning,
and the moon laughing like Sarah
hiding behind a cloud's curtain.

NOW

I am just a has been and a will be.
What *is* right now, that is the question.
My fool says I should learn from today's clouds:
"The verb 'to be' is English lightning—
lightning and thunder are happily married,
their vows are storms. Now, now, Uncle,
the plural is sweet company, fair weather,
then there is the conjugation, we are, they are,
the all or none, till 'everybody' is singular again."
Fool, my fly is open, needs to be buttoned.

I enjoy the soufflé of *la vague* and *le vague*,
the feminine "wave" and masculine "indefinite."
I relish the English Christmas pudding
of nouns made into verbs and verbs into nouns.
Since childhood I've been forested,
lost in the woods of conditional verbs,
lost in the woulds, what should I do
left wandering and wondering
where is the golden fool, the sun?
The forests one summer, inflamed by false gods,
left charcoal barrens that nourish the soil.
The trees will grow another time,
a time for rhyme, and a time to run out of time—
the hours around the clock
like hyenas around a carcass.

TIGHTROPE WALKING

Tightrope walkers know
they must look at the wire a few paces ahead,
never at their feet.
Walking the high wire of poetry
you have to look at your feet,
while you can't help keeping track
of clouds moving carefully,
a lost red-wing blackbird inside the tent
trying to get out,
a poet's son, a French acrobat,
wire behind you, the net below,
a pretty face in the crowd, cash receipts.
All this worthless information
does not make a poem.
It's as hard as selling old underwear
to write a poem about nothing.

SMILES

I argued with a dear friend, a psychiatrist
who didn't think dogs smile and dream.
I told him I thought butterflies, frogs and dogs dream
and smile—that the whole Bronx Zoo is like me,
but I don't think every Greyhound bus,
cheese, beggarman and thief is named Stanley.
I've seen trees smiling, dreaming, kissing and kissed.
I don't think the world is a mirror made by Jesus,
rather sooner or later, like Columbus,
every old sailor sees a mermaid, that Jesus
smiled and dreamed like us, and Judas
had a dog that smiled and dreamed like us.
My good dog Bozo ran wild with my shoes.
Because I sleep and dream old news,
secrets I keep from myself, I smile in deceit,
while my dog smiles, mounts a wolf at my feet.

A METAPHORIC TRAP SPRUNG

Poets, step carefully, your foot, eye, ear, love
may be caught in a metaphoric trap,
like the bear's severed foot.
Crying out or laughing is no use,
the only release is writing it off.
You don't escape fatally wounded,
you can't lick the blood away.
Learning languages helps—take *work*,
whose Chinese character includes a hand.
Too heartbroken to talk?
Every muse has eight sisters.
Where love is
or has been—words,
words spoken while making love
become flesh.

MIND

They come to mind, not of my choosing,
in several languages, women I loved,
the living and the dead, in beds here and there,
in different countries.
I remember waiting in doorways endlessly
when it seemed all love was safely abed.
Truth is, love will never come back to me from "mind"—
in my English, neuter, without gender.

CHRISTMAS 2014

Nothing I say will change anything.
I am dismayed on Christmas day.
There's sickness in my house,
almost a black Christmas.
Deep in a snowdrift, I make myself a snowmother,
the Virgin, put a snow savior in her arms.
One day, He will melt in her arms and she in His,
they will wake up a little unresurrected pond
that will fill with water lilies in spring
if I have anything to say about it,
but I have nothing to say about it.
Bring on the snapping turtles and leeches,
evergreens, bristlecones,
that may live a thousand years.
I trust trees, I have faith in butterflies and poets,
who these days and nights live days and nights.
How can God be a cannibal and a good guy?
A High Mass sings the answers to all questions.
I swear, this spring, I'll learn to look backward
and believe what I see, I will watch
them dance around a maypole, undismayed.

> *Sola una cosa tiene mala el sueño, según he oído decir,*
> *y es que se parece a la muerte, pues de un dormido a un*
> *muerto hay muy poca diferencia.*
> —*Sancho Panza*

It is 2 AM. I need to rest, sleep.
I risk being entertained by the clown of death
at a dream circus, I see half his face—
white and red likeness doesn't frighten me.
I am a lie-down comedian.
It is 2 AM. Among my last thoughts:
my wife's operable cancer . . . Marianne Moore in 1916
wore her red hair in braids . . . I don't want the clown
to wash his face, change into my street clothes.
My wife has a cancerous node.
St. Teresa read books on chivalry.
At a tender age, she and her brother agreed
to run off to the Moors' country, beg their bread
for love of God, to reach heaven beheaded.
At supper, an Avila spring or two before,
St. Teresa answered the first question,
"How is this night different from all other nights?"
It is 2 AM. Joy! Joy! William Carlos Williams
saw more than 2,000 babies pulled through
one way or another into the world. It is 2 AM.
I sat in at his poorly attended funeral
in Rutherford: no poets I recognized,
no words I remember, family, sons, Fanny,
scattered in the pews mostly old pretty ladies.

*

I must have fallen into eternity.
The telephone did not ring
but I was on the phone with Charlie Williams.
He was going to see Dylan Thomas.
I said I'd fly over. We'd go together.
Dylan was alive, no question.

Charlie was in Paris, did not have cancer,
no question. We would just have a good time.

Thank God for pleasant dreams.
It never crossed my mind to talk about God
with Dylan, but when we were coming downtown
in a taxi from the Academy with Carl Sandburg,
64 years ago, Dylan played God
receiving T. S. Eliot in heaven: "Come in.
I've read your *Four Quartets.*"
Dylan loved the stranger, wrote " . . . in praise of God,"
said he'd be "a damned fool" if he didn't.

*

Back from my entertainments, I woke up.
Half asleep, I was in bed with my wife
and Margie my dog, named after my mother.
I saw lady sunrise, naked, with all her troubles
come into the bedroom past the apple tree.
The lights of an automobile down the road
brought me to my senses. I never served time
in an overcrowded prison, shackled to no labor.
I never complained about the weather.
There are other places, names, and matters
I do not care to remember.
I read in *Don Quixote* there's an old ballad
that says King Rodrigo, alive and kicking
in a tomb filled with reptiles and vermin,
said in a low and mournful voice,
"They're eating me, they're eating me
in the place where I most sinned."
Sancho did not think the most sinful place
was the brain, the mind. He did not remember
that Jesus Christ said thinking something evil
was the same as doing it. Certainly, the squire knew
we think of doing unto others more evil than we do,
he heard the devil hides behind the cross.

FATHERS

1.

A friend told me Jesus said,
 "Go out into the fields to find your real mothers and fathers."
I thought somehow I'd done that
since I really had two fathers, none heavenly,
a subject difficult for me to talk about.
I am confused—straighten me out.
I am old and difficult under the apple boughs.
I have planted more apple trees than I can remember.

I've searched but I cannot find a text that reveals
when or how Christ's earthly father died.
I see it was from His not-blood-father, Joseph,
that Jesus was begot from patriarchs and kings—
soon the innocents were slaughtered, Joseph
took flight with the Virgin and child to Egypt
by donkey that would not eat sacred manger hay,
the beast said to have prayed when they rested.

Later, the way things happen, Joseph corrected
Aramaic speaking Jesus' Hebrew,
taught Him Torah, morning prayer, perhaps to skip
a stone out to sea. Did Joseph teach his carpenter Son
what the boy taught the rabbis? Holy riddle.
Surely Jesus sang prayers in synagogue
and at home with windows open, stopped traffic
when he sang everyday love songs.
We know Joseph had four sons of his own blood.
He compounded with his wife,
so he and Mary kissed carnally, perhaps on the Sabbath:
he must have loved her smell, touch, taste—her breasts
from which Jesus took the milk of human kindness.
His four younger brothers sucked the same nipples.

Of course Jesus, with His knowledge and direction
of everything that happens, was, is, never jealous.
His jealousy, the devil's suggestion.

No news that his Son embraced him when Joseph
was on his deathbed dying a happy death—
He might have brought Joseph a cup of hot chocolate
the dying in Mexico who worshipped snakes
took comfort from.
Chocolate had not yet come to Rome or Jerusalem.
Alas, Joseph is not buried beside his wife in Ephesus.
John the Divine is buried a few steps from Her tomb;
a stone's throw away is the Temple of Artemis,
the virgin huntress-goddess, sister of Apollo.
The way things happen, Mary visited the Greek temple,
one of the seven wonders, changed by wars into Roman.

     2.
I know a tree the shape of five question marks
when? how? why? which? where?
every word forbidden fruit.
A summer rain takes over my life
then simply abandons me.
I had a father whom most held in high regard
he deserved. Others called him evil.
My sister and I independently
were reminded of our father we called "father"
when we saw a newspaper photograph
of the decade's most famous murderer.
My mother said father was always angry,
but I had a godfather, her brother, a doctor,
beside whom for me, Gabriel, Rafael, Elijah,
and all the gods were pimps.
As a child I had to be forced to eat an apple.
I have never bit an apple since I left my father's house,
still I believe the apple does not fall far from the tree.

PSALM

God of paper and writing. God of first and last drafts,
God of dislikes, God of everyday occasions—
He is not my servant, does not work for tips.
Under the dome of the Roman Pantheon,
God in three persons carries a cross on his back
as an aging centaur, hands bound behind his back, carries Eros.
Chinese God of examinations: bloodwork, biopsy,
urine analysis, grant me the grade of *fair* in the study of dark holes,
fair in anus, self-knowledge, and the leaves of the vagina
like the pages of a book in the vision of Ezekiel.
May I also open my mouth and read the book by eating it,
swallow its meaning. My Shepherd, let me continue to just pass
in the army of the living,
keep me from the ranks of the excellent dead.
It's true I worshipped Aphrodite
who has driven me off with her slipper
after my worst ways pleased her.
I make noise for the Lord.
My Shepherd, I want, I want, I want.

THE PERFECT DEMOCRACY

I come close to the perfect democracy
a poet called "the kingdom of death."
I was created and I will die free and equal.
My soul was born on the North Atlantic
between Lithuania and Philadelphia,
city of brotherly love. I don't remember but surely
my heart can't forget being nursed, then rocked
by my mother and the Atlantic Ocean. (What a first nanny.)
These days almost everyone's a landlover,
who never spent days or weeks
looking out at nothing but endless ocean and horizon.
How can such a landlover know who he or she is
in the world and universe?

Almost everyone, when you cross the little brook
between life and death,
you will enter the democratic halls of death,
parliaments, congress, la Chambre des Députés,
take your seats before the Speaker, you will be
called to order, shrouded in your Sunday best,
perhaps a winding sheet or prayer shawl,
or you may sit, entombed, like the old Tatars,
with pipe, tobacco, and live dog;
some will have a clear view through the open roof
to the Sun and Moon, others, under the merciful eyes
of Jesus or Jehovah or both, are asleep in the Commons.
Most are "officer's mess" for batallions of maggots.
Few rest in peace. Some debating good citizens
hold hell is simply a cleptocracy, the dead
are cleaned out, without a penny's worth of anything.
Others mutter they are "never dead, not even past."
Mr. Speaker:
I salute the eight black constituents
to the Assemblée Nationale,

in the valley with the Jews who were included
in the Declaration of the Rights of Man
thanks to one vote, now a skinless finger.
Everyone knows his or her deathday.
No one sings "Happy deathday to you"
except a few still drunk on life.
Morning. A dog seems to rest its head
on smoke that smells human.
The cock calls the role. The nays have it.

O landlovers, I wish I could bring you shipboard,
surround you with blue, purple, white,
black and mountainous turquoise breakers,
bring you to their meaning and incomprehensibility,
to see what is near and beyond.
A few stand and pray
on the floor or alone in the coatrooms,
a congregation of pure Oversouls,
the odd murderer with nothing to do.

Landlover,
you may be a farmer or a gardener, bless you,
but just between you, me and the buttercups,
the ocean is coming. Question time:
Mr. Speaker, in your democracy,
are there any little deaths after death, *withouts*:
no need to have supper late or early,
no lovemaking, no music? Will I be a listener,
may I play a God-made instrument?
Surely democratic God arranges for birdsong,
winds praying in trees.

I'm filibustering. Does God eat?
I hear someone say God is a vegetarian,
another is certain God eats meat.
For centuries the best cuts were set aside for Gods.

Surely lambs were and are not sacrificed without reason.
Then God eats and, since we are made in God's image,
He defecates, urinates, wipes Himself clean.
God coughs and farts, is our Farter who art in Heaven.
I'm the Devil, you say! No, in the shadow cabinet
I'm the minister of parables. Every school child knows
Isis and other Gods of the dead are marble or bronze.
I'm trying to vote death out of office—
I say to the free man who praises his God,
"Without death, anarchy. Is God and his 42 names
protected by flights of angels, his Mom?"

The Lord swims in all oceans,
plays a kind of tag with jellyfish and whales,
He does not forget the least of the newborn.
His hand runs through, blesses many kinds of spawn.
I'm happy to have been born on the Atlantic,
my useful afterbirth thrown overboard.

In bedroom slippers, I tap-dance
up and down the stairs, hold onto the rail,
my pulse once a household member, now a guest,
cannot overstay his or her welcome.
My pulse cannot overstay his or her welcome.

THE GAMBLER

Older, I gamble with one die,
risk rolling a one-eyed snake.
I hedge my bets with the verb "to die."
The chances are I'll die some daybreak,
I prefer after breakfast and a cup of coffee
to get me through the day. It would be nice
to read again *The Gambler* of Dostoyevski,
to play with God, but "God does not roll dice,"
flip coins—heads damnation, tails grace.
"Love the stranger" trumps where the true cross is.
He cheers for peace, not war, in a horse race,
although they are both His horses,
He collects His winnings and takes His losses.

Mercy's a wild card.
Now I play numbers with fallen angels.
(God knows what the Devil feels.)
The Lord will not settle for a little human regard.
His new-fangled messengers with smartphones
text the laws, take selfies, see fire and brimstone.
I cheat at cards Yahweh deals.

Stuffed with flesh, blood, and bones,
I don't applaud any God. I lift my cap,
kick off my shoes, drop a coin in the box and clap.
I see a skyscraper as a gravestone.
Walking in New York City, forgetting is hard.
There is some reason to suppose the sap
of trees will outlast human blood by mishap.
The world shoots craps. I bet, no matter how winds fly,
a kiss will keep the world from hate, by and by.

It began, midnight. It was 1956,
I arrived in Nice by train

far from the Tiber and River Styx.
Tenth of August, no beds, with Djuna my dog,
I slept in a Hotel Negresco beach chair,
Djuna on colored stones, under my chair.
Storm clouds covered the stars.
We went into a casino to escape the rain.
Djuna died a Socialist wolf in Fascist Spain.
I still grieve for my Trastevere dog,
like a child. I'm left to speak the prologue.

But pardon, it is my wish
to honor the language. I salute the verb "to die,"
its sound and meaning from Middle English.
I play with sounds, with I and eye,
homonym roulette: morning dew,
there's do unto others and Devil his due.
Rien ne va plus. For those slated to die,
a shell game: where? when? why?
Given time, all is vanity,
the Good Shepherd will lead the universe to slaughter.
Baa, baa, baa . . . I put my money on last laughter:
there are many more stars in the day and night sky
than there are words in English.
My words contain dark matter,
invisible gravity, water dripping from the tap—
I bet my life. I'd like to catch a fish
that's been swimming in the Thames since English.
I've caught Death, the rat, in my mousetrap—
Augustine's sermon 261. No,
I take Death into the woods and let him go.

MONDAY

September, I just want to pass a pleasant day
listening in the country to my evergreen
bristlecone cousin teach a class to saplings.
I heard: be good, be good, be good,
love your neighbors in the forest—
trees, you must live in a seasonal society,
our cousinhood of woods.

Leafy branches, facing North and West
give a limosna of morning sunlight.
Brave trees, judge and stand in judgment.
There are fools who think you are ignorant
because you battle for water and sunlight,
but you know every living thing has the obligation
to protect freedom of assembly for its nation—
freedom of song for crows and nightingales,
respect for pastoral rights of brooks and waterfalls.

Dream your arboreal dream and nightmare,
terror of chainsaws, contempt for stone walls.
You have happy and tragic love affairs,
poplars and willows, arranged marriages.
The first wise gardener planted trees in pairs,
the brooks nearby taught languages.

Sometimes, trees live ghettoed in the city.
Some are Christian, celebrate the Nativity.
Most are pagan as roses and goldenrod.
The Vikings thought every tree was a God
who helped them sail longships past Cape Farewell.
Beyond wolf howls,
they sailed to a Valhalla of trees and snow owls,
to the hall of the slain, the never again,
to virgin forests, a new world,
to have intercourse with the world.

Eclipse

A ROSE

How can you run about
two minutes after you are born?
Be a horse, then you can discover
a valley, the taste of a mare's nipple,
your coat moist with her 3-year-old blood.
In a dream set partly in a horse barn,
greenhouse, outdoors classroom, I thought
universe after universe is not *here*,
is out there, out there, there, there,
there, still going . . .
Here and a rose are within my reach,
visible without wise instruments.
Our earth and sun don't matter an onion
to dark matter, places without address.
Justice is not done in the universe,
where the only evidence admissible is invisible
or with sweet deceiving countenance.
If all the world's a stage, the players have stage fright.
Ding dong, the final doorbell is ringing.
(In Middle Scottish "ding" means worthy.)
Mr. Trouble won't take his finger off
the button. I'm here, unmetaphorical.
No friend or Eurydice is like any other,
lost friends sometimes come as visitations.
Still I take up with string theory
or the rose-by-any-other-rose theory
that holds water.
A bee flew into a rose,
found darkness and silence there,
flew into another rose and another,
then bang, fires, everything.
Gravity and darkness are not dreary.
Mathematicians are heroes
who give meaning to numbers,

a wilderness of zeroes.
The thing about the cosmos
is what we cannot see is beautiful.
Not *I, you* and *me* is what I want to say.
My calling card is the periodic table.
I am thorium, the 90th element,
silvery and black.
Protons, the cosmos, black holes,
white dwarfs are never gross.
Soon after the invention of the present tense
there was comparative and superlative,
so off we went to war. We breathe in and out:
the simple past came just like that.

We believed, needed to pray, invented talk,
writing to keep accounts,
although greeting by smelling, whining,
crying, howling, served us well.
We could say *please, thank you, good morning*
and *good night, I love you,* without a word.
A child asked me a question: "Back at the start,
bang! cruel, kind, or no heart?"

ALBUM

Among family photos,
a school of smiling rainbow trout.
A magician uncle explained:
they swam across the ocean
although they were freshwater fish,
not saltwater fish. Our good fish family
studied hard underwater and learned
the scrolls, the shelves, the sudden drops.
They were taught to watch out
for sturgeon, salmon, striped bass
coming up river, some to die,
others laid eggs, then returned to the ocean.
My cousin looked for an underwater Bible
in the lily pads but never found it,
saw turtles as big as automobile tires,
but he kept looking, breaking water for heaven's sake.
Lucky he had eyes that saw in a full circle
not just straight ahead, so he did better.
They had a Watchman fish, an old fish,
too old to fertilize eggs,
every scale thick as a windscreen.
He watched for lone fish returning from war.
Somehow they became human.
They would rather be buried
than thrown overboard into any puddle.

MR. TROUBLE

Whatever the season
I add and subtract days and weeks.
I was with my dogs in the park,
I met Monsieur Troublé,
"Mr. Trouble," laughing.
"What are you laughing at?" I asked.
He spake thus: "I've read you.
I grant every birth is a nativity, holy.
Love, perhaps simply befriending,
is the answer in a world
where looking at something changes it.
Yes, eyes change the world."
"No, no," a passing angel said, *"Ave Maria*
gratia plena, Dominus tecum—
words in the Virgin's ear gave her a Son."
I said, "Then the nose, smelling changes the world.
Tasting, barely touching or lovemaking changes the world."
"Nobody is speaking for the ocean," Mr. Trouble said.

I offered: Moonlight is the traveler
and there was a full moon—
moon, mothered by winter, mothered by spring.
Day goes where night was,
after a long time I go about as music—
let's say that's what the good life is,
carrying a tune.
Moonlight sees what daylight does.
"Monkey sees," Mr. Trouble said.
"Nobody is speaking for the ocean."

158

MY MOTHER'S MEMORIAL DAY

May 19th, a sleepless night,
thirty-six years after the ocean stopped swimming,
I didn't light a candle. I wrote a letter
to my mother, put a daisy in an envelope,
mailed it express, addressed "to far places."
The letter came back *Return to sender.*
Nobody is speaking for the ocean.
I thought my mother was half ocean.

Far back as I remember,
I saw my naked mother,
the ocean swimming endlessly, wonder full.
I did not know the Chinese say "woman is half the sky";
I thought my mother half ocean, half firmament.

I was born too big. From time to time
I overheard whispering, I had injured my mother "for life."
They did not blame me. Still, my birth was a sin
like no other. It prisoned me.
I wished I was born from an egg like a pigeon.
I could not say "I'm sorry"
for what I was not allowed to know.
I believed my sin belonged only to me—
not one of the look-alikes forbidden by commandments.
I heard of penance, mine was simply crying.

At nine, I wanted to be a farmer.
I marveled at planting seeds, watching
things grow, and I wanted to be a priest
so I could hear confession, secret stories.
I could do nothing right.
To kiss was to make it "all better."

I was not a child walking in sand
with a pail and shovel looking out

at the swimming ocean. On the island of Rhodes,
on a Hellenistic street the Colossus protected,
after a Greek revolution, in a celebration
I was shot in the leg by a ricocheting bullet.
The caryatids taught me beauty without saying a word.
I swallowed the Acropolis,
a kind of Eucharist.
It never passed through my intestines.

Even so, life was an apparatus belonging to the city.
Life cleared streets, plowed snow, collected garbage,
was related to an ambulance, elevated trains.
It only made sense when I saw a field of wildflowers,
what some call the hand of God.
It took time before I took my time
reaching for what really was, is.
What is not   still is
my more than occasional companion.

ALEXANDER FU MUSING

The truth is I don't know the days of the week.
I can't tell time.
I have lived a summer,
a fall, a winter, an April, a May,
which I say because words are put in my mouth
because you-know-who is trying to sell something.
My mother rocks me to sleep, singing
a Chinese lullaby about crickets playing.
It's not easy to know so little,
but I wake to wonder, I touch wonder,
I play with wonder.
I smile at wonder.
I cry when wonder is taken from me.

TO ALEXANDER WHO WANTS TO BE A COSMOLOGIST

September 27th and 28th, two dark rainy days.
Alex was shivering, crying for no reason.
Embraced, he sobbed. It was for lack of summer.
He thought summer was longer.
"It's cold. It's already autumn."
I told him, "You simply must learn to love
autumn, winter, and spring.
We are all star children, made of the stuff of stars.
Don't cry, we are living in the golden age of stars."

TO ALEXANDER FU ON HIS BEGINNING AND 13TH BIRTHDAY

Cut from your mother, there was a first heartache,
a loneliness before your first peek
at the world, your mother's hand was a comb
for your proud hair, fresh from the womb—
born at night, you and moonlight tipped the scale
a 6lb 8oz miracle,
a sky-kicking son
born to Chinese obligation
but already American.
You were a human flower, a pink carnation.
You were not fed by sunlight and rain.
You sucked the wise milk of Han.

Your first stop, the Riverdale station,
a stuffed lion and meditation.
Out of PS 24, you will become
a full Alexander moon over the trees
before you're done. It would not please
your mother to have a moon god for a son.
She would prefer you had the grace
to be mortal, to make the world a better place.
There is a lesson in your grandmother's face:
do not forget the Way
of your ancestors. Make a wise wish
on your 13th birthday, seize the day
from history and geography.
If you lead, you will not lose the Way,
in your family's good company
where wisdom is common as a sunfish,
protected from poisonous snakes by calligraphy:
paintings of many as the few, the few as many.
You already dine on a gluten-free dish
of some dead old King's English.

In your heart, keep Fu
before Alexander and do
unto others as you would have others do
unto you.

A RED ENVELOPE

Brayed at, with an equine kiss
I've been told by my much-loved donkey
this is the Chinese Year of the Monkey,
twelve months of spring,
election lights for sale:
I fly with a broken left wing
while males and females have me by the tail.
I am an old fledgling.
Every day is precious, very dear,
I celebrate the new year
last year and next year.

CHILDREN'S SONG

"I wish I was two dogs, then I could play with me."
I am King and Queeny,
I could chase two red squirrels up a tree,
rule a kingdom on my bed,
play very alive and very dead,
question and answer, fog and dialogue,
play good dog, bad dog,
on a hot summer day
swim in and out
of a river all day,
get wetter and wetter
because R is the dog's letter,
bark and laugh
with bull, cow, and calf,
answer a moo with bark bark,
have sweet company in the dark,
play two St. Bernards in the snow,
two Chihuahuas in Mexico,
a Bloodhound and Labrador,
till Papa, hands on hips,
says, *Quiet! Quiet!*, stands at the door
while I, with my two tongues, lick my lips.
I like dog biscuits, fish and chips.
I could go to bed late and early,
I could eat a bone, one, two, three,
and never be lonely, never be lonely.

BIRTHDAY WISHES

Lovers of birthdays,
he had 99 years.
The usual toast, "a hundred years!"
would be a curse
so they gave him
a basket of Georgia peaches,
the gift of a photo:
a woman reclining naked,
her tongue showing a little,
a handkerchief, with her hair,
body odor and breath.
He and his guests
will celebrate his birthday
until there are no birthdays
anymore. Lovers of birthdays,
may circumstance, fate
bring him and you
a happier love-death
than an ancient death I recall:
Achilles, his face masked
behind a copper helmet,
slays Penthesilea,
Queen of the Amazons,
as she dies, they fall in love . . .
Lovers of birthdays,
honest readers,
there are a few
who believe her death
the best death you can have.

SPIT

I've been spit at, marching for a cause,
heard shouts, "We know who you are!" from the mob,
but I haven't done or said anything for years
worth being spit at.
I keep away from places where
if I just stood, looking as I do,
I could find spit and my killer.
I've been spit at by snakes,
grasshoppers and alpacas.
I know spit stories.
Jesus spit on mud and cured a blind man.
I heard a Welsh poet say to a Scots poet,
"I'd spit in your eye,
but there's so much spit there already
it wouldn't fit." Enough. Out of their spit
Egyptian gods made children,
while Saturn ate and spit out his sons,
we needed Eden and a virgin birth. Naked
Eve ate the mouthwatering fruit of knowledge—
mortality came with spit.

*

Spit is sometimes sad,
omnipresent, it is kept out of mind—
there's so much poetry of the senses,
does spit want to be a tear?
Spit was not made to lick postage stamps,
but without spit we die screaming
from a cracked mouth full of death.
It shows family history, has quality.
No doubt, you can get a good price
for a flask or handkerchief of royal slaver—
the proceeds given to charity.
Yes, spit anywhere can be sexual—
everything depends on the mouth.
If you can't take a little dog spit,
stay out of my house.

166

*

I did not spit in the face of John Donne.
When the yellow wind is blowing,
a Chinese poet would value Godly spit,
its rhymes and half-rhymes.
We don't have calligraphy,
but we have spitting images,
a likeness in a cradle, a little face
of a grandmother long dead.
Spit was not made for a spittoon,
but it likes to mingle in a crowd.
Spit doesn't have a song:
spit is like the morning dew,
it would be happy in a brook.
All water is made by God who took
ocean, mud and bones,
made Muslim, Christian, and Jew.

Now spit has a tune.
I want to spit to the sun and moon,
above the clouds, higher than hawks fly.
Sun and moon take spit as a compliment,
a new star. They have seen everything,
fires that gossip and sing,
how Gods can reproduce Goddesses—
Venus born out of the thigh of Zeus,
but no one has ever tried to spit so high.

WALTZ

"Whoever shall say thou fool shall be in danger of hellfire."
—Matthew 5:22

Thou fool! Three score and six years ago,
I woke after a fool's daydream—
I received a pictureless postcard special delivery
from a former girlfriend in Woman's Hospital
telling me she brought forth a daughter,
her name and weight—I suppose, pride of her husband
of 7 months, a good doctor. I saved the postcard
during years of Reconstruction, pinned to the wall—
my bedroom was full of daughters without fathers.
Sixty years later, on the internet, a blessed event:
I saw a photo of the worthy doctor husband
dancing happily with his daughter,
the picture of my mother.
I saw online she was a piano tuner,
a profession of gifted souls.
Clearly she had love for her happy stepfather.
She's childless, I do not know with whom she sleeps,
lover, husband, wife, dog, or cat,
or just *Eine Kleine Nachtmusik.*
She knows middle C from a hole in the ground,
no reason for her to know the mysterious ocean.
My father used to ask me who was I to think,
but I think she has a meantone temperament. Bless her,
she knows Pythagorean tuning, preludes and fugues
written in all 24 major and minor keys.
May she avoid the unpleasant wolf interval.

The child, mother to the man, taught me
fifths, fourths, thirds, both major and minor,
often in an ascending or descending pattern,
the beat, frequencies between notes,
then, of course, the psychoacoustic affect.

My overused ears tend to perceive
the higher notes as flat, compared to those at midrange.
I bought myself a tuning fork for Father's Day.

I think I'll go swimming, look under water
for a fathered and un-fathered daughter.
At 65, would it be better for her to know
which father is her father?
Could I explain the look on her mother's face
when her mother sometimes looked
for the Jew and poet in her Christian daughter?
Would my daughter play on her baby grand
the Great Deception Waltz
if out of terrible curiosity I told her the truth?

MY GOOD OLD SHIRT

Anything is the same old anything. I've become part of the thingness
of all things I see: for example, I am partly chair and table.
Moonless, the night seems almost as it was last moonless night.
I let my shirt, my good old shirt, lie quietly on my chair.
Not trained in any religion, I've become the thingness I see.
Angered, I have no saint.
I don't want to be awakened by Christian bells
or called to prayer by first light, when you can distinguish
a white from black thread. The sound of a ram's horn
does not call me to synagogue. I throw kisses at an elephant God
and a God of preservation. Let me be awakened by a dream—
I'm on a ship, torn open in a fog, a jolted passenger,
awake to the everyday. I sing of the universal,
the thingness of all things I see.

SILENCE

Trees and flowers elbow their neighbors
out of sunlight and rain.
Born misdirected, to better myself,
I made an "In God We Trust" soup
out of vegetable pickings, not killings,
against the recipe: devour one another
to stay alive. In another universe
God may have corrected His mistakes.
I give Him, Her, Them the benefit of doubts.
I would steal, if I had to, His gifts of fire,
air and water. I no longer take for granted
the spectacular inventions, birth and ignorance,
the failed experiment: death.

I could forget this palaver, blame it all on bang,
unbuttoned chance, personal pronouns.
How did we come to be us, the swarm, the packs,
snakes like years wrapped around each other?
Do all living things celebrate Good Fridays,
holy and unholy days and nights,
a certain thoughtfulness, like two nipples
for twins, eight for puppies and foxes?
Is *love* a good name for all this?
If not—any word.

Now, for a long dead Australian I love,
Bertie Whiting, I will consider
the just-born kangaroo: life-size earthworm
with almost legs dropped to the ground, blind "joey,"
alone in the universe, makes its way up Mama's leg
into her sack to suck—later, it jumps out,
grazes on its own half an hour—
a touch of fear,
first joy of coming back after being alone.

(A newborn Einstein on the ground,
given $E=mc^2$, could not, on his own,
make his way to his mother's tit.)
After a consistent 235 days,
the joey leaves the pouch forever,
whispers in kangaroo, "Mama, I'll never forget you."

In the world's boat, everything that is or was
causes me to praise and curse.
Praise plus curse divided by two
equals silence, not prayer.

ELEGY FOR ELIA

Three years ago, dying, in pain,
you told me to my face—"Life everlasting
is to be loved at the moment of death."
To cheer up this gathering, I recall
a fight you had with your lover husband
who said in rage, "If you go to California
I won't water your plants."

Elia, you Turkish Greek Ladino beauty,
all your life you served Dionysus
in the theater and unholy places.
He had power to protect you.
Where was the God of the grape harvest,
the theater and ritual madness,
when the laborers kept sweeping your cancer
and rotten blood as if cleaning a gutter,
tangled hoses, tubes in all your woman holes
and subway tracks? You kept your smile
with all its colors, as if you were a bug
in a bottle of formaldehyde at the hospital or studio
that once smelled of oil paints, linseed oil,
turpentine, and the perfumes you and Sappho
used a touch of in certain places.

There is still hope of deathly justice,
perhaps, perhaps, perhaps
an angel will come with a harp and sing,
the harp itself beautiful as the Brooklyn Bridge,
and flower pots on New York City roofs
your lover painted. An unknown psalm
in Hebrew in parallel rhymes:
O Elia, my Elia
your life was reason for the Lord, Ancient of Days,
with his 42 names to give thanks and praise.

Lord or not Lord, Monsieur Descartes,
silence is a sound that establishes your heart.
You made noise for the Lord,
noise is sometimes right, sometimes wrong,
war songs and love songs—
peace comes with a governance of good and evil
independent of Paradise or Hell.

Who in New York or Istanbul will deny the possibility
that a wind God, purple eagle,
will come and carry you off,
lift your body out of an oak crate,
its American dirt, its amphora,
carry you to the ancient olive trees of Smyrna.
Male or female, he will do unto you what Gods do.
We all become dust and morning dew
blown away from here to there
out there—how far? Take any number
and add a mile of zeros.
We are not resurrected, we are misdirected.
We will stand on stage again,
the congregation in the pit.
The play is called *Nothing.*
Sooner or later you, all of us,
have a second death—we are warned
like Cordelia, "Nothing will come of nothing."
Wouldn't it be nice if in the end we married France?
O star of many wonders,
 "always, always, always, always."
I forgot to say, to death there is no consolation.

GARDENS AND UNPUNCTUATED POETRY

Gardens do not need punctuation
between the lavender and peonies
baby's breath and violets
commas do not offer anything to morning glories
or devil's paintbrush or roses
the way the world is made
fragrant scarlet orchids and sweet peas
are not in apposition
the thought that gardens should have semicolons
or colons silly as street signs in a garden
Stop   No Left Turn   Dead End

Save hydrangeas from the parenthesis
the gardens of Grenada from upside down question marks
save anemones from the circumflex
the Dutch tulip from the umlaut
may Apollo protect a thousand palm trees
from a single exclamation mark
the amaryllis from the em dash
even now an Irish wart from a Roman nose

Palm trees and poems under the sky
do not need further clarification
certainly there are borders and caesuras
in poems gardens and dooryards
we see the mass slaughter of living things
there are stops worse than punctuation
some may choose to read an ancient garden
from right to left
or as a field that is plowed from the bottom of a page to the top
reading a garden or a poem depends on the reader's
need to praise or to live near flowers and certain words
he or she may want to linger a while
on a surprising verb or lily

I cheer for the first crocus pushing through the snow
proof to many God keeps his flowers and his word
I have seen fields of cornflowers and poppies
all the life they hold cut in two
by railroad tracks highways billboards oil fields
coal mines shopping centers and motels
things worse than punctuation
because the ocean was once where the garden and valley is
perhaps the reason the potato has a purple flower
the reason fish know the dances of India and Andalusia
why a gardener has written a poem about the word *the*
somehow left behind by the retreating tides

I have found gardeners on their knees
and farm workers laboring in the scorching sun
no less reverent than praying nuns
sometimes the world intrudes on gardening
poetry and punctuation
on a scorching August day a black field-hand
from my neighbor's potato field
knocked on my air-conditioned purple door
I found his distress frightening
why was he suffering like a wounded soldier
entering my life knocking on my door
when there was no war nearby
in terrible pain he said something like   got a beer
I gave him lemonade and a wet towel
little or no comfort
something like punctuation

REVIEW

A clothesline
tied from a dead ash to a weeping willow,
my old and new clothes washed clean,
on close look not washed, something to fool the eye,
my stained underwear and holy socks,
blooms of good and evil, and something to fool the ear,
dirty laundry flapping in the wind in meter.
I know bird chatterings are love calls,
"Rr" is the dog's letter.
Why don't they teach the "are"s anymore,
you are, we are, what are we to do?
Clothespinned to the line, my dirty laundry
often tells the truth, not the whole truth,
not nothing but the truth, so help me God.
Laundry makes nothing happen: it survives
in the valley of never-fooled sun and winds
where nothing is said by happenstance.
I babble, trying to honor the language:
"I am the world, a globe walking with long legs,
cities, oceans, smoking dumps around my waist."
When the music changes, the fiber optic lines tremble.
I hum the rest, I remember poets who made it new,
swam in the Yangtze, Passaic, Thames and Charles.
Like Hart Crane I wore a bathing suit with a top.
I thought describing the fat lady in the circus,
legs spread apart from the ankles up,
was the naked truth. Why are there no laughing willows?
There are giggling brooks. I heard laughter in the forest,
seven foot golden bantam corn growing in August.
It sounds like happiness, till 8 p.m. above the Hudson,
when laundry, clean and dirty, is taken in,
when the night creatures I love come out.

TEARS

Forty years ago, I wrote I would sooner disgust you than ask for your compassion. My tears are barley water. I give you my tears to wash your feet. My tears are lace on my father's face. My tears are old rags that do not fit me. My tears are spit on my face, I know spit is sexual. My tears mean no more to me than my grocery bill. My tears are produce I stand in line for. Crying makes me a child, female, shows I am a man speechless about love. I would sooner hold a porcupine than defend tears. My dogs may pull it to pieces, get a mouthful of quills . . . it's too lonely. I can't take care of it. I begin to feel the wish to kill—the thing is dangerous. I don't know what it eats. (A porcupine is the other animal that cries with tears.) I cover my eyes with my hands. I have betrayed the impossible, my porcupine—the thing's alive, smells of urine. I look for gills, see ears, I feel the weight of thorns and flesh, Christ's crown. I went into the woods that know me. The trees remembered my mother. Wildflowers taught me reality is just what is. The leaves set an example of representative democracy. The wind taught me chants and common prayer. The sunflower taught responsiveness, the dew punctuality. Oh my teachers, where did I ever learn my vices? Walking with you in the woods I learnt lust. Your lips taught me to be lazy. Your eyes taught me greed. Your touch to lie. You have burned my woods . . . cut down trees, left me only with a snake, the penalty for all those who search for paradise . . .

FOR GOOD MEASURE

He painted his faults,
what he could not see clearly,
he was the better for it.
He painted the unlikely,
the *un* of things:
unhappy, unforeseen
the uneventful everyday,
an abstract all or the everything, the fibs
"breath poor and speech unable"
the circle and straight lines
of what he called always
the ABCs of never.
He dressed without thinking about the weather,
what colors go with, dandy or maudit.
In the lift, by mistake, he nudged his neighbor
he barely knew. His hand too high,
he waved as if from across the street.
He washed his brushes
in turpentine, the sink became
a gorge of sunrise and sunset.
Friends phoned,
he answered, "Pronto,"
"Dígame," "Oui,"
on a party line,
the Coney Island of telephones.
He was proud his callers heard from one word
his preferences, he was a rubble king.

Ninety years after he was given light,
an after-dinner drunk, one time or another—*Strega,
Chartreuse, Anís de Chinchón,* calvados, grappa—
he could not remember
when he did not hear the knocking at the gate,
sleepless on port

he played the porter in *Macbeth*.
He said with his loaded brushes, he painted error,
impossible arguments—although they were studies,
his paintings taught
the mountains and deserts of hatred:
the Himalayas Atlas Alps Pyrenees, lost souls,
the Gobi Sinai and Sahara, to love their neighbors—
green valleys were children.
He was a citizen of mythos,
a migrant from the cosmos,
not part of the retinue of chaos.
He could no longer draw a circle.

One Sunday morning,
faulted, almost blind,
he wrote a letter in large script
that went up and down hill:
" . . . my darling, I can still paint what I think,
blind eagles and dumb gossips,
differences between fault, sin, mistake,
the unlikely less likely, the *un* of things,
a few remembered faces,
the anatomy of my melancholy,
dung and scat, the Dead Sea,
Chinese bridges that are also temples.
I paint changing seasons, what I don't have words for,
because no two things happen at once.
A few painters said it all,
almost all, others have their right to pleasures
every horse's ass has a right to.
Kisses for good measure."

A WALK

I saw the serpent in the garden
when I was two or three,
the bone of my head still hardening.
I walked with my father who held my hand
crossing Liberty Avenue,
talking over my head
he recited Shakespeare: tragical-comical
historical-pastoral-Samuel.
He was learning lines
he needed for an exam.
I remember my feelings, not the words.
Some forty years later, he thanked me
for the Shakespeare he remembered.
I said no, it was I who owed the debt,
kissed him without regret.

LAST MEOW

Fifty stories high,
a colossal white leopard in the wintry city
is the upper half of the Empire State Building,
thanks to twenty thousand lumen projectors,
not just a trick, but a cunning cat
with other endangered species.
I hear its cry above the city traffic.
Let the leopard take over Manhattan, meowing,
growling with hunger louder than a fire truck.
I bring rats and gallons of milk,
as I will every day, hoping it will stay.
Sometimes it holds me by the back of my neck,
carries me wherever it wants to go.
I call it Poetry. I call it my pussy cat,
my kitten I've been sleeping with all my life.
My big cat reads, respects the stone lions
in front of the 42nd Street Library.
In the main reading room it works, studies
which monuments the cats of Rome,
Paris, and Jerusalem make home—
the periphrastic reasons, causes, why.
Poetry slouches its way up Broadway
north toward the Himalayas.
It takes me through avalanche and blizzards,
the sunlight and lanterns
of the Analects, Gita, Koran, Bible.
We roll together, I discover its privates.
The gigantic cat has got me by the throat,
holds me down by a paw in the snow.
I never thought I would go like this.
I always felt death was supernatural. If I can,
I told Zhu Ming, my Christian-Buddhist cousin,
I'll come back as a butterfly in winter
so she'll know it's me.

9 CHOCOLATES

It was a shock for me to realize
I have not seen the Atlantic Ocean
for two years, not seen the truth she represents,
the beautiful and terrible world,
not embraced her or been embraced,
tasted and smelled her, knocked off my feet,
not heard her many languages.
I address her only with baby talk,
her face more familiar than any face I know,
the face of every woman I've ever known,
the most protective and life-threatening.
When I saw her every morning first thing,
there was always a kiss,
the stroking of my face and body going one way
then the slap on the way back.

I've thought I'd be buried under a loved red oak
on a day like this in August
when trees are happy and beautiful as a tree can be
except perhaps some in snow,
but now I prefer you throw me overboard
into the city of God. The Atlantic nods and smiles.
She's heard so much of my nonsense through the years,
seems to remember everything I ever said or wrote.
The tide comes in. She forgets everything I ever said or wrote.

The faces on the city streets and seabirds
all look very familiar to me.
They've got my number.
Numerology is familiar to me as chocolate.
Because nine means life in Hebrew,
I eat nine chocolates a day
from a box, its lid a painting of crawling Aristotle,
Phyllis riding his back.

Ocean around me horizon to horizon,
I'm heading east, bound for Dublin, Plymouth,
Barcelona, Venice, and Pireaus—
I've been known to trust only the stars
and my own hopeless intuition,
not instruments, even in a storm.
Always lost, I'm free, self-reliant.
The first sight of land, I think is Ireland, is Norway
—Ibsen today, not Yeats or Joyce.
Soon, using charts, I'm off to China
(after all, the Chinese invented the compass).
Finally, my body tossed overboard
into the city of the disGodded,
far from any country of prayer,
with nine chocolates in my pocket,
with the ashes of my dogs at my feet—
not Nicky, what's left of her
still under the Japanese maple.
The Atlantic nods and smiles.
Now it is easier to write than to read.

THE SEAGULL

When I was a child, before I knew the word for love
or snowstorm, before I remember a tree,
I saw a pigeon in a blizzard, knocking
against the kitchen window, trying to get in.
My first clear memory of terror,
I kept secret, my intimations
I kept secret.

This winter I hung a gray and white stuffed
felt seagull from the ring of my window shade,
a reminder of good times by the sea,
Chekhov and impossible love.
It pleases me the gull
sometimes lifts a wing in the drafty room.
Once when looking at the gull I saw
through the window a living seagull glide
toward me then disappear—what a rush of life!
I remember its here-ness, while in the room
the senseless symbol, little more than a bedroom slipper
dangled on a string.

My childhood hangs like a gull
in the distant sky,
behind loneliness,
it watches some dark thing below.
I saw before an approaching storm
the seagull stays off the ocean.
On a trawler off Montauk
I am heading home full throttle,
cleaning my catch of striped bass,
seagulls dive, fighting, desperate for the guts—
their faces inches away from mine,
every face different, a sight I never saw before.
For a few seconds, I am part of the flock—

my soul rises out of me,
struggles, surrounded by their cries.
I drift, glide off like my childhood
into the gunmetal sky.

*God Breaketh Not All Men's
Hearts Alike*
(2011)

&

Rejoicing
(2009)

REJOICING

God washed his womb in the ocean.
All things that lived in or above the sea
rejoiced that they were there.
The sand under the rocks,
the driftwood trees rejoiced.
The living, those who called to their kind,
the lucky ones, rejoiced.

When I was young and prodigal,
I dived into God's womb and the ocean.
God spoke to me as I swam
through a thousand reflections,
his face and my face touched
like Mary's cheek on the cheek of her deposed son.
God washed across my face. My face was in him.
From time to time I spit him out as I swam.

I came out of his womb dripping. I felt clean.
I knew God was cold and wet wilderness.
Shivering, I dried God off me with a towel
then I hung him on a clothesline to dry.
God and the towel seemed happy and laughing,
flapping in the wind without commandments.
From the shore I could see the horizon:
he was washing his womb in the ocean
after a day of love, before his gala night.

NIGHTINGALE

1

The nightingale never repeats its song,
sings "I want to love you,"
never "Good morning, good morning."
When it has mated
it plays hide-and-seek in song.
Some sing: "My nation is alive."
Whippoorwills and mockingbirds converse,
the nightingale pours out joy and sorrow.
When Mary was told a "sword lily,"
an iris, "might pierce through her soul,"
the nightingale was Atlas to the soul.
The nightingale does not tell lies in song,
it does not sing when it builds its nest,
when it protects its young. It has reason to weep,
sometimes flies south alone.
It seems it cannot be,
but sometimes it sings days and many nights
with its songs unanswered—
a gift to the gossiping forest.

The nightingale never repeats its song.
Does it compose
during the day to sing at night in trees
new song after new song,
write with wing and feather like the Chinese,
who paint the nightingale with a rose
calligraphy in the sky and song?
However the wind blows
for want of starlight clouds fall to their knees.
How long from is, to will be, to was—not long.
When stars disappear, the nightingale takes flight,
leaves us to birds that come at daylight,
that sing of love and heartache, and repeat their song.

2

Any bird can defeat me at song. The sky is a listener.
In Ireland, country of warblers and nightingales—
beautiful defeats. Canada, for ten summers, loons,
famous countertenors—hundreds, made me a listener.
In China, I lost to songs of joy, flocks
of green magpies overhead, omens of good fortune.
I hear everyday birds. I am ashamed I do not listen,
I go about my business, have nothing better to sing.
I am a ground feeder, a wild turkey,
sometimes a screeching Atlantic seagull
fighting with gulls over the guts of a bluefish.
I am not possible—half-male Harpy, a male Siren,
whose songs cause ladies to tie themselves to the mast
lest they throw themselves into the sea
because I sing how they and I will be remembered.
The universe is artless.
The sky is a listener, my mother now.
Call me Stanley. Give me a lake and a canoe
and I will sing the songs I've sung since I was a fledgling
confronted by the beauty of the wilderness.

SONG OF ALPHABETS

When I see Arabic headlines
like the wings of snakebirds,
Persian or Chinese notices
for the arrivals and departures of buses—
information beautiful as flights of starlings,
I cannot tell vowel from consonant,
the signs of the vulnerability of the flesh
from signs for laws and government.

The Hebrew writing on the wall
is all consonants, the vowel
the ache and joy of life
is known by heart. There are words
written in my blood I cannot read.
I can believe a cloud gave us the laws,
parted the Red Sea, gave us the flood,
the rainbow. A cloud teaches kindness,
be prepared for the worst wind, be light of spirit.
Perhaps I have seen His cloud,
an ordinary mongrel cloud
that assumes nothing, demonstrates nothing,
that comforts as a dog sleeping in the room,
a presence offering not salvation
but a little peace.

My hand has touched the ancient Mayan God
whose face is words: a limestone beasthead
of flora, serpent and numbers,
the sockets of a skull I thought were vowels.
Hurrah for English, hidden miracles,
the A and E of waking and sleeping,
the O of mouth.

Thank you, Sir, alone with your name,
for the erect L in love and open-legged V,
beautiful the Tree of Words in the forest
beside the Tree of Souls, lucky the bird
that held Alpha or Omega in his beak.

THE BATHERS

1.

In the great bronze tub of summer,
with the lions' heads cast on each side,
couples come and bathe together: each touches only
his or her lover, as he or she falls back
into the warm eucalyptus-scented waters.
It is a hot summer evening and the last
sunlight clings to the lighter and darker blues
of grapes and to the white and rose plate
on the bare marble table. Now the lovers
plunge, surface, drift—an intruding elder
would not know if there were six or two,
or be aware of the entering and withdrawing.
There is a sudden stillness of water,
the bathers whisper in the classical manner,
intimate distant things. They are forgetful
that the darkness called night is always present,
sunlight is the guest. It is the moment
of departure. They dress, by mistake exchange
some of their clothing, and linger
in the glaring night traffic of the old city.

2.

I hosed down the tub after five hundred years
of lovemaking, and my few summers.
I did not know the touch of naked bodies
would give to bronze a fragile gold patina,
or that women in love jump in their lovers' tubs.
God of tubs, take pity on solitary bathers
who scrub their flesh with rough stone
and have nothing to show for bathing
but cleanliness and disillusion.

Some believe the Gods come as swans,
showers of gold, themselves, or not at all.
I think they come as bathers: lovers,
whales fountaining, hippopotami
squatting in the mud.

IN THE RAIN

There are principles I would die for,
but not to worship this God or that. To live
I'd kneel before the Egyptian insect god, the dung beetle
who rolls a ball of mud or dung across the ground
as if he were moving the solar disc or host across the sky.
I would pray to a blue scarab inlaid in lapis lazuli
suggestive of the heavens.
The Lord is many. I sit writing at the feet of a baboon god
counterfeit to counterfeit. My Lord smiles, barks and scratches,
all prayers to him are the honking of geese.
To live I'd pray to a god with the head of a crocodile
and the body of a man or a woman: *our father who art in river,*
holy mother, dozing in mud, sunning thyself,
look on your young in danger, open your crocodile mouth,
the doors of your cathedral, let us all swim in.
We are gathered by the river, nesting on your tongue, swim us to safety.
Believers and unbelievers rejoice together in the rain.

WILDFLOWERS

What sweet company they were for an hour or night.
Yes, I kissed them, but I left them after
my crude human lying down and getting up.
I learned their purpose: their being and beauty
is entirely erotic, but that is not to know them.
I never entered them deeper than sunlight,
never ravished their petals and perfumes.
Their pollens were wasted on me.
Socrates said, "My knowledge such as it is
is nothing but a knowledge of erotic things."
Athenian, rest in your marble dust.
In the rummage and agora of my life,
on this summer evening my day is done,
the Lord is not a botanist
who art in heaven. He does not lead me
into green pastures. He is already there
delivering me from evil. Dandelions and false dandelions,
I am completely unprincipled. I lie with you
disobedient to the laws of cities.

A BLIND FISHERMAN

I teach my friend, a fisherman gone blind, to cast
true left, right or center and how far
between lily pads and the fallen cedar.
Darkness is precious, how long will darkness last?
Our bait, worms, have no professors, they live
in darkness, can be taught fear of light.
Cut into threes even sixes they live
separate lives, recoil from light.
He tells me, "I am seldom blind
when I dream, morning is anthracite,
I play blind man's bluff,
I cannot find myself,
my shoe, the sink,
tell time, but that's spilled milk and ink,
the lost and found I cannot find.
I can tell the difference between a mollusk and a whelk,
a grieving liar and a lemon rind."
Laughing, he says, "I still hope the worm will turn,
pink, lank, and warm, dined
out on apples of good fortune.
Books have a faintly legible smell.
Divorced from the sun, I am a kind
of bachelor henpecked by the night.
Sometimes I use my darkness well—
in the overcast and sunlight of my mind.
I can still wink, sing, my eyes are songs."
Darkness is precious, how long will darkness last?
He could not fish, he could not walk, he fell
in his own feces. He wept. He died where he fell.
The power of beauty to right all wrongs
is hard for me to sell.

DANGEROUS GAME

Better to wear an archaic smile
than to play with the word Time. Play with the rain,
play on a seesaw, play with your dogs awhile.
Reading your face or the cracked face of a mountain
is not reading Time, is reading only for style.
Footprints show the trace of a man, not his person.
Clocks and history are cheap imitation,
make a piece of ass of the moon and sun.
Older than darkness, Time is a grand personage
who lived before hunger and thirst, died without language—
the first player and surely the last upon the stage.
Older than space and light, time is here and not here,
loveless, close to and distant from everything.
What song would the moon sing, if it could sing?
Was there a Big Bang or a primordial clavier
when there was nothing: a restless ghost, nothing.
They say four rivers flowed out of Eden,
no tears, despite the serpent.
How can I explain Time with a pen?
Time is simply when and also then—
when darkness and light are absent,
the only survivor in the firmament,
always present.

TELL ME PRETTY MAIDEN

No wrestling with an angel,
no dancing around, no to be or not to be.
The truth is I'm stuck with this constant
simultaneous remembering and forgetting,
each jealous of the other, each the other's fool.
That's the way it is to be alive,
tell the maple tree in October
in full foliage it is not constantly
remembering and forgetting.
Tell the ocean, tell sleep, tell his brother,
tell me pretty maiden,
are there any more at home like you?

I remember when I learned
female cypresses are wide in the hips,
males narrow, I looked outside my window.
A word here, a word there
and I saw the foreplay of trees
lasting from winter to spring
to summer to autumn—longer.
A maple stands by a maple or a red oak
a hundred years, two hundred years.
While remembering, forgetting myself,
a thousand adjectives fell from trees
in woods I know.

I try to learn the language of king maples,
more difficult than Chinese: hundreds of words
for green, yellow, golden, red, as Spanish has different
verbs to be for a permanent or temporary condition,
as Greek has the dual, a part of speech for twins and pairs.
The scrub oak has twenty verbs for the English verb to be:
to be tall, to be cut down, to be lonely,
to be covered in snow, to be a taker away

of sunlight and water from saplings.
I forgot I must go back to my life of
sums and minuses, family arithmetic.
I refuse to learn by rote, I forget
the greatest poem is the human nervous system.

I could play constant simultaneous forgetting
and remembering as tragedy, comedy or farce.
The curtain rises or falls on a simple set:
a nineteenth-century oak chair and table,
a transparent glass vase with water and forget-me-nots.
An actor says: "three cheers for remembrance,"
his brother Harpo brings in three chairs.
I remember the *niñas* in Goya's brothel
wearing two wicker chairs for hats,
naked except for chiffon blouses,
smiling at their leering clientele.

The years wander off like sheep.
They don't have a dog or a shepherd.
I'm old hat, back home,
constantly, simultaneously
remembering and forgetting.
Today while I rejoiced with bathers,
love stole my clothes and left me naked.

THE RING IN MY NOSE

to Hans Magnus Enzensberger

There is a woman in all living things, a lily.
A wounded soldier dying is a woman dying in childbirth,
a dead black soldier may be the black woman
who gave birth after she was lynched.
My mother at eighty-three died singing lullabies.
For her sake, half in mourning, half in farce,
I put her wedding ring through my nose,
tied it on a string attached to a cloud
that pulls me south down the Hudson,
noses me over industrial parks,
east over Long Island suburbs once home.
A loving pig is yanked over the pine barrens,
past Shinnecock, Conscience Point, then adrift
over the shipless Atlantic. Who or what
holds the string? Father, mother, or some
old cloudy hatred? It cannot be a butterfly
that pulls me out of reason—
perhaps some phantom pain, or pleasure, lifts me to bed,
or from cloud to cloud, beyond birthdays,
till I am over China, where woman is half the sky.

GODMOTHERS

In my family the identical twin sisters
Mercy and Womb were named after words
in the Hebrew Bible spelled alike.
What luck to have two aunts,
godmothers, who kissed me on the mouth,
wished me well cautiously when I did wrong—
when I tried to right myself it was not
to disappoint them. They weren't religious, just loving.
I ached to hear them say, "There, there,"
while they held me close, my Womb, my Mercy.

On the crazy side of my family,
I had a distant cousin who got the electric chair.
They never forgave themselves.
How many times did I hear them say,
"If you wrong someone only he or she can forgive you,
not God." Mercy walked the picket lines against injustice
until her feet bled. Womb was an agitator.
If ever you hear a note of Womb or Mercy
in my voice, it is because something of those twins,
those darling girls and beautiful women,
those immigrants, lives in me.

BONE

Apollo, my canines are into the marrow.
You cannot pry my mouth open
with a railroad spike or a chisel.
My teeth may break. My jaw may break.
I will not let go. The bone is mine and was mine
since I was boning up in my mother's womb.
I will take my bone that is partly words and dreams
in and out of bed. I gnaw on it.
I'm after some otherness of bone,
words I hold in my teeth, dry nerves and fat,
that has the taste of self, marrow of dreams.

Domesticated as I am, my dog
gnaws a bone that brings him out of bondage
into the forest of his forbearers.
In wolfness, he holds onto his bone,
lets only his master open his jaws
and take the bone from him.

My bone and guts are a musical instrument
I play for my own pleasure, sometimes for friends'.
At my age I know enough to lock and unlock
my teeth, some with gold fillings.
No one will take my bone from me
till my dying breath. Beware, even then, my jaws,
by reflex or custom may lock onto your leg
as shark and barracuda sometimes do
when they lie dead in the boat.
Apollo, I know enough to challenge
only myself at music, not you.

TO A STRANGER

Señor, make me a stranger to myself.
I am ashamed of my over-familiarity
with myself. My lack of respect
for my privacy, my way of asking
"Who were you, who are you?
Why did you do or not do, think, feel
love, hate, deny, believe or disbelieve,
choose to eat or not eat this or that?"
I am tired of walking through my own shadow,
my hands feeding me, washing me, shaking as usual.
Doing lightens the burden of words.
Let me enter the forest of decaying nouns,
to spy on the morning glory that blooms one morning
and dies that afternoon, unless it has the luck
of a cloudy day when it lives 'til night.
May I go south to a Latin jungle
where the moonflower blooms,
is pollinated by night moths in moonlight—
until its petals fall at sunrise.
I do not want to know more than necessary
to find my hat and coat when leaving
a crowded restaurant.
Your will be done. Let me laugh or weep
because it is Tuesday or Wednesday
or the other way around.
Are there more Tuesdays than Wednesdays?
That is the question. Jocasta said, "O, man of doom,
God grant that you will never find out who you are."

POETS AT LUNCH

to W. S. Merwin

I said, "Nothing for the last time."
You said, "Everything for the last time."
Later I thought you made everything more
precious with "everything for the last time":
the last meditation, the last falling asleep,
the last dream before the final make believe,
the last kiss good night,
the last look out the window at the last moonlight.
Last leaves no time to hesitate.
I would drink strong coffee before my last sleep.
I'd rather remember childhood, rehearse forgiveness,
listen to birdsong or a Spanish housemaid singing,
scrubbing a tiled floor in Seville—
I'd scrub and sing myself. *O Susanna*
Susanna, quanta pena mi costi.
I would strangle the snakes of lastness
like Herakles in his crib
before I cocked my ear to Mozart for the last time.
There is not sky or clouds enough to cover
the music I would hear for the last time.
I know a bank whereon the wild thyme of
everything for the last time grows, covered with
deadly nightshade and poison hemlock.

No last, no first, thinking in the moment,
years ago, you prepared the soil in Hawaii
before you planted your palm trees, then shared
most of your days and nights with them as equals.
You built your house with a Zen room.
I made no prayer when I dug a hole
and pushed in a twelve-foot white pine,
root ball locked in green plastic netting.
I did not cut the netting, so twenty years later

a tall, beautiful, white pine died.
I lynched the roots. To save my life
I would let them seize, cut out a bear's heart,
I would partake in its flesh.
But you would die before you'd let them kill that bear.
Again, I say, "Nothing for the last time."
You say, "Everything for the last time."
Sailor, I would have killed a stranger
to save the world. Sailor, you would not.
We kissed goodbye on the cheek.
I hope not for the last time.

Home, I look into my brass telescope—
at the far end, where the moon and distant stars
should be, I see my eye looking back at me,
it's twinkling and winking like a star. I go to bed.
My dogs, donkeys and wife are sleeping. I am safe.
You are home with your wife
you met and decided to marry in four days.

REQUIEM

i

His or her life was never as close to us as now.
At the non-denominational funeral home called Truths
they hold services in the toilet.
The corpse wrapped in sanitary paper
is readied to be flushed down a large commode.
There is a bathtub full of flowers, or a shower stall,
depending upon the means and wishes of the family.
The toilet lid may bear the name, the date,
written on disposable paper,
the writing in lipstick in a chosen shade—
"ravish me red," "pink pout," "muse."
The flush turns the body around,
the head goes down first,
into the golden pipes, and then into the septic tank.
Should the body clog the pipes,
there is a hand rubber plunger.
No organ, no Bach; the sound of a Roto Rooter,
a wire snake cleans up.
In the valley of the shadow, there's a toilet –
saints and sinners, we are all manure.
Sparrows peck at us.

ii

In their houses of worship where truth sleeps,
priests, rabbis and mullahs dance for joy
because the soul is already in paradise,
while in icy Lhasa there are sky funerals,
bodies fed to vultures, the birds of the Gods.
Better to sing Holy, Holy, Holy,
wrap the body in a shroud, prayer shawl,
modest dress, or finery—
remember the ashes, perhaps still warm.
In Spain, what is left of the dough around the Host,

stamped out, not yet consecrated,
the leftovers, are a treat given children like a cookie
to be eaten with chocolate.
Words hold the soul, a small bird
protected in the hands of a child,
thrown upward free to fly into "what's next?"

BIG LEFT TOE

Now I've stubbed and broken my big left toe.
It's not like breaking a nose or a jaw,
with nine still to go, it's a comic not a tragic flaw.
Thank God Bernini curled St. Teresa's marble toe
in ecstasy. I don't give my toe a hee-haw
of praise that a friend gives his eleventh toe.
My toe has no art, it cannot pirouette.
It can follow a tune, a Mozart quartet,
draw a face in the sand, yet it is discontent
as the broken string of a musical instrument.
When my body loves, untutored,
my toe loves, wags and is not excluded.
I cut a hole in my shoe to give my toe a platform
on which to stand broken, alone in the storm.

THE MAN TREE

The man who walks through a field in December
wears a blue suit, but above his shoulders
where his head and neck should be,
an apple tree grows
stripped of its leaves by winter.
The suit he wears makes him seem human
but his branches reaching up and outward,
higher than any man, make him arboreal.
Tears flow from under his jacket
and out of his pockets, like a stream in a forest.
The man blooms in summer, bears fruit,
walks through a field of hay and wild flowers.
The man tree never says,
"*My* river, *My* waterfall."
A mounting lark never calls, "*My* . . . *My* . . ."
Except when it sings
"Come be *My*, *My* Love."
The hawk calls, "I have *My*, *My* work to do,"
then when the work is done, it shrieks with the night owl,
"It's *mine*, it's *mine*"
—is why death was invented.
Under a man tree a mother sings for a time,
"My child, my child, my tree, my tree."

VANITAS

In the sideview mirror of my car
through the morning fog I saw a human skull
that had to be my face, where the headlights
of the car behind me should have been,
or a morning star. I did not think
to step on the gas and race away from the skull
I knew wasn't behind me. Still it had me by the throat.
I can tell a raven from a crow,
a female evergreen from a male,
but I can't tell visionary bone from ghost.
I'm used to my eyes fibbing to me,
5s are sometimes 8s, 2s, 3s.
I know the Chinese character for the word "nature"
is a nose that stands for breathing—life.
I need to see an ancient nose in the mirror.

BAD JOKE

After a difficult illness, in letters to friends I wrote:
"Inside my vitals it was Stalingrad."
I could have said "Waterloo, all puns intended."
I never would have said "a holocaust inside my belly."
Only God could have the holocaust in His belly,
or, on second thought, Stalingrad inside His belly
with a million five hundred thousand dead,
among them battalions of Russian women,
everyday Russians and everyday Germans
in with the slaughtered Wehrmacht and Panzer
divisions—a few well-disciplined innocents
"On the wrong side of history" and the Volga: Dutch,
Romanians, Hungarians, the Spanish Blue Division.
They say the Lord passes days and nights on battlefields,
although I doubt He spends His time by human measure.
In His belly they were starved, frozen, gassed,
shot to death, blown to pieces,
or done in by subtler vehicles of departure.
God does not digest or belch. Yesterday, His time,
He devoured men battling with stone axes and clubs,
He downed all history and our yesterday's dead.
Are His eyes on fire without tears?
Does He evacuate? The perfect being never makes a stink.
War is the hair on His head,
the beard He strokes when He sits in judgment.
He would never have a little fat belly like Buddha.
Looking around the world, I say to God,
"Come to us all knowing or unknowing,
jealous, melancholy, wildflower baby,
who, as long as I live,
by any other name may smell as sweet."

SONG OF NO GOD

With any luck you can still find a rain god
in a cornfield, chaotic symmetry, a sacred wood,
although nothing remains of certain gods
but an octagonal vault and part of a leg. Enough.
The moon goddess doesn't weep, the sun god does not laugh.
I strike a match to light the night, a puff
of smoke, no more. I strike another to light the day
to prove I do not need a sun god anyway.
The No God inside me is not a golden calf.
My No God has two dogs: Night and Day.
They take their time, they do not come to me.
I whistle, call "stay, stay." They do what they rather.
"I'll take you in the car to run along the sea."
They race what is, what was and what will be.
They take their time and sniff an apple tree
because there in moonlight the deer gather
to eat apples and praise their heavenly father.
I pray weary of his nothingness my No God
will not call back his dogs: Night and Day,
or, for his pleasure, let slip another flood.

GLUTTON

If I could I'd gorge on Time, twirl hours on my fork
and wipe my plate clean with my daily bread,
but I am Time's pretzel, his pistachio nut.
I wish I were Time's spaghetti carbonara.
I am what he munches at the bar
waiting for the waitress to take his order,
then Time is seated wherever he is—
this godlike No God who little by little
devours me. Eat, eat, my Lord,
you will not swallow me in one gulp.
I will give you such indigestion in Paradise
with my hard head, stiff neck, broken bones,
you will wish you were never born. Eat.
You may think, Wise Guy, you can fart me out,
but what about Mount Etna, Vesuvius,
who were those nobodies?
Invisible universal glutton,
lift your little trident! Keep me off your plate!
Eat your sheep, not this Jew.

THE ICEHOUSE AND THE POND

1

Winter. The ice slept here, the father ice
with his eye sharp as ice tongs, that cold anger
under sawdust, never thanking
the wind or a cloud over the sun
for a little relief from the pain of being ice,
while the blue-eyed ice,
whose breast he sucked for coldness,
crashed into the logs that shored up the roof.
Still what shade there was came from her
who loved the snow truly, the long below-zero nights
after a snowfall that were God-given.

2

A child looked out at the pond,
the frogs, and dry cattails,
a broken oar still iced in.
Peer deep as he could through the ice
he only saw white, silver, violet, black;
there was the red gill of a fish on a nail
near the roof, but that was as rare as laughter
in the icehouse.
The flowers on the hillside confused him,
especially the mouth-red flames.

Despite crosscut saws, ice-tongs and axes,
he made his way over the frozen straw,
through the abandoned snake nest,
toward the forbidden windows, doors, slides.
He melted ever so slowly.
He was disobedient,
though in his heart he knew he was one of them
and always would be, there was nothing
that could change him under the sun

as he slipped out between the floorboards,
down the hillside.
He made his way to the red flowers, he was sure
it was his love for them that washed
him into the brook—he loved the stones,
the roots of trees, the trout swimming through him
and leaping for flies, the ferns and webs barely
touched his cheek. Part of a brook,
these days he looks back at the icehouse.
He remembers the first dank lesson:
the joy of receiving gifts being ice-picked
out of him. Old ice, palsied now.
Someone killed a water moccasin,
threw half an orange on its head.
He knows his gifts, counts his blessings.
It had become possible
for any living thing to consume him.

3

Summer. When I swim in the pond that is language
I am at best a tourist with an American accent.
I swim into deep water. I can't touch bottom.
I think grammar is down there in the mud.
I can dive down in the icy water,
touch something unborn
among the egg layers and live bearers,
the imperfect, the pluperfect,
pollywogs of words.
I swim, which signals I am not a floating oar.
Take your frog, leech, turtle, fishkind—
I devour, reproduce, live for pleasure with them.
Unlike the clouds, we are earthlings, we swimmers
the Yets, the Stills, the Howevers
half-asleep in the sun,
afraid of our kind. I make for shallow water.
I kiss waterlilies.
I think they kiss back, an old story:

God's womb holds on to my foot.
I am deep, shallow, and muddy,
I look back over my shoulder,
remember the icehouse and the warm belly of a rabbit.

MUNICH 2010

to Hans Magnus Enzensberger

I was pleased to see a one-hundred-year-old oak
and then lindens that survived the air raids.
Now the city seems to me lyrical, the smoke
of yesteryear blown God knows where.
Now sixty-five years are toast and marmalade,
are sweet and sour. The dead not here or there,
the living are here and there, have made the grade,
while grandma and grandpa fell down the hill
with another sixty million not Jack and Jill.
Thou shalt not kill is a bitter pill
to swallow. To be human is not human.
We must learn to choose the better part of human,
go back to kindergarten waking and sleeping.
Laughter is human, so is weeping.

DOGS

I built our house on Mecox Bay
out of an old barn and Greek columns,
a five-minute sail south to the North Atlantic.
In sand, along the bulkhead, I planted Montauk daisies,
red hibiscus above the sun-splashed waves.
My dogs played wolf. Swans nested, songbirds
and sea gulls lived their seemingly pagan lives.
Occasional osprey swooped in to earn a living.
All weather, times of day, seasons were welcome.
Sometimes coming out of the ocean like gods
three seasons visited in a single day.
I thought I would never sell the house,
the flowering trees I planted, the hydrangeas,
the day lilies with my dog Sancho beneath,
their blossoms something like his color.

Old, my mother and father were guests
at our bountiful table, surrounded by my dogs
Dulcie, Sancho and Horatio,
often fed from my hand and plate. Out of the blue
my mother asked, "Will you ever forgive us
for giving away your dog?" I said, "No"
and changed the subject.

I was taught from childhood to count my blessings:
at night when I called, my mother came,
good food, summers in Adirondack wilderness.
At seven I swam a mile across the lake and back
without a following boat. From an attic window
in Kew Gardens, above a maple, I read
with my dog Rhumba and pretended.
Still sometimes I went to school black and blue.
A kid of nine, I saw wonders of the ancient world:
there is a photo of me with the sphinx and a camel.

I walked along the harbor once straddled
by the fallen Colossus of Rhodes. A week later,
on the Acropolis, I was doomed and blessed
for life by Greek beauty.

I lived in a house of unnatural affection.
More than kin and more than kind,
my mother suffered from Metamorphosis:
changed from good wife, to pillow, to slave
rebuked for planting daisies along the driveway.
Still, she shared in taking down
her opinionated, overgrown thirteen-year-old
by giving away Rhumba, his old dog,
to a waitress whose face I remember.
I loved my dog for nine years. That mutt kissed
the eyes of my blind friend, came when I whistled,
gave seminars on love, intimacy and simple honesty.
Jesus said, "Father forgive them
for they know not what they do."
But Jesus never had a dog.

Thirty years later we sold our house
where I had entertained my mother and father,
buried their ashes in acid soil.
Farmer and gravedigger,
I transplanted two unmarked rocks,
Montauk daisies, my mother and father,
day lilies, my dogs, from garden to garden.
I recited prayers honoring my parents.
I only pardoned them. I never forgave them
for giving away my old dog,
despite my dog's teaching "never hold a grudge."
Of course, if my grandpas had not left
Lithuania for Philadelphia,
if we had not been free in America,
if I still managed to be born,

I would not have likely survived in Kaunas
to indulge myself in the fine distinction
between pardon and forgiveness.
I would most likely have had a roach
or a rooster for a pet, no dog—
my knowledge more Talmudic than canine.

LISTENING TO WATER

Water wanted to live.
It went to the sun,
came back laughing.
Water wanted to live.
It went to a tree
struck by lightning.
It came back laughing.
It went to blood. It went to womb.
It washed the face of every living thing.
A touch of it came to death, a mold.
A touch of it was sexual, brought life to death.
It was Jubal, inventor of music,
the flute and the lyre.

"Listen to waters," my teacher said,
"then play the slow movement
of Schubert's late *Sonata in A*,
it must sound like the first bird
that sang in the world."

THAT MORNING

I got up a little after daybreak:
I saw a Luna Moth had fallen
between the window and a torn screen.
I lifted the window, the wings broke
on the floor, became green and silver powder.
My eyes followed green, as if all green
was a single web, past the Lombardy poplars
and the lilac hedge leading to the back road.
I can believe the world
might have been the color of hide or driftwood,
but there was—and is—the gift of green,
and a second gift we can perceive the green,
although we are often blind to miracles.
There was no resurrection of green and silver wings.
They became a blue stain on an oak floor.
I wish I had done something ordinary,
performed an unknown, unseen miracle,
raised the window the night before,
let the chill November air come in.
I cannot help remembering
e.e. cummings' wife said, hearing him
choking to death in the next room,
she thought she heard moths on the window screen
attracted to the nightlight in his study.
Reader, my head is not a gravestone.
It's just that a dead poet and a Luna Moth
alighted. Mr. Death, you're not a stone wall.
You're more like a chain-link fence
I can see through to the other side. There's the rub:
You are a democracy, the land of opportunity,
the Patria. Some say you are a picnic.
Are there any gate-crashers beside the barbecue?
I'm afraid every living and once-living thing
will be asked to leave again.

The first death is just playtime.
There is a DEAD END beyond darkness
where everyone and every thing tries to turn around.
Every thing that ever lived sounds its horn.
And you, Mr. Death, are just a traffic cop.

AUTUMN

for Stanley Kunitz

In a dream after he died
I received picture postcards
from him every day for two weeks
in a single night—the picture:
blazing maples and walnut trees,
New England in full foliage.
I wept that he should write
to me and my wife in a handwriting not his
in blue ink so often.
Since I do not remember the text,
I suppose the message was:
"Every autumn you know where to find me."

THREE SONGS FOR A SINGLE STRING

1

I wish the praying wind would hire me
to help out in the valley.
In the morning when the clouds are low,
I can push clouds up toward heaven
that Muhammad said lies under the feet
of every mother.

2

You may trick a she-camel or goat
to feed on hay stuffed in the skin of her dead kid
so she will give milk to serve her master,
or an orphaned kid or camel.
In my tradition
one of the names of God is Breast.
Almighty Breast, may I be tricked to give
the love for my dead to the living.
You will have to do more than show me
a lock of hair and a glass of whiskey.

3

The ocean, stars, mountains
without their least attention
have mated with me, as they do
with all living things.
What can I do to serve them?
Give them my bones to play with.

AND THERE ARE AFRICAN LINKS/LICKS
IN EVERY LANGUAGE

So if God made us in His image*
and likeness He's a black man.
Which did He hate more,
crucifixion or slavery?
Adam and Eve were black,
Cain and Abel black.
Somewhere there was
a white man in the woodpile.

Maybe God, come back,
had to drink at a Negro fountain—
wasn't what he meant by dividing the waters.
Black Jesus or Jehovah's voice
walked in the cool of the day.

Not that whites invented slavery,
they just made more money at it,
made it a Christian virtue,
found when they got a taste for it,
like good whiskey, watering it down a little
is better than nothing.

Do I see the Father come again,
sunning Himself,
passing the time of day
or night on street corners
out of a job?
If in the beginning was the Word,
we know the Word was African.

* DNA evidence proves all human beings have an early black/African heritage.

SAND

My scarred tongue has been everywhere
my finger has been and for longer.
My tongue is gentle, my heart's cousin.
I have no time for ornament
thinking why the wind does this or that.
The afternoon breakers roll ashore,
there is little left in the sand,
a shell where my face was.
I spit out more sand than truth.
I go to my garden. I save the day
with dirty hands. Rain, rain, rain,
I'm sure the rain means more to the garden
than to sand. Then I remember creatures that live
with their mouths wide open, their tongues in sand,
that we first made love in a bed of Atlantic sand.

ON BEES DISAPPEARING IN AMERICA AND EUROPE BUT NOT IN BRITAIN

Someone is playing tricks on flowers and blossoming trees;
now you see, now you don't see bees, wasps and hornets.
This summer, the hives and nests are empty,
pollen and nectar dry, untouched, unsucked in the cup.
Perhaps gunsmoke and lies did them in.
Bees are royalists, perhaps a little democracy
did them in. I can tell a bumblebee from a hummingbird,
how Samson found bees in a lion's carcass.
I remember Psalm 118:
The nations compassed me about like bees;
they are quenched as the fire of thorns:
for in the name of the Lord I will destroy them.
—a passage St. Augustine read as referring to Christ's capture.
Yes, I am grateful for the gift of black ants
to peonies, the sexy winds of summer, while insecticides
stop and question butterflies who lost their memory
in fields and gardens of America.
Hail Britannia, where queens and drones still prosper,
kept alive, I think, in public and private gardens
by Shakespeare in the air.

DOWN RIVER

to Zhou Ming

She remembered her dad's kissing-her-everywhere game,
her puppy pushed off the bed, not much about her old flame.
She could see his pointed eyebrows, heard, "No rain,
no rainbow." She remembered her Uncle James had a game
of pretending to throw his granddaughter out the window.
Why did she remember that, and what did that have to do
with the forced-upon-her pleasure and pain
of her dad's finger-inside-her game?
She banished herself for his smell and saliva on her pillow.
Smells can lie, but saliva's true as rain.
What she could not remember they would do again:
he is there, sure as hyacinths are blue.
She buried his ashes under a weeping willow
and went down river in a boat she could not row.

THE GIANT BATHERS

You asked me how I would kill time
three hours before my next appointment.
I did not want to lose a moment.
I remember the day was resplendent.

Three hours before my next appointment
my senses were not working wisely or too well.
I remember the day was resplendent.
I hurried to Cézanne's sad naked bathers.

My senses were not working wisely or too well.
The French still make love from cinq à sept.
I hurried to Cézanne's sad naked bathers,
and two rejoicing bathers, their sex covered over.

The French still make love from cinq à sept.
In a room with sixty sad naked bathers,
and two rejoicing naked bathers, their sex covered over,
time was not wasting me.

In a room with sixty sad naked bathers,
nearby, a wine bottle standing on blue nothing.
Time was not wasting me.
Beyond reason, a black scribble in a blue-and-white sky.

Nearby, a wine bottle standing on blue nothing.
Such scribbling defies the laws of nature.
Beyond reason, a black scribble in a blue-and-white sky.
I stayed until I was ordered out.
Such scribbling defies the laws of nature.
You asked me how I would kill time.
I stayed until I was ordered out.
I did not want to lose a moment.

CRUELTY AND LOVE

Cruelty will not fool me,
love will not fool me,
but unexpected kindness
like disappointment
startles me into being a dog.
I lick the face of kindness,
roll over on my back
offer my throat to disappointment,
bark or just whine from time to time
throughout the night.

SLEEP

These days I doze off, sleep longer.
Sleep drags me off, first by inches,
then by yards—
now miles closer to eternity,
that is another name for poverty.
So sleep steals my wallet.
It should be shackled, jailed,
allowed a period of recreation,
time off for good behavior,
paroled. As for me, I have life to live,
work to do, books to read.
Think of me as one of those
old Portuguese wines.
Let me get dusty, decant me
after one hundred years;
do not put me on ice.
Drink me in the garden
on a summer evening. Get drunk.

PLEASE

Please may be a town in Oklahoma,
but in my GI track doctor's waiting room
an old man in a wheelchair
kept repeating the word please:
pleaseplease   please   please   please
without stop at intervals endlessly.
I thought his "pleases" had different meanings:
Please,   please says, "help, the pain is killing me!"
Then there were pleadings to have a shot,
one I thought a prayer, useless without praise.
Could he crash into paradise with one word?
I remember the cries of sailors screaming in pain
without words or legs or arms,
the pain coming from limbs not there.
"Phantom." *Please   please.   Please.*
I think every living thing no matter how rude
has a way of asking   *please   please   please.*
Please is not like a telephone that keeps ringing.
At the American Hotel, "Lady Lowell" cried, "Please,
please kill me. Please, please kill me,"
while eating steak. I said "no," she said "why not?"
I said, "because tomorrow's Thursday."

A WOLF'S SONG

I take my hat off to St. Francis
who signed a pact with a wolf
before a notary: the town
of Gubbio would feed it,
the wolf would have no need
to eat children. If you need proof of this,
there are paintings of St. Francis
holding the paw of a wolf
beside the notary—in the distance
that shows the past, at the edge of a forest,
the remains of a child.

I would sign a pact with a wolf,
I kiss him good night.
We share blueberries.
We mix our blood to seal the bargain.
To those who would kill me with pleasure,
I say, "Look: the howl of a wolf
comforts me. What's the matter?
I will hold your hand, make
your favorite dish your mother cooked."

I see a grenade flying my way, a deadly sparrow.
I hide my head under a poem,
I hear obscenities in languages entangled
like flowers along the Amazon.
What can I offer compared to the pleasures of killing?
A wolf's song. I swear before a notary,
"I'll ask the ancient goddess Breast
to wash their steps with milk."
Peace is an erratic boulder
left behind by a glacier,
different from the surrounding landscape.
I will shake hands with a rock.

ON WILLIAM BLAKE'S DRAWING,
"THE GHOST OF A FLEA"

Blake drew a giant flea inhabited
by the soul of a man,
"bloodthirsty to access,"
usually, "providentially confined"
to the size and form of a flea.
This ghost flea is an inhuman giant,
its face and body part man's, part flea's,
drawn in pencil and gold leaf on mahogany,
tongue curled out of its mouth—
it clutches a bowl of blood
out of which it feeds.
On a heavy wooden plank,
near the feet of the giant ghost
is an almost invisible second flea,
a common flea. A dream of madness produces fleas.
Flea-bitten by wars and slavery, God's messengers
visited Blake every day, found if the poet prayed at all
he kneeled or stood in what he called
"the seven synagogues of Satan."
Many days, the Angels of God brought and returned
the same message made human by Blake:
Every thing that lives is holy.
Afflicted, Blake rejoiced to see his dead brother
clapping his hands on his way to heaven,
while Jehovah held naked Jerusalem
in His arms, pressing her to Him,
holding her buttocks firmly in both hands.

A GLANCE AT TURNER

His last words, "The Sun is God."
He found truth in color,
the Book of Revelation useful.
He cried out against the four angels
to whom it was given to hurt the earth and sea.
He followed a guiding star, a flight to Egypt,
a donkey burdened with the Word
and the Christian nation.
He gave a damn,
more than the sun, moon or darkness cared.
With a palette knife and thumb prints,
he answered the question,
"If God is the sun, what is the sunset?"
—proof the most pious death is by a kiss?
On his palette, primary colors,
something like never-before words,
his dead father, his mother in a madhouse.
He picked cherries with Claude and Poussin,
knew Rembrandt sometimes painted with his own feces,
that beauty may stink to heaven.
His own suffering never washed out of his brushes,
his Last Judgment, an angel with a sword, standing in the sun.
He did not know Blake's *Last Judgment*,
almost black from working and reworking.
God breaketh not all men's hearts alike.
Blake saw God sitting at the window,
Turner tried to pour sorrow out the window.
In the distant sky, beyond the stars there is
no Venice, no Titian, the Sun of Death shines.

CAPRICCIO

Better if I had said in song what I wanted
from a lady beneath her window or in a car
or when she passed twirling a parasol.
I saw Goya knew about suffering.
He etched a baby a woman held by its wrists
and ankles, its anus used as a bellows
to flame up the fire. I was Goya's child.

It was just after dark, someone
reproached me for lingering,
I smelled smoke, there was an air
of constant discourtesy. I smelled something
sour, like the dirty yellow smoke of a paper mill.
Roads were out. Two colossal figures like me,
Goya's boys, stood in the middle of a valley,
one with a club, the other swinging a rock on a rope.
In the distance, the crowd divided, moved
in opposite directions, dark figures on foot
speaking useless languages.
I heard a woman screaming, her hand
reached out was half the size of her body.
Under cement arches I saw a heap
of corpses, Jews with amazed faces;
some still alive raised their heads in protest.

I thought changing my shirt
for a clean one was the right thing to do.
I couldn't close open wounds
with flaming iron like an old soldier.
La Verbena of Seville is a burial party.
On a summer Sunday afternoon,
if the sky is a family, the clouds and I are
useless brothers. To find out what
access to the unknown I might have

I played a blind philosopher who had fifty-eight years,
led by a street-wise, seventeenth-century
Neapolitan kid. I told the boy who led me
by a fold of my cape, *I live like the dreamer*
who in sleep seems to act and speak
but waking has said and done nothing.
I live in total darkness
where the most ordinary things must be imagined
and the unknown becomes less extraordinary.

I said nothing that made anything better,
so I put what I wrote away,
not wanting to be barely entertaining.
I think I lived between always and never.
I wanted to forget that. I was like a dog,
chin on a rock, looking up at the sky.

CLOUDS

Two beautiful women in the sky kissing,
their arms and legs wrapped around each other,
one has wings, is an angel. Her lover's left hand
is deep in her feathers. Her lover's right hand
reaches deep inside her. Their tongues
are pink, gentle, rough, or hard.
The miracle is that a cloud can kiss,
that if one cloud has wings and is wrapped
around the other, the other is helpless.
Now they are rolling over each other.
I wish I could carve 'Stanley'
on the white marble bluff. I am in Cardiff.
I sleep at the Angel Hotel.

OVER DRINKS

The day is a lion across the horizon,
the forests, a thorn in its foot,
it gnaws on hapless years, its stomach full.
The lion rolls on its back kicking the heavens.
The lion of Judah is part of its pride, its mate—
some say the favorite.

Furthest from the truth: the night, the universe
is a black Labrador pup biting
as if we were its mother's teat.
Lear's fool says, "Truth's a dog must to kennel . . ."
One day the mind will dream up an equation
for reality—I may grasp in my mouth
as a bitch holds her pup
or some, an after-dinner mint. It's true the night
is the same for the sun, the rose and us,
I mouth metaphors for memory like the zoo,
put lovers in cages with primates and reptiles.
I remember a mother sea lion feeding her young—
balancing a spinning world on the tip of her nose.
There is still time to rejoice in it all.
The Irish say, over drinks, "The night is still a pup."

I'LL BE BACK TO YOU

I'll be back to you very, very soon, English.
I'm going back to Yiddish Russian, my grandmother's tongue.
I'm not a traitor, I just need my grandmother.
America, I'll be back. My friend, speak to me in Gaelic,
I'll understand.

to Paul Muldoon

THE WILD DOGS OF SAN MIGUEL DE ALLENDE

At the school in the Plaza Hotel, Mexico,
I taught the young and old what I could:
Learn from the starving dogs of San Miguel
how to see and listen. Do not waste a word
or a syllable, they are loaves and fishes,
enough to feed five thousand. No lies:
angels are specific, the devil generalizes.
We know there is mythological bread.
When you use what is called a metaphor
it is just an alibi, unless you knead it
like a baker kneads dough to make it rise
to bread, or cake, to—whatever, the devil's word.
Then use it. That's what you do for a living.

In the hills of San Miguel there are snakes
that once were walking sticks. Saint Hubert
was converted when he saw a stag
with a crucifix between its antlers.
Who has not seen a starving dog in headlights
running with a crucifix in its mouth?
At night when the wind dies down, some who listen
hear the Virgin weeping. She knows starving dogs
at the foot of the cross, snarling at evil,
licked up her son's pooling blood while He suffered,
and after, when she held Him, licked His wounds.

Any dog can nose a rat in the anus of the rich,
mercy in the asshole of the poor. Red-haired
Judas fed his good dog under the table.
The starving dogs of San Miguel de Allende
will carry off your sorrows if you put your trust in them,
or feed them from your hand.
Easier to speak for wild dogs than the poor.

THE UNICORN

Here is a lady with a unicorn in her lap,
a holy mother with a unicorn,
a symbol of Christ the Savior,
a black horse with a yellow horn and yellow tail.
I see the Lady with a unicorn, a savior who is not Christ,
but poetry. She kisses the beast
who licks her face. The unicorn
pokes its horn in her neck, a sign of love,
closes its eyes, falls asleep in her arms,
forgets all suffering.

In a heartbeat, heart beating so hard
you can hear it, the beast awakens,
runs about the house, kissing books and sharpening its horn,
today on free forms. Rising on its back legs
it stands on Shakespeare—
showing its golden penis, it ejaculates,
then grazes in "the valley of its saying,"
on Góngora, Lorca, the Psalms,
washing and feeding the poorest of the poor,
until, with the excuse that it is in love,
or loveless, it returns to the barn, the library—
weeping because it is only a metaphor,
captured in the lap of the virgin.

FOR MY GODMOTHER, TWENTY YEARS LATER

Give me a death like hers without tears,
those flies on a summer day about a carcass—
about the house medicine, Mozart, and good cheer.
My song: life is short, art long, death longer.
My doctor uncle covered her with kisses.
When her life was a goldfinch in his hand,
on a feeder and birdbath outside her window:
larks sang, splashed and fed above the sparrows.
A blue jay militaire drove them away.
Then, a bird of prey, a necessary reprimand
screamed overhead without mercy. Instead
of terror, it was met at her window
by the warbler of good cheer that sometimes sings for the dead.
I whistle for it to come and nest near my window.

THE MESSIAH COMES TO VENICE

He rode into the city unrecognized on a lion,
wore a pointed hat with fool's bells,
whetting his knife on his lion's haunch. Someone shouted,
"He made the laws before he made the world!"
His hand dripping oils, the rider pointed at the voice.
"I want my bond, since I made the laws before the world."
The lion bowed its head.
"Christians, Muslims, Jews, I will teach you to be content,
one as the other. Know this law:
you must first be one, then the other,
Jew play Christian and Muslim, Muslim play Jew
and Christian. Christian, wear my gabardine, then be a Turk.
That is my bond, the pound of flesh I cut from your heart.
You must learn to leave the meat of your life behind,
as an infant cut from its mother—
whatever the nothingness you call years.
Kick me, spit on me, or praise me—no matter.
I stand for judgment.
Now play your parts. Change gods, change gods,
then do the dance you call *your days*."
A lion is swimming in the Grand Canal.

SQUEEZING THE LEMON

If the table and chandelier
made for Wright's mile-high building
had "social relations, hapless and unheard,"
according to your lyrical experiment,
where might you go then to tell your story?
Where, *où*, *¿dónde?*, *dove*, *nali* in sexual Chinese
nali nali also meaning "you're welcome"? Nowhere.
A "confessional poem"? Sooner waterboarding.
If there were a San Francisco earthquake,
would *Varieties of Religious Experience* fall off the shelf?
Did your mother speak for a year without a noun or verb
except in the last sentence? With barely a taste of self,
we are like prisoners in San Quentin,
salt and sugar taken off our tables,
two in a cell playing husband or wife on alternate weeks.
In a wink, you join with the one action that is death,
the broken nose of stars—
the last line of an unfinished style,
the last syllable of meaning squeezed out of a lemon.

THE HUDSON RIVER

A child of seven, I swam across the Hudson
at her source and rise in the Adirondacks,
at Lake Tear of the Clouds. I had her
where she is golden and sandy, ten yards wide,
as generations of swimmers have had her
in deep and shallow waters. I have spent many nights
beside worldly rivers. The Hudson is provincial,
sometimes like an overworked mother,
daughter, or servant. Her eyes and shoreline
show years of disappointment and disrespect.
Damn those who defame her.
She is indifferent to me—still, I have had her
it seems all my life. I fall asleep beside her.
Often I awake half-dreaming.
I see the Hudson is naked.
In the torn clouds I see a little boat with a light
on top of the mast. Is the light her navel or nipples?
I say that, but I know you can 'have' a mother,
not a river, not any other woman.
Swimming in the Hudson I learned I can love a woman,
"have" her, and she may believe I "have" her too,
and that she can "have" me for a greater or lesser price,
but we cannot keep anything but our word.
I bet my tongue on that.

ANATOMY LESSONS

i

At Piazza Santa Croce
I bought a print for less than the cost of a gelato,
an etching made when vivisection was a sin:
a battle in a vineyard: long-haired naked men
against long-haired naked men, Tuscans
cut open, dissected with sabers, crossbows and axes.
They do not fight half lusting for each other.
They do not take pleasure in their nakedness as bathers do
or fight for a cause, city or God,
or over a lover removed from the scene.
There is the artist's cause—to show flesh unresurrected,
how men look, stripped to bones and innards.

ii

With their book on love, *The Neck-Ring of the Dove,*
Muslims came to Florence from Córdoba,
dressed lords and ladies in gold and silver
brocades and taffetas—their poet-physicians taught
how naked bodies looked in life and death,
kissed and torn to pieces on earth, in hell and paradise.

iii

These days they pass a camera with ease
down the throat and out the anus, taking silent movies
of what was thought divine. Note: the sacred heart,
masked surgeons watch vital signs, seldom genuflect.
There is the poetry of sonar imaging, the heart, the kidneys,
the diseased prostate doomed to shipwreck
in the blood and urine of mothering seas.
X-rated and X-rayed, the body is sacred, love is still an art
some call "praying": lying down, standing up, or on their knees,
whatever the place, the time of day or night they please,
when the body lets the soul do whatever it please.

FEBRUARY

to Arnold Cooper

A week ago my friend, a physician, phoned
to say he has lung cancer, "not much time
so come on over." I brought him some borscht
I cooked and about a tablespoon of good cheer.
We kissed goodbye as usual.
Then it was as if
we walked out in deep snow.
He was still in bedroom slippers.
March was a long way off, the snow
much too deep for crocuses to push through.
Then it was as if he laughed,
"I lost a slipper. Poor snow."
I put his bare foot in my woolen hat.
We talked about February and books
as if it were a summer day. I thought,
"No better mirror than an old friend."
He said, "In my work I've done what I wanted to do."
A branch broke off a sycamore, fell
into the snow for no reason.
The buildings of New York's skyline seemed empty
of human beings, gigantic glass and steel gravestones.

These words are obsolete.
We had an early summer. He died the ninth of June,
directed toward eternity like a swan in flight,
Katherine and Melissa at either wing.
Surrounded by love, he landed in his garden—ashes now.

Hibiscus, roses, day lilies: hold firm!

SPACE POEM

Universe after universe opens outward
as an ocean seen from shore,
where the waves and breakers do not roll toward shore.
They break outward toward
a region from which nothing, not even light, escapes.
I am there, beyond numbers and humdrum words,
billions of light-years away
with lightless, darkened, sun-filled,
begotten, misbegotten, dirtless stars
playing as puppies on planetary tits—
still not beyond what is. I think I heard
Emilia Bassano playing the virginal.
A caterpillar, I write riding a leaf in space.
I have only left or right.
I beg for east or west, north or south.
The maple leaf I ride blows out to a universe inferred
into and beyond amoral black holes
through its interaction with other matter,
unlike the moral silences between words.
The clouds I touch are as hot as the ovens of Auschwitz
and as cold as the gulags of Siberia,
temperatures I know from picture books.
I eat away on my leaf. I call from nowhere:
Sweetheart, have dinner. I won't be back in time.

THE GRAMMARIAN

I say, to be silly,
Death is a grammarian.
He needs the simple past,
the *passato remoto*, the *passé composé*,
the *le* in Chinese added
to any verb in the present
that makes it past.
In the pluperfect houses of worship
death hangs around,
is thought to be undone.
Sometimes he is welcome.
I thank him for the simple present
and his patience.

ONLYNESS

to J.B.

Your Onlyness, your first commandment was:
"Forget about me. It's the passerby that matters."
Was that my neighbor? I followed him into the crowd
but lost him. I barely saw his face.
My book of uncommon prayer commands:
'You shall love the stranger as yourself.'
Those without a spine with crooked hearts?
I saw a snake cut open, its heart exactly like mine.
He was a passerby. We did not walk the same,
but All-knowing Onlyness, You saw we danced alike.
I love the garter snake and the *fer-de-lance*,
but I cannot love my neighbors equally. At school I sang:
"Trust thou in Your Onlyness, He shall establish your heart."

When years hunted as wolves in snow,
before the forests were poetry, the plowed fields fiction,
I was something like an Arctic lizard
that lived ten months a year under ice,
a dew of reptile-antifreeze in my skin.
You did that. Then one day You chose to make me human.
Your Onlyness, what did You ever do I knew the reason for?
What did I ever do I knew the reason for?
The rat holds her young tenderly as Our Lady,
sings a lullaby in a sewer pipe.
I am among the passersby.
I live with the music I love, that faceless beauty.
I think Your Holy Ghost is every living thing.

SEVENTH CHILD

Seventh child
crippled by polio
backward
born to my grandparents,
my mother's side
in their fifties.
When my grandmother died
my aunt did not speak
for seven weeks, till she met a stranger
to whom she could pass on
the evil eye.
She wrote *Bessie*
and her address
in her prayer book
so God would know
where to find her.
I was her infant lover.
She played with my
personal pronoun I.
I will bury
her prayer book in my garden,
a fallen leaf to mark
the text for the day:
The palm tree protested,
Do not cut down
the cedar. Both of us
are from the same root.

EYE

I owe much to my distant relative
the recently discovered
primordial ocean creature
an Eye surrounded
by a few transparent
gelatinous arms and wings.
The Eye prospered,
found food, avoided danger,
read shoals, corals, ocean bottom,
floated
out to sea, looking,
looking. Before there was hearing
or smell, an Eye swam,
saw. The evidence
is still insufficient
under sand, sunken mountains,
hidden perhaps in our salt tears.
Before primordial syntax
or love at first sight,
my ancestor, my ancestor saw!

FOR GEORGIE

Today, flying from Munich to Rome,
I saw Venice through Tiepolo clouds.
I knew Venus and Mars
were making love down there.
Two days ago, my dog died,
ate poison,
her insides were cut to pieces.
You Doges, Popes,
Admiral Jehovah,
Admiral Jesus, Zeus, Satan,
whoever is up to it,
I'll give you Venice, the Titians, Bellinis, Tiepolos,
the piazzas and palaces—*un affare.*
It's all yours. Give me back my dog.

CHORUS

Today I saw proof in the dusty theater
of my Y chromosomes: 7,000 years
before King David my ancestors wore
his invisible star, G2a(P15).
Out of Ethiopia or Tanzania
they hunted and gathered their way north,
ice ages before what we now call years,
past Ephesus, the Black Sea, to Iberia.
Some lingered behind, found figs and grapes
they shared with larks and wolves.
My Betters, I am a child of your hungers.
Ancient, present, and future Silences,
I invite all of you to a fish soup dinner.
Call me a ship, a freighter and crew, adrift.
My joys and sorrows are battened down.
In my hold is the dry rot of things "better left unsaid."
Drifting? I am on my old course: I need
to wake up not knowing where I am.
Call it love of wilderness, Elijah, chance,
my North Star. Waves teach me winds.
I follow Aphrodite and Venus, those streetwalkers.
I read my slips of the tongue as if they are charts.
My rudder is for waving goodbye.
Pardon, Silences. What is this? Sooner or later
a message in a bottle thrown into the sea.
I am still at sea. God knows I love a storm.

PEACE

The trade of war is over, there are no more battles,
but simple murder is still in.
The No God, Time, creeps his way,
universe after universe, like a great snapping turtle
opening its mouth, wagging its tongue
to look like a worm or leech
so deceived hungry fish, every living thing
swims in to feed. Quarks long for dark holes,
atoms butter up molecules, protons do unto neutrons
what they would have neutrons do unto them.
The trade of war has been over so long,
the meaning of war in the O.E.D. is now "nonsense."
In the Russian Efron Encyclopedia,
war, *voina*, means "dog shit";
in the Littré, *guerre* is "a verse form, obsolete";
in Germany, *Krieg* has become "a whipped-cream pastry";
Sea of Words, the Chinese dictionary,
has war, *zhan zheng*, as "making love in public,"
while war in Arabic and Hebrew, with the same
Semitic throat, *harb* and *milchamah*, is defined
as "anything our distant grandfathers ate
we no longer find tempting—like the eyes of sheep."
And lions eat grass.

ANONYMOUS POET

to Jean Garrigue

Sometimes I would see her with her lovers
walking through the Village, the wind
strapped about her ankles.
Simply being, she fought
against the enemies of love and poetry
like Achilles in wrath.
Her tongue was not a lake,
but it lifted her lovers
with the gentle strength of a lake
that lifts a cove of waterlilies—
her blue eyes, the sky above them—
till night fell and the mysteries began.
My friend I love, poet I love,
if you are not reading or writing tonight
on your Underwood typewriter,
if no one is kissing you, death is real.

HOTEL ROOM BIRTHDAY PARTY, FLORENCE

Mirror, mirror on the wall,
who's that old guy in my room?
In the red nightshirt on my bed
I'm a kabuki extra. If I please
I can marry all
to nothing, snow to maple trees,
leap for joy over my head,
play bride and bridegroom,
an old and young shadow on the wall.
I can play a decapitated head
laughing in its basket of flies.
There are no clocks in paradise,
a dog's tail keeps time instead.
(Today be foolish for my sake.)
Which comes last, sunset or sunrise?
Nightfall or daybreak?
The day is Puccini's,
the street is for madrigals,
the celebration in the cathedral:
a skull beside a loaf of bread,
but for my grandmother's sake
it's a portion of *torta della nonna* I take.
It is a double portion of everything I want.

A mirror is a stage: I'm all the comedies
of my father's house and one of the tragedies.
I draw my boyhood face
in blood and charcoal
I hold my masks in place—
all the worse for wear
with a little spit behind the ear,
and because this is my birthday
like a donkey in its stall
let fall what may.
To be alive is not everything
but it is a very good beginning.

THEN

In our graves we become
children again
then we are grandchildren
then great-grandchildren
and so on, name after name
till we are nameless
free as the birds to sing
songs without words
mating calls, warnings
simple trills, for no reason,
that call the day is glorious.

SATYR SONG

> *"I want a hero: an uncommon want . . ."*
> —Byron, Don Juan

A common satyr and poet, I want a hero
who reaches up to the matter beneath
the stanza: eight lines, ten syllables or so,
as into underpants, who rhymes *faith*
and *death, hello* if he cares to with *Galileo*,
who recanted, but fathered before his death
Natural Philosophy and three natural daughters
baptized in the Arno's muddy waters.

I cheer for *love*, what some call *vice*,
what some call *sin*, some simply pleasure,
humping, romance, odd ways of making nice,
taking advantage of, taking the measure.
One wife's passion is another's sacrifice,
one man's poison is another's cure.
A little fornication rights all wrongs,
there are no commandments in the Song of Songs.

We are made of water, earth, air, and fire
in the image of the One you-know-Who,
whose hair in the wind is Hebrew barbed wire.
On the first day when the sun was brand new,
creation a blast, He simply took a flyer,
since in darkness there was little to do,
He made us—to drown us in the ocean
of the last full measure of devotion.

Not every lady returns from the dance
with the guy who brought her, anything written
by man or woman in honest ink may rinse
away in tears. Love's not an altered kitten
in the master's lap, fed on white mice.

For every French kiss there is a France,
for every bugger there is a Britain,
for every time I bite, twice I'm bitten.

I like heels, their music on the floor, not bare human feet.
Mozart loved to hear the sound of hoof beats
on oak, marble—Köchel 44,
his concerto for woodwinds and satyr hooves,
brought satyrs to court before the Emperor.
Today you hear such music, such hooves
in Andalusian caves and orange groves,
in Greek cafes, and on the Mount of Olives.

When a boy, I first saw my lower half:
my goat hooves, my pecker, I shook in terror,
called it "my sock apple tree" for a laugh.
How many would eat my apples to the core,
would I father a kid, a faun, a calf—
I stood helpless before the mirror,
the living proof of the Creator's error,
erotic errata, a kid who pees on the floor?

My mother told me Jesus was a satyr
so I wouldn't feel bad at Christmas without a tree,
that God was a lover, not a hater,
to button up my overcoat when the wind is free
(she said she'd tell me about the Devil later),
to take good care of myself, she belonged to me.
She taught me to be silly, and to be good,
which brightened the night sky of my childhood.

Further, she explained, "Be true to your phallus.
Live in the wilderness. The future is now, not eternity."
I loved the Aurora Borealis.
Hell was the city, heaven the country,
the woods, a field of wildflowers, my place.

One kiss in the country is worth ten in the city,
whatever the weather, I took nymphs at random,
one at a time, in circles or in tandem.

Now, the question is, how can a good wife
live with a circumcised satyr from Queens
who thinks sin is cutting spaghetti with a knife,
childbirth the parable of spilled beans.
To understand this mystery, this hieroglyph,
each day she needs a Rosetta Stone, she preens
burrs, hay and lice from my graying plumage,
gently combs the old madness from my rage.

Centaurs teach, satyrs are autodidacts.
I have horns, not rays of light like Moses,
following the heart is my business, not facts,
or lines of reason. I chase the scent of roses,
waterfalls, meanings that fall through the cracks.
The day composes and decomposes—
love after love—I pay attention to rhyme,
to sunrise and sunset, not silly-billy time.

I have no time for clocks that tie up time's
two legs so the Gods only hop and jump—
sure to stumble on "is" or simple rhymes
for "was." My god makes the grasshopper jump,
frogs croak, the sun go down while the moon climbs
up to darkness. Love made the first atom jump.
I am entangled by love and untangled—
love the enchanting, love the newfangled.

When I heard the great god Pan was dead,
I asked did he die three deaths for us: goat,
man, and God, the hand of Saturn on his head?
He taught the ways of imperfection. Devout
Pan, you died so we might know Lust instead

265

of moderation, so we who cannot fly can float,
free as you taught us, our drunken hooves unsure,
walking the giddy clouds above our pasture.

The trick was not to know myself, I was not
human, so I could only pretend to be
a gentleman, a fish out of water, a What-
is-That?, a centaur, a mule, a donkey.
Let me be a well-written sentence, not
a blot on the human page, not poetry,
a satyr, a freak of nature, a growth,
a knot on a tree, a goat of my word, an oath.

I said, "I will never forget you, dear,"
but what is my never, never, never worth?
Once my "never" was worth fifty years;
you could take it to the bank, a piece of earth
you could mortgage. Now my life is in arrears,
it is late December, there is a dearth
of everything, years, months, days are hostile.
I will remember you, love, a little while.

My lady's touch has a way of whispering:
"It is summer, a perfect day, cloud
after cloud." The world's a good-for-nothing
and a good-for-something. It is right that a hungry crowd
of seagulls attacks a fluke as if it were the world.
In the lucky world, still on the wing,
love whispers, "It is summer, a perfect day."
May my lady's touch have its way.

A SATYR'S COMPLAINT

It means little to me now when I am rusting away
that at dawn gods still roll out of our human beds,
that once I entered down the center aisle
at the Comédie Française, the Artemis of Ephesus
on my arm, all eyes on her rows of breasts and me.
"Who is the master of her ninety nipples?"
the public whispered. No one noticed I was in fact
a bronze satyr, my goat feet, my tail, my erect penis.
I loved confusion, chaos was paradise.
I found happiness, so to speak, on the ramps
and scaffolding of the Tower of Babel,
I danced holding a tambourine above my head
made from a brass Turkish sieve I called *time*.
Water, sacramental wine, ink once words, passed through.
In old Rome, I played the flute, but at the first sight
of my combed, perfumed, and throbbing lower half,
Lucretia thrust a dagger through her heart.
Later in Pisa, when on the Piazza a colossal
New Testament was carved in marble in Greek—
chapter and verse, I danced across Matthew, John,
Mark and Luke, leapt to Revelation, stars flashing
from my hooves. In the Basilica, virgins
lined up on their knees in white for first communion.
A proper satyr, I took half a dozen from behind.
The wafers danced on their tongues. Beautiful,
the little hearts of blood on white lace.
The Tower of Pisa leaned away from me in disgust.
I shouted back at the mob of tourists who attacked me:
*You will never put out the fires of hell
with a nineteenth-century American candle-snuffer.*
The devil is no one, a French-Canadian plaster loon.
Frightened by my mythological smell
a bronze horse reared up, broke away
from his handler. Mares turned their hindquarters

to the north wind, bred foals without the aid of stallions.
Born for blasphemy and lust, uncircumcised half-goat,
I made my way to the Holy Land.
I am proud my bronze prick was the clapper
in many a Jewish, Christian and Muslim belle.
I must have done something right,
Jew, Christian and Muslim chased after me
throwing stones: onyx, opals, diorite,
the glass eyes of their god.
I hid in the cold lawless night of Sinai,
my companions a snail, a lamprey eel skeleton.
Wise man, remember every giraffe farts above your head.
What have I stolen from myself, I thought.
How can I pay myself back in kind?
The sun and moon survive absolutely without conscience.

DIARY OF A SATYR

WHEN I was a child, I moved my pillow to a different part of the bed each night because I liked the feeling of not knowing where I was when I woke up. From the beginning I yearned for the nomadic life. I wandered, grazed like a goat on a hill—the move from grazing to exploring was just a leap over a fence. In my seventh year, I had a revelation. A teacher asked me a question. I knew the answer. Miss Green, a horse-faced redhead, asked the 3A class of P.S. 99, Kew Gardens, Queens, a long way from Byzantium: "What are you going to do in life?" Most of the answers remain a blur, but someone said she was going to be a novelist and someone said he'd write a play, or for the movies. I remember waiting; I was last to answer: "I am certain I am a poet." Then Miss Green said, "I knew it. You, Stanley, are a bronze satyr," and she whacked my erect penis with a twelve-inch Board of Education wooden ruler.

I ran home in a fury at my parents. They had never told me I was a satyr. My mother's explanation: "You know what a hard time I had giving birth to you. Why do you think every time I hit you it hurts my hand? You had whooping cough the first six months of your life. The doctor said no human being could survive that. Even so, when you were three months old in your crib, you knocked your five-year-old sister unconscious. Nothing ever fits you, not your shoes, not your pants, not your shirts, nothing. Your feet always hang off the bed." How many times did I hear my mother say, "That kid doesn't know his own strength. You'll injure somebody for life. Don't hit. Don't hit. The other kids, gentile and Jew, lie. You are mythological."

After the revelation, at dinner, I saw my father—a public high school principal—as an angry centaur. Most evenings he was out herding his mares and women together for song, smell, and conversation. At our dinner table, I knew if I didn't speak, no one would. My fifth summer, my father went to Europe "alone," mostly, I think, to Venice and Vienna. By watching others, I taught myself to swim. When he returned I couldn't look him in the eye. He brought back presents: a wooden bowl that, when lifted, played a Viennese waltz, a bronze ashtray of a boy peeing, after the fountain in Brussels, a silver top on a plunger I could never figure out, a blue necklace for my mother, some etchings of Venetian views and one of Beethoven. We lived in an apartment as desolate as Beethoven's jaw.

Still, on February 7, 1935, with my father on sabbatical leave, we set out as a family aboard the *S.S. Statendam*, heading for the stormy waters of the Atlantic, then southeast to the sunny Mediterranean. It was the first of many voyages I would take under different circumstances from the moral north to the warm south. For the first time, I heard the Roman languages of satyrs and satires, then Greek, Hebrew, Arabic, and Turkish. I heard rolling r's, strange j's and h's, sometimes silent, throated on olives, anchovies and garlic. Until that February, I had entered a house of worship only on special occasions—a Protestant Adirondack church in summer, to attend films—a synagogue, only once, to tell my grandmother on Yom Kippur that my mother was waiting outside in a car—I was thrown out for not wearing a hat, or perhaps because I was a satyr. My mother offered me hers, a brown, broad-brimmed hat with a veil that I refused to wear. Within a month, this satyr stood before the *Nightwatch* in Amsterdam. I read "Franco Franco Franco" on a wall in Malaga, I rode a camel beside the Sphinx, toured the Basilica of San Marco in Venice, watched men praying at The Wailing Wall; I entered the Church of the Nativity and the Holy Sepulcher, heard the "good news" for the first time. I took off my shoes, heard my hooves echo on the green rugs and tiles in the mosque of Santa Sophia and the Blue Mosque. I was photographed with the caryatids on the Acropolis, ran through the Parthenon on a windy February or March day, the Greek sun so bright against the white marble it hurt my eyes.

A few days later, on the Island of Rhodes, I was proud to be nicked in the leg by a ricocheted bullet in a post-revolutionary celebration. When I told the story throughout my childhood, I was shot in the leg in a Greek Revolution; I said I had a scar to prove it—and I do. That spring, I wandered off alone into the red light district of Algiers. An auburn-haired, tattooed lady smelling of flowers and sweat kissed me for nothing behind a beaded curtain. She touched a naked breast to my lips—I was in paradise. My mother thought I was lost. Soon, in Cairo, late at night, I roused most of the hotel attendants, claiming I had leprosy. I was covered with volcanoes of blood, my only comfort a black dragoman, tribal scars on his face, until my parents returned from a performance of belly dancers and made the discovery that I had been bitten by an army of fire ants. I would not forget the poverty and disease in the slums of Cairo, the crack of whips over the donkeys and horses. I was nine years old, eight years younger than the Soviet Union, changed forever.

Aboard the *Statendam*, I played chess with a thirteen-year-old kid named Matthew. He wore white knickers and traveled with his grandmother. I last saw him crying, kicking and spitting at my father, who was beating the dickens out of him. I never, in the two-month voyage, saw Matthew or his grandmother again. I asked my mother if Dad threw them overboard; she said, "You're exaggerating again." My father said, "To ask questions is a sign of intelligence, but you ask too many questions. Your mother is the Tower of Babel. You and she are two of a kind."

Now that I could accept and was proud of being a bronze satyr, I remembered when I was a baby in my Aunt Bessie's arms, I took her breasts out of her blouse, thinking, "I am pretending to be just a baby, but I am really out for a feel." I wish I had been photographed, then with my little victorious, evil satyr smile, instead of the family photo of me in a baby carriage reaching for a cloud. In our family, the beginning of civilization was understood to be the moment Abraham sacrificed the ram instead of his firstborn son. I started one dinner's conversation with "I think it would have been better to kill Isaac than the ram. I think the ram stands for me. Daddy, you know there's a very thin line between the good shepherd and the butcher."

"Who are you to think!" Whack went my father's Board of Education ruler, a thirty-six-inch weapon. My mother threatened to stab herself in the heart with a kitchen knife like a bronze Lucretia. We were a family of atheists; still, we celebrated an occasional seder with uncles, aunts, and their children, most of whom kept away from me, lest I molest them. What could I do to liven up the evening? I planted a snail and a skeleton of an eel under the parsley and horseradish on my father's seder plate. The moment he passed out the horseradish, everyone saw the snail and eel's skeleton. I said, "Horseradish rhymes with Kaddish." Lightning, my father reached

271

out for me, but he missed. I was ordered out of the house, into the world of wild things.

I had planned one last, beautiful gesture. My mother and Aunt Mabel had a friendly contest, who could make the lightest matzo balls. My mother always lost. I had found my aunt's matzo balls laid out on a platter in the kitchen. I took our little collection of stones and jewels from Jerusalem, and one by one I thrust them into the center of each matzo ball: diorite, opal, quartz, limestone, sandstone, onyx. I watched through the window as the matzo balls were served with a spoon, one by one, into the chicken soup. My aunt had a big and loyal constituency that typically gulped their food. Hypocrites, they swallowed the matzo balls with such comments as, "Light as air!" "Like perfume," until my cousin Audrey cried, "I broke a tooth on a rock!" I danced my little goat dance outside for joy. For the first and only time in her life, my dear mother was declared a winner.

Whatever the weather, the smoke of battle never cleared. In November, on the anniversary of my grandfather's death, my mother lit a Yartzheit memorial candle in a glass. I believe she prayed. "What would happen," I asked, "if I blew out the flame?" My mother's face saddened that I should ask such an unspeakable question, but she knew my ways. "That would be a sin." She almost never used that word. Now I knew there was a second sin—the first, the greater sin, wasting food. A proper satyr, sin was my pie in the sky. I knew that in one evening Alcibiades had cut the penises off half the herms in Athens. I scouted the neighborhood, and in one evening, with our nineteenth-century American candlesnuffer, I put out the flames of seven Yahrzeit candles. I came across a magazine called *Twice a Year* that introduced me to Rimbaud, Lorca, Wallace Stevens; they taught me how to survive. Out of a bar of Ivory soap I carved a Virgin Mother with a baby satyr in her lap, then another virgin with a unicorn in her lap. My thought was the unicorn represented, not Christ, but my savior—poetry. I cut school and went two or three days a week to the main reading room of the Forty-second Street Library (a satyr among lions), or the Museum of Modern Art, or to the Apollo Theater to see foreign films. I smoked five-cent Headline cigars. One romantic evening I called my father a sadist (the first shot of the fourth Punic War). It was then I was banished from Jackson

Heights forever.

Hard years. I learned to disguise myself to earn a living. Wherever I went I carried my desperately thin production of poems and Wallace Stevens. I was sure Hitler was anti-satyr. I joined the Navy at seventeen. A sword wound and the G.I. Bill got me through college in style. I had a recurring nightmare that, like the satyr Marsyas, I was flayed—just for being a satyr, for no reason at all, not for challenging Apollo at music. I leapt around graduate women's dorms, broke windows and doors. Police were called. I was expelled for "subversive activity." Now history: I was hired by a detective agency to spy on organizing workers. I became a counterspy for Local 65. I sang in a band, played the bass, waited on tables; I was a sailor on a Greek merchant ship (I got the job through Rae Dalven, the translator of Cavafy); I grazed a while at New Directions; for mysterious reasons, Dylan Thomas and I became passionate friends—I loved his poetry and his deep-throated Christianity. I remember his saying "the truth doesn't hurt." He could and would talk intimately to anyone, regardless of class or education, not a habit of American or English intellectuals. He drank, he told me, because he wasn't useful, which I understood to mean he could not relieve human suffering. Anyone who really cared about him knew how profoundly and simply Christian he was. Dickens was a favorite teacher. He gave away the shirt off his back. The turtleneck sweater Dylan wore in that picture was mine, knitted for me by my Aunt Tilly. We discovered an Italian funeral home on Bleecker Street where, after the bars closed at 4 a.m., we drank whiskey on a gold and onyx coffin. He introduced me to Theodore Roethke, his second-favorite living American poet. His favorite was e.e. cummings— "he can write about anything." Dylan, Ted and I spent an evening with townspeople from Laugharne, trolls who whitewashed the town. What a concert of Welsh accents and laughter. Dylan had his boathouse, Roethke his greenhouse, I had my apartment house in Queens.

I met a blond, green-eyed Catalan beauty named Ana Maria. Full of Spanish poetry and Catalan republican-heretical-anarchistic tragedy, she was a great bad-weather friend. After Barnard College she sailed off to Spain; I followed, after writing a poem called "Sailing from the United States." (I earned the money to follow by wild luck—an old 8th Street satyr who knew I loved painting gave me an El Greco to sell, a crucifixion with a view of Toledo.) We married at the American Consulate in Tangiers. Our witnesses—her mother and two virgin sisters. There was blood on the floor. It turned out that one of her sisters had been given a metal garter with nails by a nun at the Colegio del Sagrado Corazón because the nun thought Ana Maria was marrying an American Protestant. A miracle: the sister who wore the garter and shed her blood at my wedding found her way to Philadelphia, married an orthodox Jew, a painter. They both died too soon and are buried on a hillside overlooking Haifa.

I knew in Rome there was a tradition of centaur teachers—why not satyrs? I made my way to pagan Rome. I taught English and tutored. We lived facing the temple of the Vestal Virgins across the Tiber. I decided, one August evening, to have a mythological picnic, a cookout for my mythological friends. Of course, it had to be beside the river, on the embankment of the Tiber, because the hippocamps were half-horse, half-fish; the tritons were half-man, half fish. There were nymphs and maenads. The great god Pan himself came—and the Artemis of Ephesus on a sacred barge. (You understand I could not serve my famous fish soup.) A giraffe crashed the party. He said he was a tree, a sycamore among men, lonely since his nesting birds flew south. He said he envied trees that can lean over a river and see their reflection. Madness, I thought, to have a private mythology, but I knew to speak to him I had to accept his metaphor. The symposium began. How did it feel to a man to make love to a fish, how did it feel to a horse to make love to a fish? What was love? Someone complimented Artemis on the beauty of her many breasts. A harpy screeched, "She has no nipples; they are the testicles of sacrificed bulls." We all came out of darkness, hatched from a single egg that was love the enchanting, the brilliant. When we departed, we kissed goodbye in our several heartfelt ways. Some wept because the sirens, as usual, sang their song of how we would be remembered.

I spent years in Rome, happy to eat the leftovers of the gods, reading and writing, trying to make a living holding four jobs simultaneously. More than once, drunk on Frascati, I bathed in the Bernini fountain of the four rivers. On summer evenings, I drank from the Nile with a marble tiger. I corresponded with my mother. I received one letter from my father I carried around a while. Finally

I destroyed it, lest God should see it. Out of the blue, I received a postcard from my father, "We will be in Pisa on August 18, 1956, at the Hotel Cavellieri, if you care to see us." Signed, "Pop." Never, not once in my life, did I call my father "Pop." I arrived on the appointed day, shocked to see how much they had aged. They were fifty-eight. We had lunch in the piazza, the pages of the Bible flapping in the wind. A little peeved that I had learned Italian and Spanish in the passing years, my father taught himself passing Italian and Spanish to go with his Greek, Latin, and French. He had more than enough Italian to order, as usual, exactly what he wanted. He insisted on having his spaghetti with cinnamon and sugar, no doubt a Litvak recipe out of his mother's kitchen. My mother said my hair was getting straight; did that have anything to do with the Leaning Tower of Pisa? Oh, how I miss my mother's questions. My father spent a cordial week in Italy, my mother another month at our apartment in Trastevere. She slept in a room I usually rented out, in a bed just vacated by Christopher Isherwood and friend. If she had known, would she have slept a wink? My father said, in wishing me goodbye, "If you had only been a bronze horse rearing up once in a while, I could have handled you." What was our mettle, a word I misspelled in my head as m-e-t-a-l? What we were really made of, the years would prove.

Coming out of his thoughts, my father said abruptly, "What I know of poetry I owe to you."

"How so?" I asked suspiciously.

"When I was studying for my principal's exam when you were two or three, I had to memorize passages from Shakespeare. On walks, I would recite the great speeches over your head, and repeat them out loud until I had them: *Hamlet, King Lear, The Tempest.*"

I said, "Perhaps what I know of poetry I owe to you."

He started reciting "O, what a rogue and peasant slave am I" with his large, tin ear. I finished it. I kissed him and said, "Thanks a lot." (A well-known actress from a famous acting family once put me down with "I saw my father play King Lear when I was ten. You couldn't possibly understand the difference between that and studying Shakespeare at Yale." I informed her that I began my Shakespeare studies when I was two.)

I met Ted Roethke again in Rome when I was munching on the

review *Botteghe Oscure*. We both had passed dangers. We hit it off. We met again two years later by chance at a Pinter play in London when I was heading back to the States after Rome fell. We joined up to see *Hamlet* and Gielgud in *The Tempest* (we did not drown our books). Eight seasons passed. Ted and Beatrice came to stay with me at 57th Street at a barn I was living in. I gave Ted big breakfasts and my homburg, he gave me his famous raccoon skin coat. He liked the fish and turtle tank in my small dining room. He told me he was once in love with a snake. Ted brought me to dinner at Stanley Kunitz's. I remember that first long, long, long evening. Thinking back, I didn't quite know how lucky I was. They were in their fifties, Stanley had almost fifty years to go, Ted had six. Dylan had crossed the Styx a handful of years before. On still another evening, not after death, Roethke came with his not-quite-finished manuscript of *The Far Field*. He went off one evening to show it to Stanley Kunitz. He put on a blue serge suit and my homburg for the occasion. Just before dawn, he rolled back in. "What did Stanley say?" I asked.

"He liked it a lot." Then a look of pain crossed his face and I knew that Ted, who had been in the mood to be crowned heavyweight champion and nothing less, was disheartened. I thought Kunitz had found something not quite right, that he had been demanding and not just celebratory. Suddenly, Ted said, talking half to me and half to the world, "Stanley Kunitz is the most honest man in America." I told this story in an introduction to a book of Kunitz conversations. More years. Roethke long dead, after a formal Roethke celebration at which Kunitz, an aged ex–Roethke sweetheart and I were the only three people in the room who knew him, Kunitz asked me to repeat the story at dinner to a young poet. I was pleased my story had touched Stanley.

When my father was soon to die, he spent his last hours in a fury that he hadn't died a year before when he'd wanted to. His doctor kept saying to me, "He's made of stainless steel. He's made of stainless steel." I understood my bronze self was just a chip off the old block, a mere alloy of tin and copper. What is a satyr, a Turkish brass sieve without moral outrage, a chamber pot that lets the urine through beside my father's moral steel.

My mother divorced my father six months before her death. On her birthday, a month to the day before she died, she saw her second great-granddaughter, who, to her joy, was named after her. She never knew she had a grandson. My sister sent our mother's ashes through the U.S. mail. My parents are buried in a garden I made in Water Mill, the graves two unmarked stones, surrounded by Montauk daisies and pink mallow. I didn't think my mother would want the stones too close. Last spring, a swan nested right on the graves. When the eggs hatched, the mother swan paraded with her six grey cygnets in the bay in front of our house. When I approached, they all jumped on their mother's back, and she swam away with them to safety. My mother would have liked that.

A History of Color
(2003)

A HISTORY OF COLOR

What is heaven but the history of color,
dyes washed out of laundry, cloth and cloud,
mystical rouge, lipstick, eyeshadow? Harlot nature,
explain the color of tongue, lips, nipples,
against Death, come-ons of labia, penis, the anus,
the concupiscent color wheels of insects and birds,
explain why Christian gold and blue tempt the kneeling,
why Muslim green is miraculous in the desert,
why the personification of the rainbow is Iris,
why Aphrodite, the mother of Eros, married
the god of fire, why *Adam* in Hebrew
comes out of the redness of earth . . .
The cosmos and impatiens I planted this June
may outlast me, these yellow, pink and blue annuals
do not sell indulgences, a rose ravishes a rose.
The silver and purple pollen that has blown on the roof
of my car concludes a sacred conversation.

Against Death washerwomen and philosophers
sought a fixative for colors to replace unstable substances
like saliva, urine and blood, the long process of boiling,
washing and rinsing. It is Death who works
with clean hands and a pure heart. Against him
Phoenician red-purple dyes taken from sea snails, the colors
fixed by exposing wool to air of the morning seas near Sidon,
or the sunlight and winds on the limestone cliffs of Crete—
all lost, which explains a limestone coastline
changed into mountains of pink-veined marble,
the discarded bodies of gods.
Of course Phoenician purple made for gods
and heroes cannot be produced nowadays.
Virgil thought purple was the color of the soul—
all lost. Anyone can see the arithmetic when purple
was pegged to the quantity and price of seashells.

Remember
the common gray and white seagull looked down
at the Roman Republic, at the brick red and terra-cotta
dominant after the pale yellow stone of the Greek world,
into the glare of the Empire's white marble.
The sapphire and onyx housefly that circled
the jeweled crowns of Byzantium buzzed prayers,
thinks what it thinks, survives. Under a Greek sky
the churches held Christ alive to supplicants,
a dove alighted on a hand torn by nails.
In holy light and darkness
the presence of Christ is cupped in gold.
Death holds, whether you believe Christ
is there before you or not, you will not see Him later—
sooner prick the night sky with a needle to find the moon.

2

I fight Death with peppermints, a sweet to recall
the Dark Ages before the word Orange existed.
In illuminated manuscripts St. Jerome,
his robes egg-red, is seen translating in the desert,
a golden lion at his feet—
or he is tied to a column naked in a dream,
flagellated for reading satires and Pliny's
Natural History that describes
the colors used by Apelles, the Greek master,
a painting of grapes so true to life
birds would alight on them to feed.
Death, you tourist, you've seen it all and better before,
your taste: whipped saints sucking chastity's thumb,
while you eat your candy of diseased and undernourished infants.
On an afternoon when death seemed no more than a newspaper
in a language I could not read, I remember
looking down at Jerusalem from the Mount of Olives,
that my friend said: "Jerusalem is a harlot,

everyone who passes leaves a gift."
Do birds of prey sing madrigals?
Outside the walls of Jerusalem, the crusaders
dumped mounts of dead Muslims
and their green banners, the severed heads of Jews,
some still wrapped in prayer shawls,
while the Christian dead sprawled near the place of a skull
which is called in Hebrew Golgotha.
Among the living, blood and blood-soaked prayers,
on the land of God's broken promises—a flagged javelin
stuck into the Holy Sepulcher as into a wild boar.

Hauled back by the *Franks*, colors never seen in Europe,
wonders of Islam, taffetas, organdies, brocades, damasks.
Gold-threaded cloth that seemed made for the Queen of Heaven
was copied in Italy on certain paintings of Our Lady,
on her blue robes in gold in Arabic:
"There is no God but God, Muhammad is His Prophet"—
for whom but Death to read?
Wrapped in a looted prayer rug,
an idea seized by Aquinas: the separation of faith and reason.
Later nicked from the library of Baghdad:
the invention of paper brought from China
by pilgrims on a hajj, looted rhyme, lenses,
notes on removing cataracts.
Certain veils would be lifted from the eyes of Europe,
all only for Death to see.
Within sight of Giotto's white, green and pink marble bell tower
that sounded the promise of Paradise,
plants and insects were used for dyes made from oak gall,
bastard saffron, beetle, canary weed, cockroach,
the fixative was fermented piss from a young boy
or a man drunk on red wine, while the painters
mixed their pigments with egg yolks and albumen,
gold with lime, garlic, wax and casein
that dried hard as adamantine, buffed with a polished agate
or a wolf's tooth.

At the time of the Plague, while the dead
lay unattended in the streets of Europe,
the yellow flag hung out more often than washing,
someone cloistered wrote a text
on making red from cinnabar, saffron from crocus,
each page an illumined example.
At the Last Supper the disciples sat dead at table.
Still, by the late fifteenth century
color was seen as ornament,
almost parallel to the colors of rhetoric,
blue was moving away from its place describing
the vaults of heaven to the changing sky of everyday.
Does it matter to heaven if a sleeve is blue or red or black?
In Venice Titian found adding lead-white to azurite-blue
changed a blue sleeve to satin.

3

I think the absence of color is like a life without love.
A master can draw every passion with a pencil, but light,
shadow and dark cannot reveal the lavender iris
between the opened thighs of a girl still almost a child,
or, before life was through with her, the red and purple
pomegranate at the center of her being.

Against Death on an English day Newton discovered
a single ray of white light refracted,
decomposed into a spectrum of colors,
and that he could reconstruct the totality,
mischievously reverse the process,
then produce white light again—which perhaps is why
last century, in a painting by Max Ernst,
the Holy Mother is spanking the baby Jesus.

Goethe found a like proof on a sunny summer day—
the birds, I suppose, as usual devouring insects
courting to the last moment of life.

While sitting by a crystal pool watching
soldiers fishing for trout, the poet was taken
by spectrums of color refracted from a ceramic shard
at the bottom of the pool, then from the tails of swimming trout
catching fire and disappearing,
until a rush of thirsty horses, tired and dirtied by war,
muddied the waters.

A heroic tenor sings to the exploding sun:
"Every war is a new dawning"—Fascist music.
Death would etch Saturn devouring his children on coins,
if someone would take his money.
Of course his IOU is good as gold.

Turner had sailors lash him to the mast
to see into a storm, then he painted slavers
throwing overboard the dead and dying,
sharks swimming through shades of red.
Later he painted the atheist Avalanche, then heaven
in truthful colors: *Rain, Steam, Speed.*
"Portraits of nothing and very like," they said, "tinted steam."
Turner kept most of his paintings to leave to England,
his *Burning of the Houses of Parliament.*

Against oblivion a still life of two red apples
stands for a beautiful woman. On her shoulder
the bruise of a painter's brush—she is no more
than a still life of peasant shoes.
"You will not keep apples or shoes or France," Death says.
A child chooses an object first for color,
then for form, in rooms with mother, father,
Death, and all the relatives of being.

4

Now this coloratura moves offstage
to the present, which is a kind of intermission.
My friend Mark Rothko painted a last canvas,

gray and yellow, then took a kitchen knife, half cut off his wrists
bound and knotted behind his back
(a trick of the mind Seneca never mastered)
to throw off Eros, who rode his back and whipped him
even after he was dead, till Eros, the little Greek,
was covered with blood of the Song of Songs.
Now Rothko is a study of color, a purple chapel,
a still river where he looks for his mother and father.

Death, you tourist with too much luggage,
you can distinguish the living from your dead.
Can you tell Poseidon's trident from a cake fork,
the living from the living,
winter from summer, autumn from spring?
In a sunless world, even bats nurse their young,
hang upside down looking for heaven,
make love in a world where the lion, afraid of no beast,
runs in terror from a white chicken. Such are your winnings.
Death, I think you take your greatest pleasure
in watching us murdering in great numbers
in ways even you have not planned.
They say in paradise every third thought is of earth
and a woman with a child at her breast.

RANSOM

Death is not Prime Minister or resplendent,
not eternal darkness, silence, or heaven-sent.
Death is an unrepresentative form of government,
a dead mother and father who rule without consent,
a drone in every flower, the Queen in her hive.
They have a room in every house, pay no rent.
Silent at dinner, they deceive, connive,
as the clock ticks. They never say, "Live and let live."
How many times have I tried to sing them to sleep?
Eternal bride and bridegroom,
I do what I do to make my death handsome,
to make them proud, to win a faceless smile by a leaping
somersault to childhood. I pay ransom
to my kidnappers who tie me to their bed—to weep
in their pillow, to sleep, to dream, to do or undo,
to *twinkle twinkle* in their firmament of two.

Silly to think there was a death: a father and mother
before there was time. Perhaps there was a single egg,
like the egg that hatched love, or something profane, other,
an indebtedness to which we should not pray, but beg
for more time. Or do we take a steel shovel and dig,
dig up a God, a Father who had a Holy Mother.
Perhaps love and death were married beneath a single egg,
a sign of resurrection like the butterfly.
Mothers and fathers live until their children die.

HEART WORK

No moon is as precisely round as the surgeon's light
I see in the center of my heart.
Dangling in a lake of blood, a stainless steel hook,
unbaited, is fishing in my heart for clots.
Across the moon I see a familiar dragonfly,
a certain peace comes of that. Then the dragonfly
gives death or gives birth to a spider it becomes—
they are fishing in my heart with a bare hook,
without a worm—they didn't even fish like that
when the Iroquois owned Manhattan.
Shall I die looking into my heart, seeing so little,
will the table I lie on become a barge, floating
endlessly down river, or a garbage scow?

There is a storm over the lake.
There are night creatures about me:
a Chinese doctor's face I like and a raccoon I like,
I hear a woman reciting numbers growing larger and larger
which I take as bad news—I think I see a turtle,
then on the surface an asp or coral snake.
One bite from a coral snake in Mexico,
you'll take a machete and cut off your arm
if you want to live. I would do that if it would help.

I say, "It's a miracle." The Chinese doctor and the moon
look down on me, and say silently, "Who is this idiot?"
I tell myself, if I lie still enough I'll have a chance,
if I keep my eyes open they will not close forever.
I recall that Muhammad was born from a blood clot.
If I'm smiling, my smile must be like a scissors opening,
a knife is praying to a knife.
Little did I know, in a day, on a Walkman,
I would hear Mozart's second piano concerto,

that I would see a flock of Canada geese flying south
down the East River past the smokestacks of Long Island City.
I had forgotten the beauty in the world.
I remember. I remember.

TO MY FRIEND BORN BLIND

You told me your blindness is not seeing
even the shades of black called darkness.
You felt useless as a mirror until you made a poem
useful as a dog with bells around its neck.
Sometimes you wake to the wind moving through different trees.
A child, you loved to touch your mother's face,
you wished the world were ocean,
you could hear, smell, and taste, knew that it was blue.
Trees had a smell you called green, apples red.
How could the flag be red-white-and-blue?
You laugh when I tell you "drink to me only with thine eyes"
is a love song, that some who see
only make love in the dark. You wish you could see as a bat.
Mozart you say is the great equalizer, the truest democrat,
you always preferred a dog to a cane.
When in Braille you first read, "the disciples asked,
'Rabbi, who sinned, this man or his parents, that he was born blind?'
Jesus answered, 'Neither hath this man sinned nor his parents,
but that the works of God should be revealed in him ...'
and he spat on the ground and healed the man
with his spit and mud"—you waited awhile, then read on.
Blind in dreams, you touch, taste, smell and hear—
see nothing, nightmares like crowds are the more terrible
because you never see what terrifies you.
Since childhood it was an act of faith
to believe the sun and moon were in the sky,
it pleased you the sun is a fire the sighted cannot look into . . .
It is late. As always you, my imaginary friend,
take me by the hand and lead me to bed.

SUBWAY TOKEN

If Walt Whitman were alive, young and still living in Brooklyn,
he would have seen the burning Trade Center,
and if he were old and still in Camden, New Jersey,
he would have seen men jumping out from a hundred stories up,
some holding hands, believers and nonbelievers
who prefer a leap of faith to a death in an ocean of fire.
Walt could have seen women falling from the sun,
although the sun has no offices.
True in the heavens there often has been a kind of tit for tat,
not just thunder for lightning:
where there is grandeur observed, something human, trivial.

The South Tower fell like the old Whitman,
although it was second to be struck,
then the North Tower like the young Whitman.
What history, what hallucination?
Anyone could see the towers fell like the great poet,
with three thousand people from eighty-seven countries,
and three hundred and forty-three firefighters
into the irrational fires that burned for ninety days.
None of the dead lived in a boarding house
as would be likely in Whitman's time.
History, hallucination?
A life goes up in flame like a page of Bible paper.
You could not pile books so high, not good books,
as this grand canyon of steel and concrete body parts,
my city's broken backbone pushed out through her throat.

THE CELLIST

to Daniel Stern

You cherished your silent beautiful cello
after your shoulder joint wore out.
You would not play dead like that entombed Jew.
You could not stop hearing music in your head:
a disease. Whatever the conversation
or dream, you hear the chamber music you played—
the *Archduke Trio*, concerti in your head
in the Monday, Tuesday, everyday world—
the first cousin of a religious experience.
Sometimes I ask: "What music is playing now?"
The evening program, however sublime, always seems painful.
You sold your cello to pay a doctor's bill.
It could have happened in a Balzac story—
wherever you are, outside in the street Balzac is standing,
winter and summer, fat and naked beneath his bronze cloak.

We are hanging on to life by a cello string.
I take the A string that carries the lyric, you the G
for darkness and light, both holding on to Dear life,
to D for Darling, Divertimento, and Don't let go.
Our C string sounds at the bottom of a well.
The Great Concertmaster is playing us
for the hell of it. We are his cello.
His bow the tails of a hundred white horses.
Maestro, keep playing, an aire on any string will do,
Mozart, Bach, jazz, a little street music.
Sing us or pluck a note from time to time,
or a chord with one turn of the wrist
to accommodate the curve of the bridge.
Practice, practice, practice. O Concertmaster,
a question we, the cello, ask with our undersong
of lust: "Do we love the world more than one person?"
—again with a turn of the wrist
to accommodate the bridge over the dark river.

THE GOOD SHEPHERD

Because he would not abandon the flock for a lost sheep
after the others had bedded down for the night,
he turned back, searched the thickets and gullies.
Sleepless, while the flock dozed in the morning mist
he searched the pastures up ahead. Winter nearing,
our wool heavy with brambles, ropes of muddy ice,
he did not abandon the lost sheep, even when the snows came.

Still, I knew there was only a thin line
between the good shepherd and the butcher.
How many lambs had put their heads between the shepherd's knees,
closed their eyes, offering their neck to the knife?
Familiar—the quick thuds of the club doing its work.
More than once at night I saw the halo coming.
I ran like a deer and hid among rocks,
or I crawled under a bush, my heart in thorns.

During the day I lived my life in clover
watching out for the halo.
I swore on the day the good shepherd catches hold,
trying to wrestle me to the ground and bind my feet,
I will buck like a ram and bite like a wolf,
although I taste the famous blood
I will break loose! I will race under the gates of heaven,
Back to the mortal fields, my flock, my stubbled grass and mud.

SONG OF AN IMAGINARY ARAB

Until they killed my brother who killed you,
there were readers who read and smiled at:
From the rock of my heart a horse rose
that I should ride to follow them
the night they left by taxi
from the Damascus gate and fled toward Bombay.
My heart threw me off.
If only I had robes white enough,
but my robes were full of ashes and dust.
The rouge, lipstick and eyeshadows
you left on my flesh, I washed off before prayer.
My heart was gone, it looked back at me
from a distance, its reins bitten through.

Until they killed my brother who killed you,
there were readers who read and smiled at:
It is written, man was created from a blood clot.
When I am put in the grave and those who question the dead ask me,
"Was the blood drawn from the finger of God
or the heart or His tongue?"
I will not answer. I will say, "I have heard music so beautiful
it seemed the blood of the Lord."
I know there is profit in God's word, in prayer rugs, in silk and wool,
blood of the lamb and spit of the worm.
A man who rose from barber to physician,
I prize most my grandmother's brass tray, pure as the sun
without etching or design, where I first saw the angel of mathematics,
the stateless angel of astronomy.

Let an old Palestinian grandmother sit in the sun
beside an old Jewish grandmother; I'll bring them sage tea,
that in Hebrew is called something like "Miriam," because when Mary
was pregnant with Jesus sage tea comforted her.
The Jew said, "Respect is more important than the Talmud."

I was admiring the girl on the balcony in Ramallah
when the shrapnel hit me in the head. I did not have time
to make the break between my thoughts
and the attack on my head.
I thought it was a flower pot that fell off the balcony.
"Allahu akhbar!" I shouted. Someday the horse will fly.

Until they killed my brother who killed you,
there were readers who read and smiled at:
Love now is more dangerous than hate.

A FALL

for Stanley Kunitz

The mouth on his forehead is stitched and smiling,
his head is crowned with bandages,
his broken nose: Michelangelo's slave marble.
Like the last minutes of summer sunset
his cheekbones and eyes are lavender and black.
The face that hit the cement sidewalk of 12th Street
with the full force of his gravity does not frown.
I refuse to see what I know. I kiss the mouth of sorrow,
I rejoice that he is alive. I am drinking his gin
as if I were the English Consul,
he Lorca's gypsy nun chased by the wind.

In his sitting room that is part greenhouse
we are on the sea of poetry in a familiar squall.
I must speak louder now above the wind.
We are on the green and mountainous Atlantic,
yes, there is a "cargo of roses," a reason to smile.
Blaaah, blaaah. It is time to hold hands.
I hear the cries of poets washed overboard in my throat.
He says he is the oldest poet who ever lived,
fifteen years older than King Lear.
Now we are two old fishermen mending nets,
untying knots, hoping for fair weather—
then at sea between Emerson's "Over-soul"
and "The tear is an intellectual thing."
At Saint Vincent's I will visit his love who broke her hip.
He says, "One step closer, I would have caught her."
I will come Tuesday to cook, bring a new poem.
In his easy chair, his fist on the tiller, life is north northeast,
he heads windward, a hummingbird
blown out on the North Atlantic
struggling toward land to kiss a flower.

THE CELESTIAL FOX

1

Death is a celestial fox that leaps out of his coffin:
tonight his tail sweeps away insects,
which the religious read as a sign:
the fox kills but does not end their lives.
Sometimes he stops, noses the air,
sings, showing his teeth.
I wish I just owed him money.

2

When my two dogs and I run on the beach
innocently thinking we hunt the fox
because we see two eyes in the ocean
where the fox crouches at the foot of a great wave,
my dogs jump in barking at nothing I can see,
while the fox leaps into its true lair,
the moist den of every sexual act.
There he waits, waits with that I-told-you-so grin.

3

I am a great cunt waiting for death to fuck me
between the golden thighs of endless morning,
swaddled in labia. American,
architect of my own destiny,
he shall not flatter me or marry me,
he shall not suck me or finger fuck me
though I am wet as the Mississippi,
death shall not slip it in.

THE FALCON

My son carries my ghost on his shoulder, a falcon,
I am careful not to dig in my claws. I play
I am his father owl, sometimes sparrow, a hummingbird
in his ear. I told him from my first chirp:
"Be an American democratic Jew mensch-bird."
When he was a child in Italy I was a migrant bird
with a nest in America. When I flew home
he cried, *"Perche, perche?"* I wept
not wanting him to have a distant bird
or a sea captain for a father.
How many times did I cross the Atlantic
in the worst weather to perch outside his window?
What kind of nest could I make in Italy
on a hotel balcony? When he needed to be held
his mother and nannies took turns. When he reached out
to me he often fell. He said *I know I know* to everything
I might have taught him. I fought for his life
with one wing tied behind my back—
for his name, school, and to have his hair cut
in a man's barber shop, not a salon for signoras.
"Lose to him! Lose to him!" his mother screamed.
I was the only one in his life
who would not throw a footrace
he could win in a year, fair and square.
How could a small boy spend so much time
laughing and talking to a father in restaurants?
He complained in Bologna I took him to six museums,
in Florence four, in Espagna *mille e tre.*
We laughed at those rare Italian birds
who don't find themselves sleeping forever
on a bed of polenta—preening, displaying,
making a *bella figura.* An omen in his life.

I flew him to an English meadow
to study Dante, then Shakespeare's Histories
in a king maple overlooking the Hudson,
the cast: himself, me, my mate the beautiful Jane bird.

What are years? Not a herd of cattle,
perhaps a flock of birds passing overhead.
Sometimes I hear him chirping my song
louder than I ever sang it.
One day, when the heavenly dogs and hell dogs
find me behind a bush and fight over me,
may one with a soft mouth break from the pack
and take most of me to his Master. Let Him say, "Good dog,
good dog, what a peculiar kind of bird is this,
with his gray curly feathers and strange beak?
Have I ever heard him sing?" May it dawn upon Him,
I am the bird with the human son.

JUDAS

Judas, patron saint of bankers,
I run a piggy bank, audit myself.
Why is my search for gifts brought to the Magi,
expenses deducted for travel, called "a journey"?
There is a difference between writing, rewriting
and cooking the books. Accounting in the dark
I have mortgaged more than my house,
my heart pays usurious interest.
Where is such a price paid? I have faith
in the Secretary of Treasury.
For my "losses carried forward half a century,"
I say only the last five years are deductible.
Judas, your God with his small coins
of good and evil, lends himself to fictions.
I am in the market for bracelets,
chains, necklaces and rings of illumination.

AN ARGUMENT WITH MY WIFE

When you said you wanted to be useful
as the days of the week, I said, "God bless you."
Then you said you would not trade our Sundays
or Moondays, useful for two thousand years,
for the Seven Wonders of the ancient world.
I said, "Endless are the wonders I can say 'ah' to,
and the 'Ah' that is in heaven. Yes, I've heard
the 'ah, ah' that comforts a baby."
Then you said, "Go make a living on metaphors
for 'ah,'" that I was your lunatic husband,
that I secretly want to be the Lighthouse
of Alexandria, a seventy-fathom-high
collaboration of art and science
in the Greek Egyptian sky, a mirror of light
that can be seen ten days out to sea.
Further, you complained, I see myself
standing on a rock beside Poseidon,
my right hand around his "terrible trident,"
surrounded by all the wonders of Greek Africa
offering me a bed as a welcome guest.

Ah, today is Monday. I want little more
than to be a hand-mirror you carry
in your purse with a hankie
to stop my hemorrhaging humility.

GRACE

In the great iron pot of the universe
there is *pot-au-feu* for dinner:
gravity, galaxies, darkness, plasma;
my host, my dearest and least dear father,
sits at table without conversation,
rhetoric or grammar—none I comprehend.
I am thankful for much that I swallow
and for tonight's guests: the great what is
in front of me, to my left the face of a clam,
to my right the sky brought down to its knees.
Hungry, I rush through "God is memory."
I am thankful I am not green as parsley,
I put my red and white checked napkin under my chin,
I eat with the manners of Saturn.

EL SOL

If *the sun is money*, as you say,
the ocean has deep pockets.
Three miles down there's still a little flickering,
small change in the deep—eight miles further
the sun is broke, flat as a flounder.
In Lima it rains once a year;
people are hot and tired of too much money.
While in sunny Spain anarchists in the Civil War
made leaves money. *Duros* and *pesetas* were out.
Olive trees cashed in.
Your typical wallet *portafoglio* held oak leaves,
olive leaves, and laurel. On rare occasions
a newspaper photo of Lorca was found
among the leaves. (Some things never change:
Cuentos verdes are still dirty jokes,
Judías, Jewish women, *Judías verdes*, green beans.)
When anarchists burned the churches,
if caught they sometimes confessed to the priests
before they were shot against a sunrise of money.
Would to Allah leaves were still money,
paintings of Adam with money over his privates.
In 1909 anarchists protesting conscription to Africa
dug nuns from their graves and danced
with those money-covered nuns in the streets of Barcelona.
The sun is the root of all evil. Sun talks.
Blake pointed out, some see the sun as a golden guinea.
He saw it as the heavenly host crying, *holy, holy, holy.*

TSUNAMI SONG

A father is teaching his daughter to swim
in the Indian Ocean,
near them a fisherman throws his net,
silver and pink fish leap out of reach,
the child, wearing water wings,
loves her accomplishment,
squeals and laughs.
The father is happy teaching his daughter
something useful that will give her joy
the rest of her life. He says, "Come to me."
When the great stone ocean falls from the sky,
for a second, the rest of her life,
the child thinks she is swimming—
then she is a pebble in the deep.
The father, reaching for his daughter,
disappears, a shard of blue glass.
Like a seagull the water wings fly
to the foot of the mountain.
Despite a broken wing
it tries to rise from the sand.

I walk along the North Atlantic
with my wife and two dogs.
A horseshoe crab writes in the sand
the sun disappears,
everything darkness with no one to see it,
the moon a skull in the sky.

CHINA SONG

I did not say: *The peach blossoms are not as white*
as plum blossoms. I said: *They are beautiful, beautiful.*
The peach blossoms fell into a rage,
their faces redder and redder with accusation.
But I intended no harm, no offense.
There was no reason for anger.
Pity me on my birthday, the first day of summer,
when flowers have their ways completely beyond me.

I remember when the Chinese for "how do you do?"
was "have you eaten today?"
I tell Alexander Fu this summer
"I will take you to the ocean."
The ocean has English and Chinese waves.
He reaches out and catches a white button on my shirt.
I explain my shirt isn't the ocean.
I tell him my button isn't the moon.

From the crowd below the Chinese guillotine
I noticed the eyes of a severed head
for some seconds responded to calls of the victim's name.
Left to itself, the head does not roll away in shame
or modesty. The lips do not utter a word.
It is the eyes like a child at school that respond.

BEAUTY IS NOT EASY

What are they but cattle, these butterflies,
their purple hides torn by barbed wire,
scarred blue, yellow and scarlet.
If they are not marked for slaughter
I cannot tell to whom they belong.
They are just stray cattle.
The sun does not witness,
the clouds do not testify.
Beauty does not need a public defender,
but I would listen to a serious defense
of beauty—tell me what happens to the carcass,
the choice cuts, everything useful:
hide, bones, intestines, fat.
Then talk to me of butterflies.

SONG FOR A LOST RIVER

Now there are four rivers: once there were five,
one has left without tears or a bird cry,
rivers leave their beds, have nothing else to give,
when a lover goes, love does not die—
in an empty bed love will survive.
Love, the sweet invisible spy,
is lucky: it has tears and laughter,
for a while, past, present and hereafter.

RAINBOWS AND CIRCUMCISION *

1

He might have made some other sign,
but it fitted his purpose to use sunlight
behind rain to make his sign of the covenant,
a rainbow above the flood. What was in the sky
was suddenly moral, moonlight and passing clouds
were merely beautiful.

We answer the rainbow with an infant son,
cut a touch of ignorant flesh away.
The wordless infant stands on the Book
that separates him by the width of the pages
from the bookless ground.

Rainbow and mother tell me who I am.
We might have used another sign,
a red dot on the forehead, or a scar on the cheek,
to show the world who we are,
but our sign is intimate, for ourselves
and those who see us naked—like poetry.

2

Once in Rome, on a winter day after a rare snowfall,
I stood on a hill above the snow-covered arches,
columns and palm trees of the pillaged Forum.
Against a dark purple sky suddenly opened
by shafts of sunlight, I saw two rainbows.
To see all that at the same time, and two rainbows,
was a pagan and religious thing: holy,
it was like the thunderous beauty of a psalm, and like
peeking through the keyhole with the masturbating slaves,
watching Hector mounted on Andromache. O rainbows!

*Rainbow and circumcision: each is a biblical sign of the Covenant.

I HAVE COME TO JERUSALEM

I have come to Jerusalem
because I have a right to,
bringing my family who did not come with me,
who never thought I would bring them here.
I carry them as a sleeping child to bed.
Who of them would not forgive me?
I have come to Jerusalem to dream
I found my mother's mother by chance,
white-haired and beautiful, frightened behind a column,
in a large reception room filled with strangers
wearing overcoats. After forty-two years
I had to explain who I was. "I'm Stanley,
your grandson." We kissed and hugged and laughed,
she said we were a modern family,
one of the first to ride on trains.
I hadn't seen before how much she looked like
her great-great-granddaughter. I remembered
that in her house I thumped her piano,
I saw my first painting, a garden, by her lost son.
I remembered the smells of her bedroom:
lace-covered pillows, a face-powdered Old Testament.
Then my dead mother and father came into the room.
I showed them who I'd found and gave everybody chocolates,
we spoke of what was new
and they called me only by my secret name.

JERUSALEM: EASTER, PASSOVER

1

The first days of April in the fields—
a congregation of nameless green,
those with delicate faces have come
and the thorn and thistle,
trees in purple bloom,
some lifting broken branches.
After a rain the true believers:
cacti surrounded by yellow flowers,
green harps and solitary scholars.
By late afternoon a nation of flowers: *Taioun,*
the bitter sexual smell of Israel,
with its Arabic name, the flowering red clusters
they call *Blood of the Maccabees,*
the lilies of Saint Catherine, cool to touch,
beside a tree named *The Killing Father,*
with its thin red bark of testimony.
In the sand a face of rusted iron
has two missing eyes.

2

There are not flowers enough to tell,
over heavy electronic gear
under the Arab-Israeli moon,
the words of those who see in the Dome of the Rock
a footprint of the Prophet's horse,
or hear the parallel reasoning
of King David's psalms and harp,
or touch the empty tomb.
It is beyond a wheat field to tell
Christ performed two miracles: first he rose,
and then he convinced many that he rose.
For the roadside cornflower
that is only what it is,

it is too much to answer
why the world is so, or so, or other.
It is beyond the reach
or craft of flowers to name
the plagues visited on Egypt,
or to bloom into saying why
at the Passover table Jews discard
a drop of wine for each plague, not to drink
the full glass of their enemy's suffering.
It is not enough to be carried off by the wind,
to feed the birds, and honey the bees.

3

On this bright Easter morning
smelling of Arab bread,
what if God simply changed his mind
and called out into the city,
"Thou shalt not kill," and, like an angry father,
"I will not say it another time!"
They are praying too much in Jerusalem,
reading and praying beside street fires,
too much holy bread, leavened and unleavened,
the children kick a ball of fire,
play Islamic and Jewish games:
scissors cut paper, paper covers rock, rock breaks scissors.
I catch myself almost praying
for the first time in my life,
to a God I treat like a nettle
on my trouser cuff.
Let rock build houses,
writing cover paper, scissors cut suits.

4

The wind and sunlight commingle
with the walls of Jerusalem,
are worked and reworked, are lifted up,
have spirit, are written,

while stones I pick up in the field
at random have almost no spirit,
are not written.

Is happiness a red ribbon on a white horse,
or the black Arabian stallion
I saw tethered in the courtyard of the old city?
What a relief to see someone repair
an old frying pan with a hammer,
anvil and charcoal fire, a utensil worth keeping.
God, why not keep us? Make me useful.

A GUEST IN JERUSALEM

On the grapes and oranges you gave me on a white plate: worry,
in the kitchen, day worry, in the bedroom, night worry
about a child getting killed; worry in the everyday gardens
of Jerusalem, on geraniums and roses from the time they bloom
in December, long as they live. In the desert wind
playing over the hair on a child's head and arms, worry.
In the morning you put on a soiled or clean shirt of worry,
drink its tea, eat its bread and honey. I wish you the luxury
of worrying about aging or money, instead of a child getting killed,
that no mother or father should know the sorrow
that comes when there is nothing to worry about anymore.

EXCHANGE OF GIFTS

You gave me Jerusalem marble,
gypsum from the Judean desert,
granite from the Sinai,
a collection of biblical rock.
I gave you a side of smoked salmon,
a tape of the *Magic Flute*—
my lox was full of history and silence,
your stones tasted of firstness
and lastness, Jewish cooking.

You took me to a synagogue where a small boy came up to me
and asked me to dance him on my shoulders.
So we danced around Genesis and the Song
of Solomon. He clapped his hands to be riding
the biggest horse in Judea. I cantered lightly
around Deuteronomy, whirled around the Psalms,
Kings and Job. I leapt into the sweaty
life-loving, Book-loving air of happiness.

Breathless I kissed the child and put him down,
but another child climbed up my back.
I danced this one around Proverbs and that one
around Exodus and Ecclesiastes, till a child came up to me
who was a fat horse himself, and I had to halt.

What could I give you after that?
—When I left, a bottle of wine, half a bottle of oil,
some tomatoes and onions, my love.

THE LOUSE

In a room overlooking Jerusalem,
I felt something like a leaf on my forehead—
I picked off a louse,
squashed it between the labyrinths
of my index finger and my thumb.
I have faith every louse in Jerusalem
has come through hair and feather:
Jew, Muslim, Christian
from wing to head to beard to crotch,
from cat's ear to rat's balls . . .
At the Jerusalem wall between Heaven and Hell
the unprepared are given skullcaps—
I refused a clean, gray paper cap,
the kind given children in different colors
at birthday parties with other favors;
I picked dusty black rayon someone left behind
despite my friend's warning: "You may get lice."
Whatever the time of day, a little before fear,
the sun hurt my eyes. I kissed the wall
but had nothing further to say to it . . .
My louse's cousins have spent time among hyena packs,
nestled in carrion, under pus, lip to lip with maggots.
Surely Christ, who suffered crucifixion,
felt the bite of the louse. My fingers are Roman soldiers
if the louse I squashed had a trace of Christ's blood.
I have faith King David after all his adventures
had an itch in the groin, a louse danced with him.
Once a winged horse with a peacock's tail
and a woman's face flew into this city from Arabia
with a prophet on its back.
We all can use a little sacred preening and combing.
I should be grateful for another louse.

WORK SONG

As full of Christianity
as the sea is salt,
the English tongue
my mother and father spoke,
so rich in Germanic tree and God worship
and old Romantic Catholic nouns,
does not quite work for me
at family burials or other,
as we say in English,
sacramental moments.

Although I know the Pater Noster
and Stabat Mater as popular songs,
I am surprised, when close friends
speak Hebrew, that I understand nothing.
Something in me expects to understand them
without the least effort,
as a bird knows song.
There is a language of prayers unsaid
I cannot speak.
A man can count himself lucky these days to be alive,
an instrument of ten strings,
or to be carried gently off by sleep and death.

What of belief? Like the tides
there is and is not a temple of words
on which work continues.
Unsynagogued, unschooled, but lettered,
I drag a block of uncut marble—
I have seen prayers pushed

into the crevices of the Western Wall,
books stacked against the boulders,
ordinary men standing beside prophets and scoundrels.
I know the great stoneworkers can show the wind in marble,
ecstasy, blood, a button left undone.

BABIES

Babies, babies,
before you can see more than light or darkness,
before your mothers have kissed your heads,
I come to you with news of dead and dying friends.
You so close to the miracle of life,
lend me a miracle to bring to my friend.
Babies, babies.
Once Death was a baby, he grasped God's little finger
to keep from falling—kicking and chortling
on his back, unbaptized, uncircumcised,
but invited to share sunlight and darkness
with the rest of us. Mother Death would nurse him,
comfort and wash him when he soiled himself
in the arms of the mourners and the heartbroken.

Older, Death took his place
at table beside his mother—her "angel."
They ate and drank from each other's mouth and fingers,
laughed at their private jokes. He could play
any musical instrument, knew all music by heart,
all birdsong, the purr, growl, snort, or whine
of each and every animal.
The story goes that, fat with eternal life,
older than his mother, he devoured her,
far from light or darkness.

Babies, at the moment of your first uncertain breath,
when your mother's magic blood is still upon you,
I come to you, the helpless ones still coughing
from miracles of birth.
Babies hardly heavier than clouds,
in desperation, for my friend, for a lark
I hold up the sac you broke through
as if it were Saint Veronica's Veil—

but no face is on it, no blood.
I hold up a heavy sack of useless words.
I shake a rattle to catch your eye or first smile.

PRAISE

for Yehuda Amichai

1

Snow clouds shadow the bay, on the ice the odd fallen gull.
I try to keep my friend from dying by remembering
his childhood of praise to God, who needs us all. Würzburg:
the grownups are inside saying prayers for the dead,
the children are sent out to play—their laughter
more sacred than prayer. After dark his father
blesses and kisses him *gute Nacht.* He wakes
to go to school with children who stayed behind
and were murdered before promotion.

Now his wife lies beside him.
He may die with her head on his pillow.
He sings in his sleep:
"Her breasts are white sheep that appear on the mountain,
her belly is like a heap of wheat set about with lilies."
Awake, he says, as if telling me a secret:
"When metaphor and reality come together, death occurs."
His life is a light, fresh snow blowing across the bay.

2

A year later in Jerusalem, he carries a fallen soldier
on his back, himself. The text for the day begins:
"He slew a lion in the pit in a time of snow."
Seconds, minutes, hours are flesh,
he tells me he is being cut to pieces—
if they had not made him turn in his rifle . . .
He sees I cannot bear more of that.
Yet a little sleep, a little slumber, a little folding
of hands in sleep and we drink to *life.*
Chilled in desert heat, what keeps him alive:
soldiers—his wife, his son and daughter,

320

perhaps the ashes of a girl he loved in childhood.
Outside their window
a Sun Bird and Dead Sea Sparrow fly
from everlasting to everlasting.
Later he covers my head with his hands, blessing me,
later unable to walk alone he holds onto my hand
with so much strength he comforts me.

NEAR MACHPELAH/HEBRON

It was not a dream: a poet
led me down into the earth
where the sea in another age
had hollowed out a mountain.
He led me into a cave of marble cloud:
colossal backs, shoulders, thighs of reclining Gods.
Just above us a battlefield four thousand years old,
some olive trees and wild flowers.
I cannot believe these Gods need
more than an occasional lizard
or the sacrifice of a dove that comes to them
through jags and crevices.
Madness to think the Gods
are invisible, in us, and worth fighting for
—if they want anything, I suppose,
it is for the sea to come back again.

TO ARIEL, MY ARABIST FRIEND

In a museum forty years after it happened
I saw a snapshot of my lost brother,
a Hellenistic Jew, sitting in a lifeboat,
wordless, a few yards from the shoreline of Palestine,
behind him a rusty sinking freighter,
his two years in a displaced persons' camp,
his two years in Treblinka.
With him in the boat, half a dozen Jews,
tired to death and hopeful, my brother
sat in the middle, somehow a little apart,
in a good overcoat, his gloved hands
in his pockets, thumbs out, his tilted fedora
brim up, a clean handkerchief in his breast pocket
as our mother taught him, still the *boulevardier*,
the *flâneur*. Knee deep in the water
to meet the boat and help them in, Mr. Kraus
from Frankfurt, giving the newcomers his card,
directing them to his Viennese pastry shop,
the best in Palestine.
My brother washed more than one death
out of his handkerchief. For me as a child
his handkerchief was a white mouse
he set free in Europe's worst winter,
when it became inhuman to love.

Ariel, whose language am I speaking?

A VISIT TO THE DEVIL'S MUSEUM IN KAUNAS

I put on my Mosaic horns, a pointed beard,
my goat-hoof feet—my nose, eyes, hair and ears
are just right—and walk the streets of the old ghetto.
In May under the giant lilac and blooming chestnut trees
I am the only dirty word in the Lithuanian language.
I taxi to the death camp and to the forest
where only the birds are gay, freight trains still screech,
scream and stop. I have origins here, not roots,
origins among the ashes of shoemakers
and scholars, below the roots of these Christmas trees,
and below the pits filled with charred splinters of bone
covered with fathoms of concrete. But I am the devil,
I know in the city someone wears the good gold watch
given to him by a mother to save her infant
thrown in a sewer. Someone still tells time by that watch,
I think it is the town clock.

Perhaps Lithuanian that has three words for soul
needs more words for murder—murder as bread:
"Please pass the murder and butter" gets you to:
"The wine you are drinking is my blood,
the murder you are eating is my body."
Who planted the lilac and chestnut trees?
Whose woods are these? I think I know.
I do my little devil dance,
my goat hooves click on the stone streets.
Das Lied von der Erde
ist Murder, Murder, Murder.

GHETTO THEATER, VILNIUS, 1941

Perhaps the players chose to wear something
about the person, a spoon, or since it was autumn
a large gold maple leaf that looked like a star of David
pinned to a shirt or blouse. The play was *One Can't Know Anything.*
Someone shouted: "You are play-acting in a cemetery!"
But they went on: "To sit, to stand, to lie on the ground,
is it better to close or open your eyes, to listen or not,
to speak or not to speak? Those are the questions."
Then a grave song: "I knew him well, Horatio.
Here hung the lips I have kissed I know not how often . . .
My Lord, I have some remembrances of yours."

Fifty-six years later in a sandlot where for three hundred years
the Great Synagogue stood, I watch children playing.
Perhaps God shows himself as hide and seek,
as wrestling, laughter, as children falling,
cutting their knees, and the rush of tears.

CHINESE PRAYER

God of Walls and Ditches, every man's friend,
although you may be banqueting in heaven
on the peaches of immortality
that ripen once every three thousand years,
protect a child I love in China
and on her visits to the United States,
if your powers reach this far, this locality.
You will know her because she is nine years old,
already a beauty and an artist. She needs more
than the natural protection of a tree on a hot day.
You have so many papers,
more than the God of Examinations,
more than the God of Salaries,
who is not for me, because I am self-employed.
It may help you find her to know her mother
was once my bookkeeper,
her brother is a God in the family,
who at six still does not wipe his bottom.
Protect her from feeling worthless.
She is the most silent of children.
She has given me so many drawings and masks,
today I offered her fifty dollars for a painting.
Without a smile she answered,
"How much do you get for a metaphor?"
Sir, here is a little something to keep the incense burning,
remember her to the Almighty God whose character is Jade.

THE STARTLING

When I saw the Greek hunter
painted on the fifth-century red-figured pot
was changed into a startled fawn
because he watched a goddess bathe naked,
and that his own dogs tore him to pieces,
I had already changed from myself
to another self, further apart
than man from fawn.
When coming out of my self, I woke you
in the middle of the night to carry you off
to the sea; I stopped three times
to ravish you; you took me beyond my life,
raced me from great distance to great distance,
till helpless I fell in your lap
and said I was near death.
You lifted the heavy beast's head,
still snorting and groaning, kissed me
and washed your blood from my face,
stroked me and called me "sweet one"—
then you sang your siren song,
told me how I would be remembered,
that sleep and death were brothers,
that the sirens defeated by poetry
were changed into the great boulders
on which the city of Naples,
so well known to lovers, was founded.
I kissed you and you asked gently,
since you were young and I was not,
what Dido asked Aeneas
who was soon to go to war:
"Will you leave me without a son
of your name?"

A RIFF FOR SIDNEY BECHET

That night in Florence,
forty-five years ago,
I heard him play
like "honey on a razor,"
he could get maple syrup
out of a white pine,
out of a sycamore,
out of an old copper beech.
I remember that summer
Michelangelo's marble
naked woman's breasts,
reclining Dawn's nipples—
exactly like the flesh I ached for.
How could Dawn behind her clouds hurt me?
The sunrise bitch was never mine.
He brought her down. In twelve bars of burnt sugar,
she was his if he wanted her.

THE LOST BROTHER

I knew that tree was my lost brother
when I heard he was cut down
at four thousand eight hundred sixty-two years;
I knew we had the same mother.
His death pained me. I made up a story.
I realized, when I saw his photograph,
he was an evergreen, a bristlecone like me
who had lived from an early age
with a certain amount of dieback,
at impossible locations, at elevations
over 10,000 feet in extreme weather.
His company: other conifers,
the rosy finch, the rock wren, the raven and,
blue and silver insects that fed mostly off each other.
Some years bighorn sheep visited in summer—
he was entertained by red bats, black-tailed jackrabbits,
horned lizards, the creatures old and young he sheltered.
Beside him in the shade, pink mountain pennyroyal—
to his south, white angelica.
I am prepared to live as long as he did
(it would please our mother),
live with clouds and those I love
suffering with God.
Sooner or later, some bag of wind will cut me down.

ELEGY FOR A 5,000-YEAR-OLD TREE

That tree was a teacher, whatever the weather—
everyday birds, hawks and osprey nested
in its branches, nations of common insects
fought in its gullies, while generations of deer
scraped their antlers against it in rutting season.
Looking up to its crown, it seemed higher than the Brooklyn Bridge
from a ferry passing beneath—some were frightened.
Few understood the tree's gentleness with bees and butterflies,
its hospitality to rodents, lavender and Lad's-love,
that for centuries horned lizards, toads
and snakes hid in its dens—the joys and sorrows it found
in heavy rains and snows, its heroism
at the timberline, its lifelong love of clouds.
The golden-mantled squirrel survives.

Curious to find the ancient tree's age, an "arborist"
chose to count its rings by drilling with a diamond-tipped corer.
Putting his back into the drill, as if the tree were marble,
he quickly passed through American history,
knot and counter-knot, to the age of Mozart,
through the Baroque, through Shakespearian grain,
through a charcoal cave where lightning struck,
through the time of Jesus and Buddha's enlightenment,
through the guano of owls, the Olmec.
In the era of the prophets, the drill broke—
what could a tree person do? After clearing away young trees,
to save his drill, he appealed to forest rangers.
It took five, with orange hydraulic saws, to fell the great tree.
When they counted rings, it took them hours, some five thousand rings.
The tree they killed was the oldest known living thing on earth.
Where can you weep for the tree that had wept and laughed
beyond all human consequence? No one could agree
what poured out: butterflies or troupes of prima ballerinas,

old men or unemployed youths who never found a purpose,
newspapers, folios, books, leaflets or turtles
with ancient Chinese writing on their backs.
A madman shouted that God had carried the tree to heaven.
Everyone let him rave. Some say the fallen tree began to shudder
and sing a requiem for all the slaughtered, innocent multitudes.
Lingering for a moment before they disappeared,
two shadows searched for their young.
Or were they two readers in the Warsaw ghetto
stopping to buy a book out of a discarded baby carriage?

THE LAST JUDGMENT

Pushing up through a hole in the red marble floor of heaven
a black prisoner sentenced to death,
shows his tattooed resurrected flesh:
a blue tear under the outside corners of his eyes,
on his arm two copulating dragons,
their eyes a woman's breasts,
a pierced bleeding heart on his back the size of an eagle,
his chest bears the face of Christ.
Anathema, it cannot be true such unlikely flesh rises to heaven.

Now in the maw of heaven
I see poor losers shrouded with eternal ink—
it's a little like whistling against Bach's *B-minor Mass*,
there is so much ecclesiastical counterfeit money around:
the anti-Christ silver dollar, the St. Sebastian dime.
Asleep on the marble floor a drowned sailor,
at his knee a cock, his wrists ringed with barbed wire;
a woman walks in circles,
her body still scented with the lilies of death,
her mouth the shape of her lovemaking,
a wolf's head on her shoulder,
its nose nestled between her breasts.
Beneath a huge egg hanging from a cord,
a woman who seems to be mad
says she will die if she sleeps alone,
a vine of tiny roses runs down both sides of her belly
to her bush still moist, a large bee put where the hair begins—
on her back, lovers beneath a tree in full foliage
and the motto: *God is the name of my desire.*
Anathema, it cannot be true such unlikely flesh rises to heaven.
Is it true Jewish children with tattooed numbers on their arms
keep their religion even in heaven?
I look at my own flesh with the dyes of age,
the craquelure of love and caprichos. How many nights

332

have I fallen asleep to the beat of the oars in a boat
with the adult passengers: summer, winter, autumn, spring—
not knowing who is the designer, who the boatman,
the needles writing all night like dreams,
awaking, as all of us, to an uncompleted world,
to the *Behold I am standing before Thy face.*

SOME FLOWERS

for Irving Howe

In a world where you are asleep with your fathers,
in that part of the forest where trees read,
your tree still reads to us. Tonight your branches bend over
Conrad, Trotsky, Saba,
the evergreen Irish.

Joyce hated flowers,
his wife put a houseplant on his grave.
There are no socialist flowers
yet the balmiest wind favors
a more even distribution of wealth.
Some have seen among the flowers religious orders,
proved a rose a Christian,
while of course they pruned away the Jew.

It is easier for me to believe flowers
know something about wages and hours,
a fair day's pay for a fair day's work in the sun,
than to believe in the resurrection of the flesh.

When you died, the Amalgamated Clothing Workers
of America published a notice
of their mourning and sent flowers.
Your last sweet note that reached me after your death,
I left on the dashboard in a book,
the way they used to press dry flowers.
As I drove along in Canada,
it flew out of the window—
I thought it was a bill.

ROMANCE

I was not Eros with a limp, or sleepwalking,
even so on a December Sunday afternoon
sunning itself on a footbridge that was three planks
over a meandering dry stream,
I saw a small green snake that was perhaps a year
twist away at the first sight of me into the tall reeds
of the future, with time enough to found a nation.
I crossed the same planks, the heavy serpent
of old age oozed along behind me.
The sunlight on the bridge and the two snakes
were a sundial beyond the indications
of the world's Christian calendar.
Then I passed green fields of winter rye
already six inches high despite the early snow.
I whispered to myself:
Verde, que te quiero verde. Verde viento . . .
Follow the heart, follow the heart!

2002, ALAS

Where are the birthday poems
for Stalin and Hitler,
the angelhair tarts for Franco?
Where are the sweets of yesteryear,
the party hats? Our revels are not over!
They are shooting rifles in the air
for bin Laden and Saddam.
Happy children
are making bombs of themselves
as never before.
Dreams of mass murder have only begun:
daydreams and wet dreams.
But where is the pastry?
Where are the poems?
Coming, coming, the children sing.
Coming, coming.

SEPTEMBER 11TH: A FABLE

You caterpillars, who want to eat
until there is not one familiar leaf on our living tree,
in New York there are bees that will bore into your belly,
sleep with your striped velvet over their eyes,
with their feet on your heart,
that, waking, will eat their way out of your soft belly.
I promise you would prefer
the quick sharp beak of a crow.
Become a butterfly.

A DENTIST

Today I am Saddam Hussein's U.S. Army dentist.
I open his mouth, the color of a mop that has scrubbed blood
from a prison floor. His soul, the smell of his breath,
rises up in my face: vomit and eau de cologne.
It isn't every day I have a mass murderer in my chair.
I whistle for courage the staccato opening bars
of the overture to *The Marriage of Figaro*,
when my drill hits his nerve I hold every note.
He gives me a look of contempt that says
you are only a Jew dentist, not a torturer.
I put the removable bridge of his soul back
in his mouth and tell him to rinse.
Alas, I remember George Washington
had five slaves' teeth pulled out to fix in his bridge.

WEDDING INVITATION

I leap high as I can for joy, higher than you think I can.
My son writes he is marrying in September in Fiesole,
I leap over my dogs, whom he invited,
although they don't understand weddings.
You, dear reader, are also invited,
after all the funerals I brought you to.
I've often played a drum major in a brass band called hope—
even when the band wasn't there. I suggest to my son
he ready his foot to break the wineglass
in memory of the destruction of the Temple. If he doesn't care to,
I'll leave the wineglass around, so it may break
by happy accident. I never broke a wineglass
except when it fell off the table, or in rage. My best advice:
the usual public vows are not for nothing, when there's a problem
talk it over. I hope family history does not weigh heavier than love
and honorable intention. Bless you both,
now let the centaurs and Russian dancers in.

SONG OF IMPERFECTION

Whom can I tell? Who cares?
I see the shell of a snail protected by a flaw
in its design: white is time, blue-green is rot,
something emerging in the rough dust, the unused
part of a shape that is furious and calm.
In aging grasses, knotted with their being,
the snail draws near the east bank of the pond,
not because that is where the morning sun is,
but out of coastal preference, raising
a tawny knotted counterwhirl
like a lion cub against its mother's haunch,
anus of a star. But let the conch stand
in the warm mud, with its horn become an eye,
suffering the passion of any snail:
a hopeful birth, a death, an empty tomb.
I'd walk with this horned eye, lip-foot after lip-foot,
beyond the dry wall of my life, backward
into the sacramental mud, where the soul begins to reason—
as on that afternoon Aristotle dissecting
squid proclaimed "the eternity of the world."
There is not a thing on earth without a star
that beats upon it and tells it to grow.

GOOD NEWS SONG

I had just written "good and evil, each
indebted to the other and the gift of life"
when the call came—conceived in liberty
and dedicated to the proposition
that all men are created equal—
I'm going to have grandchildren,
conceived three weeks ago, "likely twins"
already revolving around the sun, young but not silly,
holding on to their mother for dear life.
Bienvenito! May you speak the honest tongue
of my grandparents and great-grandparents,
and Latin, Greek and Chinese.
Honor your father and mother, read left to right
and right to left. Make peace.

POST-SURGERY SONG

My surgeon went harrowing like Christ in Hell,
dug a virtuous pagan tumor from my kidney.
"What do I look like inside?" I asked. "Just like every other,
except the distance from your kidney to your heart."
"Aah," I thought, "I have a certain lonely alley inside,
like the Vicolo della Bella Donna in Florence."
I thought I knew the catechism of the bladder,
the daily questions and answers, until blood clots
clogged my drain, once a Roman fountain.
My bladder swelled as if giving birth,
then for all the world—a razor blade in the anus.
I cried uncle. Christ and surgeon,
if you believe merely thinking it
is the same as driving in the nails,
leave my wound! Physician, heal Thyself.

HOT NEWS, STALE NEWS

Herodotus tells us in an election year
Peisistratus, the Athenian tyrant,
wanting the protection of a god,
got the biggest beautiful woman he could find,
dressed her in silver and gold armor,
proclaimed her the goddess Athena
and drove through the streets of Athens
with the goddess at his side.
In our elections, every candidate
wants to be photographed
going to or coming from Jesus.
One declared, "Jesus is in my heart,"
but when he refused to stay
the death warrants for a hundred or so,
his Jesus was silent.

Our presidential candidates,
like Roman emperors,
favor the death penalty,
but in two thousand years there is a difference.
No candidate would do it for fun, or think death
a competent sentence for cutting down trees
or killing deer, as in 18th century England.
It's not all blood and circus:
when Camus asked de Gaulle,
"What can a writer do for France?"
The President replied: "Write well!"
Have you heard what's new on the Rialto:
since Pope John Paul declared anti-Semitism a sin,
hell has been so crowded,
you can't find a decent room there at a hotel.

THE FILM CRITIC IMAGINAIRE

He found his good wife weeping alone
when their friend's infidelity was discovered.
She had long pretended her husband's playing around
was like filmmaking: a take here, a take there,
out of sequence, everything but their life together
would end up on the cutting room floor.
Now she wept at breakfast,
forgot to pick up his suit at the cleaners,
and wept over that.
Angered, he realized his friend's infidelity
had held a full-length mirror to his own,
that the friend's behavior was unacceptable:
he had inconvenienced the distinguished critic,
the reader, the Anglophile, the man of the left.
For some days, my life was a fly buzzing around his head—
he swatted with the *Times.*

FACING THE RED SEA

Lord of Crops, Prince of Cereals, Queen of Coffee and Milk,
I'm sunning myself on a balcony in January.
Yesterday, I crossed the Negev to where I am.
Just over the brim of my coffee cup is the Red Sea.
Looking straight ahead, I see Saudi Arabia,
but Mecca, the Kaaba I cannot see. Without moving my head,
to the left I study the continuous limestone
coastline from Eilat, Israel to Jordon, Aqaba.
From the corner of my right eye:
Egypt 500 meters down the way.
Good News: the bus drivers of Jordan, Israel, and Egypt
are making deals. The bad news is purple mountains,
the Negev, the Arabian Desert, Sinai, the sun and Red Sea
don't make deals. To trade a little Koran for a little Torah,
a little Torah for a little New Testament,
you need poets or Marx Brothers.
I think Byzantine fish on the coral reefs below
are willing to make deals in Hebrew, Arabic, Aramaic,
Greek, Latin, Turkish, even in Suez English.
They eat, are eaten, add, subtract, and multiply.
Christ, what stories they could tell,
passed down from fish to fish,
but their purple, red, and blue tails only fan the waters.
I like to think that poetry does a little more—
Arabic, Hebrew, and Provençal made a deal for rhyme.
Tomorrow I will drive to Saint Catherine's Monastery,
to the foot of God-Trodden Mount Sinai.
Such information is less than sand,
has the weight of a few syllables.
These days only a few old timers and two timers
live behind / within the prison bars of rhyme,
talk behind them. A deal can be made between forms of life
that can live locked in stone. Perhaps the deal is that hatred
has to be desalinated, but English and my tongue
will never lick the salt out of the Red Sea.

THE FAMILY

After P.A. Cuadra

Maria, sister,
it was the end of days.
Everything collapsed and we were left
in the street with what we wore,
twelve brothers and sisters trembling
and Mama wanting to put her arms around each of us.
At that moment, we were suffocating in the dust, listening
to the death rattle of the world.
At that moment I was thinking, "Papa,"
you understand, you already know
the ways of our father,
"I'm going to look for him," I said,
my poor mother screaming,
the brothers and sisters weeping.
But what can you do when everything falls,
when time succumbs, what remains
except looking for your father?
How often we said to him, "Father,
charity begins at home."
He, you know, always in the clouds,
always giving to everyone,
but demanding of us.
I ran through those black streets
while the whole city rose up
in dust and lamentation.
The shadows threw stones at me.
I felt rage, the deaf rage of a son
against a father
who abandons him,
and I blamed him
as if he were the author of Tenebrae,
the fist of destruction.
It may be—I thought—he's helping others. And so it was.

Do you remember Juan,
the caretaker? Remember
Juan, the one who left him with all the work in the field
and ran off with a prostitute?
I came across our father with his hands bleeding
rescuing Juan,
I saw him carrying Juan.
He looked at me with his gentle eyes: "Help me!"
he said. I should have shouted,
"Father, Father,
why have you abandoned us?"
It's useless! You know how he is,
he always
abandons the flock
for a lost sheep.

IT CAME DOWN TO THIS

to Arnold Cooper

A mile from the Atlantic,
in your living room with the books and flowers
and the painting of fields behind your house
facing Mecox Bay, home to some two hundred swans,
fifty of which I have known since they were born,
it came down to this: I saw the room a little tilted
and you saw it straight, and when you proved it with a ruler
and leveler I fought back. The ruler might be wrong,
I have no faith an inch is equal to any other inch.
There are no equal numbers,
there is just an agreement as to what they mean.
I pity the violinist who just plays the notes.
But the roof of your house is not a sonata,
or your apple tree a violin, whoever plucks the fruit.
And worse, you, old friend, know better than I
the uniqueness of human beings
you measured hoping to prove me right. I remember
once when we had caught a stringer full of bass
I tied them to the oarlock with a double hitch
I learned in the navy. When we came ashore
my knot had slipped—the trophy fish gone.
Even that, you forgave me with an archaic smile.
We are the same age, equals before the law,
but one will slip away under the water lilies
before the other. Whoever slips away first,
proving me right about the ceiling, the roof, and inches—
the other shall hold a kind of grudge.

THE BLACK MAPLE

After an Atlantic hurricane,
no curled brine-drenched leaf
was at first to Katherine's eyes
a Monarch butterfly,
yet she telephoned the news:
flights of deceived Monarchs
had dropped down on her Black Maple
till she could not tell
leaf from butterfly.
In the morning when I arrived
only the tree of metaphor was there,
the butterflies gone to Mexico.
Katherine and her lover, soon to marry,
returned to Manhattan
to practice medicine and music.
Left behind by so much storm and flutter,
I have almost lost count of the seasons.

DARK CLOUDS

From whose breast does the milk of madness course?
I or he, an 18-year-old boy makes up his address,
the deaths of his parents still alive, his father's suicide.
I woo or he woos a girl, feigning coming blindness,
asked what he would farm—*rifles*, he smiles.
I or he memorized Milton.
I or he never learned to say a prayer out loud
so God would hear us. Speaking to ourselves
as if to the Lord, he and I are two persons,
three, four, five, a multitude
climbing out of the mouth of a Leviathan.
My mother's breast wept, losing its milk.
He and I became the nurslings of dark clouds.

HOW I GOT TED ROETHKE'S RACCOON-SKIN COAT

I gave my friend a lovely naked woman
dancing with a tambourine above her head,
a red terra-cotta plaque by Renoir.
With a laugh he gave me ten dead raccoons,
a blue and gold lining: his raccoon-skin coat,
made for hard Michigan winters and football games,
with a pocket inside for a whiskey flask.
Later, I sent to Seattle my English homburg
that flew cheering for him across America.
He told me to keep his blue pajamas
he left behind, sent back love and this:
"Robert Traill Spence Lowell
lays on his effects with a trowel,
I put them with Ginsberg's *Howl*,
the works of Robert Traill Spence Lowell."

FOR VIRGINIA ON HER 90TH BIRTHDAY

We know at ninety sometimes it aches to sing
or to sit in any chair, that words, music, love, and poetry
sometimes trip over each other.
Virginia, teach me not to walk steadily into the grave,
but to trip over it, to do the funny dance of the good long life.
It's easy as one, two, three. But what is one,
what is two, and where is three?
A good death is like a black butterfly
born too soon during a mild winter.

JUNE 21ST

Just when I think I am about to be tilted
on a table for death to eat—my friend arrives
playing a harmonica. It is my birthday.
He sings a little song that is a poem
written for the occasion.
How does he know the day I was born
the midwife laughed, enthusiastic
over the size of my head, chest and penis?
My mother must have told him.

My years are sheep, I shepherd them night and day,
I live with their "ba-ba."
They much prefer his harmonica to a panpipe.
Some years graze near me, others wander
across the valley out of sight.
I have two dogs, one dog can't do the job.
My 57th year keeps mounting my early years,
my 63rd year is giving it hard to my 57th,
my dogs are running in circles, barking for joy.

OVIDIAN FOLLIES

1. PHAETON

Canto I

News reached Helios the Sun God,
as sounds of war, prayers,
the distant traffic of the world sometimes does:
a handsome boy was nearing the sun in a chariot,
in danger of catching fire. The boy had passed through
India, asking anyone old enough to be wise:
"Can the Sun God be my father?"
School friends had made fun of the fatherless boy,
although his mother Clymene explained
she met Helios by chance in an orchard.
"I loved him because he made the flowers bloom.
March became summer in an hour. The Sun
bit into me and the orchard—as if we were one apple,
and you were born."

Phaeton's chariot arrived at the palace barely singed.
The God of Fire had turned his face away.
He met his son at the flaming doorway.
"Before you ask, Phaeton, what your mother said is true.
You are my son. To celebrate our meeting
I will stock the northern lakes with sunfish."
The God noticed the boy's hair was flaming red.
He had his father's sunrise.
Phaeton badmouthed the God:
"Where were you when I needed you to teach me
everyday lessons? I think you are a father
for a day." The God erupted,
"Who are you to think sunny? Still, there's sunrise
in you; ask me a favor, I will grant it—
I swear on the River Styx."

Phaeton grinned. "What I ask is your chariot.
I want to drive the winged horses for a day—
the car with the gold pulpit and axle,
the chrysolite wheels and silver spokes.
Keep your word to the River Styx and me."

The Sun God's voice darkened, "Yes.
Since the dawn of time that I am, there has been a form
in the sky, an eagle the size of an oak on its shoulder.
From the creature's entrails, you hear screams
of every living creature being devoured by their fathers.
Out of a vent in its tail leaks a dreck of fathers and sons.
That creature would be called "the Master of Creation"
if Zeus did not hold it back, spike it with lightning.
Passing that monster that begat itself,
without me the winged horses
will panic, snap the reins you hanker for
made of gold hair left on my pillow."
The Sun God knew his words were useless.
The Hours were leading out the four winged horses.
"Phaeton, be a bright dawn, the hope of the world.
Drive westward, pyramids on your left. No horse
or boy ever learned from whippings or floods.
Look, the moon, my poor sister, is pale as a dove—
do not cause a drought. Because of me
there is no God of Disappointment."
The Sun God was mumbling now, afraid of his son's fate.
The boy jumped into his father's chariot,
shouted, "I'll be back tonight."

Canto II

Rising from the East like any other day
Phaeton opened the night clouds with his whip,
turning them to fire. The horses knew
they were carrying a light, mortal thing that had no history.
Noon. The horses high in the heavens,

half a sky off course, smelled mares below,
dragged the godless flaming chariot earthward,
let off fountains of urine in Phaeton's face.
Phaeton's knees shook. He had to urinate.
He wished he never knew who his father was.
He wished his father had broken his oath.
He wished he were a bastard again.
Where is East, where is West? Who is North, who is South?
Now the eagle the size of an oak was coming toward him.

A wheel broke off, rolled in flames through Africa.
Crete and Sicily were under water, the Arctic—mud.
China was a flaming paper lantern,
rivers promised swans for coming summer boiled.
The world's olive groves, some sacred, were hissing embers.
Parnassus was blackened marble.
The Earth Goddess called to Zeus,
"Oh my great lover, all my harvests,
all the years of laboring, good farmers I blessed, gone,
the pain of the plough I bore, come to nothing.
Strike down the sun's vainglorious boy!"
Zeus smacked Phaeton out of the burning clouds.
Helios the helpless Sun God wept.
For the first time since chaos he took off his golden helmet.
He felt like a coal miner in a pit. In darkness he shouted,
"Zeus, you bugger, you seducer of mortal wives
and boys, disguise yourself as the great prick you are
and piss out the fires. Zeus, may you be deposed by Jews,
Christians, Muslims, Hindus, Baptists and Buddhists.
I owe nothing to the world. I see the living live by stealing fire.
Since I was the Dawn of Time, I labored.
How often I found my bright work dull.
Don't you think I wanted to command the Sea,
make War, or Music?"

Zeus mumbled, "My thunderbolt is not a question mark."
Every God and Goddess yawned. The Sun's flaming tears fell
into what rivers were left on Earth, making amber
that would one day become gifts between lovers,
recalled in the Canticle of Canticles, the Song of Songs.

Canto III

After years of darkness, Helios took pity on the Earth Goddess,
with Eros on his shoulder, he turned his face toward Earth.
There was sunlight, good tempests and good blizzards.
The Earth bloomed. There were crops and farm houses,
oil lamps, fires under soup kettles, marble cities, slums again.
An old Greek, not an oracle, only a clever fellow
said: "These days, you almost never see a naked swimmer—
the Earth is filling with burning dumps and battlefields—
an insult to the Earth Goddess."
Someone shouted across the port of Athens,
"You will never crucify Apollo!" The Greek wrote in a letter:
"The Sun can never be made to look ridiculous.
You cannot get a hook into a Leviathan,
catch him with a line, or carry him to market.
You cannot get a word out of him, or have a covenant with him.
Sooner battle the Leviathan than the Sun."
The Sun had long since called back his winged horses,
whipped them and drowned them in flames.
Now every day is like every other to the Sun.

2. CRITON

Among ancient trees, there stood a colossal Oak
that protected others for a thousand years.
When earthquakes levelled temples and their marble Gods,
the Sacred Oak protected the Greek countryside.
Even when lightning seized it by the throat,
it sheltered fieldworkers, orchards, nests and hives.
How many lovers had slept below its branches?
In summer, but especially in winter
when there was snow, birds and butterflies
alighted on its branches in such numbers
passing armies would lay down their weapons
surrendering, it seemed, to beauty.
Profane Criton, the Tyrant, in need of timber,
drove away lovers, gave orders to his slaves
to cut down the colossal Oak. He boasted,
"The great tree may be the one the Goddess loves most,
it may be the Goddess herself, but this tree has lived only
to be useful to me, for ships and a banquet hall."
Then Criton killed two slaves who refused his command.
Taking up the axe himself, he swung in fury.
The Oak trembled, groaned, the green leaves
turned pale, then black, the tree moaned,
blood pouring out where the branches joined the trunk,
as from a bull's throat cut for sacrifice,
blood pulsing from its mouth. The Tyrant and slaves
heard a voice: "A nymph loved by Demeter,
I live in the wood; I say to all who love green,
worthless Criton will soon die
—my last consolation."
Still, he struck blows for pleasure,
till the weeping oak chained by ropes and tackles
manned by an army of whipped slaves,
fell with the roar of a great waterfall in spring.
Butterflies, lovers, birds, snakes and rabbits,

wild cats and bears flew out of the tree
to save themselves—some without their young.
The falling giant broke the backs of a thousand trees.
Voices came from everywhere, in Greek and shrill Persian:
"We have never ploughed a field or picked a fig
without permission of the Goddess of Harvest.
Punish this zero to the left. Punish him!"
Demeter nodded Yes—the fields and forest trembled.
"I sentence him to endless Famine!" (Of course,
she could not speak to Famine because Fate
never allows the Goddesses of Harvest and Famine to meet.)
In her place, Harvest sent a messenger
saying, "Go where the earth is salt and bones,
where nothing lives but cold, pallor and fear.
Go to the screeching hag Goddess Famine.
Tell her I will put in a word for her where it counts
if she crawls inside Criton, hides in his body,
lets nothing give him nourishment." The Goddess smiled.
"Take my chariot of winged dragons to make the distance shorter."
In Scythia on a crag of the frozen Caucuses,
where the dragons could only steady the chariot
by continually beating their wings, the messenger found Famine.
If not for a bleeding jaw and her diseased eyes,
he would not have distinguished Famine
from the pink gravel and ice around her.
Her skin so tight, so transparent,
her stomach seemed a skull.
He thought Famine's throat covered with brine sang—then Famine,
knowing Zeus loved the goddess of Harvest, took her bargain.
Like a silver crab, on three broken wings
that once were elbows,
she crawled the great distance to Criton,
sleeping away his last moments of satisfaction
in a purple and gold room without a household god.
Famine locked her scaled arms around him.
Her breath that smelled of human waste spilled

on his face and in him, her broken teeth
stabbing his throat with the needles of endless hunger.
Then, her good work done, she turned back
from a country of green fields and flowering orchards
to her fatherland, the mountains and valleys
of bones, salt and ice.
Sleep, with its soft wings still caressed Criton,
soothed him, but now in his sleep he dreamed of feasting:
but his jaws bit into nothing, his parched throat swallowed nothing.
His mouth full of sewage his tongue struggled to escape.
Yet he woke famished.
He summoned a legion of servants and slaves,
ordered them to slaughter his cattle, to heap before him
meats cooked or raw, fish, fowl and frogs.
Whatever he ate, his stomach
shouted in pain and anger.
He swallowed rabbits whole and turtles in their shells
and he groaned, "I am starving, I am starving."
Night and day he ate what would feed a city, a nation
but the more he ate, the more he craved.
He starved as fire burns straw, crawling to dry branches,
from fallen trees to flaming forests.
Then, as an ocean eats a coastline, he hungered,
cliff by cliff, mountain by mountain,
he sucked out the marrow—all this was to him
less than a black olive, a dry fig.
His stomach was a gorge cut by a dry river.
Starving and moneyless, he called on his daughter,
sold her for five sheep. She looked toward the sea,
crying out to Poseidon, who had once been her lover,
"Remember, oh God, three nights in summer, save me."
Poseidon, quick as a fish takes to water
when dropped from a fisherman's net, disguised her as a fisherman,
red-eyed from the sun, skin becoming coral,
so the slavemaster did not know her,
saying to her simply, dumbfounded,

"Fisherman, where is the slave girl I paid for?"
She answered, "I swear, may Poseidon not watch every net I cast,
no one's been here but me." The fool went off with his deceived dog.
Then Poseidon's trident gave her back her own form.
Starving Criton, seeing that his daughter had the gift
to change her form, sold her over and over again
to barbarians. But she walked away,
now a mare, now a heifer, now a sheep, now a lion,
now a dove, now an eagle
till there was no food for her father to buy
till there was nothing, nothing at all—
only his own flesh for his teeth to gnaw.
He licked his fingers then ate them,
then his hands, then his wrists, then elbows,
his trotters and sex, he swallowed his own ears
and lips and tongue, portion by portion,
he consumed his own body, his whole self.
Demeter, who does not allow a field to be planted
without her permission, had made clear her will.

POPE PIUS XII ANNOUNCED HE WAS VISITED BY CHRIST ON HIS SICKBED

An easy bus ride or short walk through Rome,
sewer of Heaven that flushed Christ home,
a grave-faced Christ visited the Pope,
his Irish sheets changed, already rancid,
cross in fist, his eyes in a backward slope;
that day I do not remember what I did,
Christ's voice echoed under St. Peter's Dome,
Neptune to ocean, the Holy Ghost to foam,
He strode out on the lifeless shore. Lift the host,
sea bells clang the presence of the Holy Ghost
along the Tiber, a headless angel sings
with collars of bees about his throat, Christ king,
and bees swarm out of their golden hive
into Italian Spring. What lives
that hunted on the Mount of Olives
for a younger, unaging Christ? Not the dead,
the dead have buried the dead,
the living celebrate the living
for a younger Christ, on Easter Sunday,
almost the first day of spring, a display
of miracles, bread and wine on the table,
the ordinary adorable.

There's farce, silly, and turnabout.
Once in Heaven, you can get thrown out,
ask some questions, raising doubt.
Was Christ appearing enough?
Did the Lord say anything off the cuff?
Did He choose to play it rough,
say, in sacred conversation, *Pacelli,*
you hammered in another nail
when you mystically waved "sieg heil!"?
Did you genuflect when you danced the hoochie coochie
with Il Duce?

Did Christ come to Rome for a last laugh?
I'm sure the Pope believed what he saw.
Soon after, I do not think Pacelli went to hell,
heaven, or that he got his what for.
I believe at this late date
I shall have the same fate.

PROPHECY I

An oracle told me
an elephant in a zoo
will pick up a child higher
than he has ever been
on a swing or a seesaw—
the trunk an S
over the elephant's head.
His father will drop
his ice cream cone,
the kid will wave to the world
hello, goodbye—
then he's thrown *swoosh* across the moat.
That's the way it will happen.
You will call the mother
saying, "Darling,
I have something to tell you . . ."
the taste of chocolate
still in your mouth.
And you are the father
and you are the child.

STOWAWAY

1

Aging, I am a stowaway in the hold of my being.
Even memory is a finger to my lips.
Once I entered down the center aisle
at the Comédie Française, the Artemis of Ephesus
on my arm, all eyes on her rows of breasts and me.
"Who is this master of her ninety nipples?"
the public whispered.
Now the ocean is my audience,
I see in secret my last secret.

2

Mid-December, my old felt hat that I could have imagined
myself leaving behind in a restaurant for eternity
blew out into the Atlantic. The damn thing so familiar
I saw myself wearing it even into the deep,
an aging Narcissus, in white foam and northern sunlight,
on my way to becoming a conch. It is like seeing music
this growing from flesh and bone into seashell:
undulating salts become a purple mantle,
and the almost translucent
bivalve of memory and forgetting closes.

HERMAPHRODITES IN THE GARDEN

1.

After the lesson of the serpent there is the lesson
of the slug and the snail—hermaphrodites,
they prosper on or under leaves, green or dead,
perhaps within the flower. See how slowly
on a windless day the clouds move over the garden
while the slug and the snail, little by little, pursue
their kind. Each pair with four sexes
knows to whom it belongs, as a horse knows
where each of its four feet is on a narrow path:
two straight below the eyes, two a length behind.
There is cause and reason for,
but in the garden, mostly life befalls.
Each male female lies with a male female,
folds and unfolds, enters and withdraws.
On some seventh day after a seventh day they rest,
too plural for narratives, or dreams, or parables,
after their season. One by one they simply die—
in no special order each sex leaves the other
without comfort or desire.

2.

I open my hands of shadow and shell that covered my face—
they offered little protection from shame or the world.
I return to the garden, time's mash of flowers,
stigmas and anthers in sunlight and fragrant rain.
Human, singular, the slug of my tongue
moves from crevice to crevice, while my ear,
distant cousin of a snail, follows the breathing
and pink trillium of a woman who is beautiful
as the garden is beautiful, beyond joy and sorrow,
where every part of every flower is joy and sorrow.
I, lost in beauty, cannot tell which is which,
the body's fragrant symmetry from its rhymes.
I am surrounded by your moist providence.
A red and purple sunrise blinds me.

THE BLANKET

The man who never prays
accepts that the wheat field in summer
kneels in prayer when the wind blows across it,
that the wordless rain and snow
protect the world from blasphemy.
His wife covers him with a blanket
on a cold night—it is, perhaps, a prayer?
The man who never prays says kindness and prayer
are close, but not as close as sleep and death.
He does not observe the Days of Awe,
all days are equally holy to him.
In late September, he goes swimming
in the ocean, surrounded by divine intervention.

Asleep in the Garden
(1998)

&

The Intelligence of Clouds
(1989)

HANNIBAL CROSSING THE ALPS

He urged his starving elephants upward into the snows,
the barges still smelling of Mediterranean brine,
packed with huddled troops, men of Carthage
in ice-covered armor, some wearing desert sandals
wrapped in leaves, elephants up to their necks in snow,
trumpeting, their trunks grabbing at crumbling clouds of snow.
The colossal gray boulders swayed, moved upward,
some tumbled back into the echoing ravines.
An avalanche, forests of ice fell on Africa.
In the morning soldiers gathered remnants of red and blue silk,
dry sardines and beans, gold goblets still sandy
from desert victories, live turtles meant for soup,
a tangle of chained goats and sheep meant for sacrifice.

O you runners, walkers, horsemen, riders of bicycles,
men of sense and small gesture, commuters like me,
remember Hannibal came down from the Alps
into the warm belly of Italy, and conquered.
It was twenty years later in another place,
after errors of administration and alliance,
that he poisoned himself. What is remembered?
His colossal head asleep on the sand of Tunis,
a few dates, confusion between victories and defeats,
his elephants.

ANNUNCIATION

I saw a virgin who did not want to be
impregnated by words—but I do,
or did I see her pushing off the unwanted angel
when it was over, her humped-back cat hissing,
sensing perhaps the human, inhuman, natural son.
The loudest sound I ever heard came from within my ear:
babble and chaos, twins inside me, as if word and verb
from the beginning were without pause, stop, caesura—
all words meaningless, life without time and weather.
Did I hear my death conceived inside my ear,
like a child some call "the Savior"?

THE POET

He stared at a word and saw his face,
in every noun and every verb—his own face.
He could understand if he saw his face
in words like ocean, or on a blank page
or in anything that might mirror him,
but he saw his own face in *buts* and *ands*,
in *neither nor*, in *which* and *whose* and *what*.
In the names of others living and dead
he saw his own face.
The moment his senses came into play,
at the very edge of any perception, in light or darkness,
the word became his flesh
with his obscene mouth, his poisonous eyes.
Secretly he drew close to certain words
he hoped might not be his face, words he misspelled
in languages he barely knew, but every letter
was hair and tooth. What was not his face
was wordlessness—wordless tears, wordless laughter—
that never came to vowel or consonant.

THE SWIMMER

I remember her first as a swimmer:
I saw my mother swimming in a green and white bathing suit,
her arms reaching out across giant ocean waves,
swimming through the breakers of the Atlantic.
I stood on the shore,
knowing almost nothing, unable to go to her—
dumbfounded by the wonder of it,
It happened long before I could dress myself.
I was a little older than the weeping Chinese child
sitting alone in the rubble of Nanking—
barely old enough to be read to,
not able to tell time or count.
When I had that kind of knowledge, in her old age
she showed me herself naked, the tubes and the sack.
An hour later she said, "I must have been crazy."
Then she swam off again and never came back.
For a few days I awoke as that child again.
Now I have learned a kind of independence.
It is mostly in dreams she comes back, younger or older,
sometimes fresh from the joy of the swim.

LETTER TO AN UNKNOWN

Five centimeters, already Chinese,
in your mother's womb, pre-intellectual,
about sixty days. Sounds can see you,
music can see you. Fu Xu, your father,
I introduce you to him, he is a painter
already saving for your education, preparing
to carry you on his shoulders to museums.
Zhu Ming, your mother, holds you close
as it is possible to hold a being close,
rare as an Empress, Freudian Chinese therapist,
she will teach you the joys and sorrows
of writing Chinese. May you spend
many happy years washing ink from your hands.
You have made the Great Wall of China bleed.
Who am I? Something like a tree
outside your window: after you are born,
shade in summer, in winter my branches
heavy with snow will almost touch the ground,
may shelter deer, bear, and you.

ALEXANDER FU

Surrounded by a great Chinese wall of love,
he is already three weeks old and has a name.
His mother combs his hair with her hand, nurses him.
Soon he will learn the tragic news: the world is not all love.
He has already begun to earn a living,
a little of his poopoo was just put in a flower pot.
The least part of him bears the seal of his Manufacturer.

ALEXANDER'S FIRST BATTLE

Now that you are looking over the edge of the world,
who will blame you for refusing to exchange
your mother's warm breast for rubber and warm glass?
Will you ever again be content? There will be laughter
and music, the solace of small talk, the solace
of art or science, twelve-year-old whiskey.
You will search the earth through hard years
to find somewhere in a timeless bed, or Venice,
or God forbid in the back seat of a car,
the return of such contentment. Alexander,
fight the bottle, fight it with all your being.
I will fight at your side.

ALEXANDER FU TO STANLEY

Big fool, my ancestors understood
we live in two societies: time and that other society
with its classes and orders, which you, Mr. America,
like to think you can ascend or descend at will.
Do I, a baby,
have to tell you there are laws that are not legislated,
judges neither appointed nor elected?
You are wetting your pants to talk to me.
Did it ever cross your mind I like to be ten months old,
going on eleven? You are trying to rob me of my infancy
because I have all the time in the world, and you don't.
On this May evening passing round the world
I probably have more diapers on the shelf
than you have years to go. I wish every time I shit
you'd have another year. Now that's an honest wish,
better than blowing out candles.
(Secretly you want to learn from me.)
You say I look like a prophet. Did it ever cross your mind
I would just like to be a bore like you?
Stop thinking about the Jew, Christian, Buddhist, Taoist thing!
The Long March wasn't from Kovno to Queens.
In summa: you are old and I am young,
that's the way it should be. I have better things to think about
than are dreamt of in your toilet-trained world.

LETTER TO ALEXANDER FU, SEVEN YEARS OLD

A few days after your first birthday,
we had lunch on soup I made for grown-ups,
your father took you from your mother's arms,
carried you around our house to show you the sights;
he passed a painting of barren Sarah offering Hagar
to Abraham, old as I am. Then he stopped
before a half-naked lady looking in a mirror,
her two faces made you laugh.
In the library he showed you a family
resting on a hillside while their donkey grazed.
He did not tell you who they were, or that they were
on their way to Egypt.
He explained in Chinese and English:
"In this kind of painting, you must show the source of light.
The sunlight is behind the olive tree, the donkey
and sleeping father are in shade."
He named the colors, showed you a rainbow over a river.
You clapped hands and danced in his arms,
screeched so loud for joy, the dogs barked.
Next he came to an archangel with black wings
leading a boy carrying a fish.
He didn't tell you the boy will take fish gall,
put it into his father's eyes and cure his blindness.
Your father is a Chinese artist with a green card,
you are an American citizen in his arms.

Six years have passed. I read this letter to Alexander,
asked him what it meant.
He said, "It means Daddy likes me.
He should have explained in English before Chinese.
Abraham lived a hundred years,
had a baby and made God laugh.
God tells the heart what to do,
the heart tells the brain what to do.
I like that story, I want to take it home."

TO ANGELINA, ALEXANDER'S COUSIN, WHOSE CHINESE NAME MEANS HAPPINESS

She lies naked, five days old,
a chance that history might be kindness and love,
a chance the size and strength of her hands—
the rarest Chinese-American beauty,
certain to break hearts.
May she teach her children Mandarin,
Tu Fu and calligraphy,
however busy the city.

May she know the joy of singing,
may she play a musical instrument,
may she find her own way in the wilderness.
Under the seven halts in the sky,
may she and her brother who is four
having sucked from the breast
of one mother, swear on her dark nipple
to be true to her nature.

I remember an ancient Chinese poet
saw a nine-year-old beauty
in a rose garden.
No one near the child
would speak except in whispers—
such was the power and burden of beauty.

After ten ancient years
the poet returned to marry her.
Later, the French and British
in Beijing ravished the sacred garden,
pillaged the Summer Palace.
It was not enough for the Brits

to have roses bloom at Westminster in December . . .
Angelina, you are five days old
and I have some 28,000 days.
If I were not married, I would wait.

APRIL, BEIJING

Some of the self-containment of my old face
has been sandblasted away. The "yellow wind"
is blowing and my mouth and face burn
from the Gobi dust that scorches the city
after its historic passage over the Great Wall.
When I was young, I hosed the Atlantic salt
off my body—the salt was young too.

In China, "ashes to ashes and dust to dust"
means something more; work, no matter how cruel,
is part prophecy. Workers in fields
that were Chinese eight thousand years ago,
their plows and terraces a kind of calligraphy,
face the living and the dead, whose windy fortress
takes on a mortal form: the Great Wall.
Even here the North Wind abducts a beauty.
Never before have I heard ancient laughter.
In China, I can taste the dust on my own grave
like salt. The winter coal dust shadows every wall
and window, darkens the lattice and the rose,
offers its gray society to the blue cornflower,
the saffron crocus, the red poppy.

                    The moon
brushed by calligraphy, poetry and clouds,
touched, lowered toward mortality—
to silk, to science, to paper,
requires that the word and painting respond
more intimately to each other, when the heart
is loneliest and in need of a mother,
when the ocean is drifting away,
when the mountains seem further off.
The birds sing in the dark before sunrise
because sunlight is delayed by dust and the sound

of a poet grinding his own ink from stone
according to the moon's teaching.
I am happy to be here, even if I can't breathe.
The emperor of time falls from a tree,
the dust rises.

CHINA POEM

On a red banner across the center of a cave house
there is painted in gold Chinese letters:
"Strive to Build Socialist Spiritual Civilization."
On the right side hangs a red banner saying,
"Intellectuals: Cleaning Shithouses for Ten Years
in the Cultural Revolution Clears the Head."
Down the left side is pasted
a lantern-thin red and black paper-saying,
"When Spring Comes Back, the Earth is Green."

Down the hill is China: the people give little importance
to what they call "spring couplets," the paper-sayings
pasted with wheat-flour and water above the lintels
and down the sills of peasant houses. They seldom notice
they enter and depart through the doors of poetry.
An ancient story is told in calligraphy.

DOG

Until the rain takes over my life I'll never change,
although I know by heart the Lord's Prayer
and the prayer Christ prayed to his father
in John, chapter 17, sanctifying himself.
Trying to convert me would be like teaching a dog to drive a car
just because it likes to go out for a drive.
On the other hand I am a dog that has been well treated
by his master. He kisses me and I lick his face. When he can
he lets me off the leash in the woods or at the beach.
I often sleep in his bed.

ON TRYING TO REMEMBER TWO CHINESE POEMS

I've forgotten the book, the poet,
the beauty of calligraphy,
the poems made to be seen and read out loud,
two lost songs on hanging scrolls
stolen by foreigners . . .

White as frost,
a piece of freshly woven silk
made a fan, a bright moon.
She, or my lady, kept a fan nearby,
its motion a gentle summer breeze . . .
He dreaded the coming of autumn
when the north wind breaks the summer heat
and the fan is dropped unwanted
into a lacquer box,
its short term of favor ended.

A catalog of beds:
riverbed, flower bed, family bed.
My mother died when I was three,
dreadful to be a child in baby clothes.
I climbed into her bed and tried to nurse,
clutching her body with all my strength;
not knowing she was dead I spoke to her,
called to her. I remember thinking,
before, when I wept and ached for her,
although she was sick she came to me,
she whispered and caressed me,
then the lamp went out
and my mother coughed by the chilly window.
. . . A night of restless birds.

Without warning
a great forest fire, a devouring flaming wind,
rolling mountains of fire
with nothing to stop them but the sea.
Woman is half the sky.

POSTCARD TO WALT WHITMAN FROM SIENA

Today I walked along the vaulted hall
of a Renaissance hospital opposite the Duomo
and I thought of you, Walt Whitman, in your forties,
writing letters for the wounded and dying.
This October Italian morning is clean as the air of Montauk.
In the sunlit galleries among medieval painters
there is a kind of gossip about the life of Christ
—the artists did not sign their names,
worked for the honor of illumination,
gold leaf, not leaves of grass.
I remember you sang Italian arias
and "The Star-Spangled Banner" in your bathtub.
To wash the horribly wounded and the dying,
you did not need to think of them as Jesus.
Walt, I saw a cradle that was a church that you could rock.
Yesterday at five o'clock I heard the rosary
up to the "joys and sorrows" of the Virgin, had coffee,
then returned for the litany, metaphors about the Virgin:
star of the sea, lily of the valley, tower of ivory—
like you and your America.
Walt, I know you and the Virgin Mother
have conversation with the poor.
I try to listen.

A POOR WOMAN

She felt ashamed. She was only a poor woman
no different from any other. Whom could she ask to forgive her?
She was taught in childhood if you wrong someone
only the person you wrong can forgive you, not God.
She could sew and sell her sewing. Fruit of the womb,
He was not her only son, He was not His own Father.
People found it easier to believe after the parables
the first miracle, the water to wine,
His going to hell, His suffering, the rising.
She wept. His flesh tore like paper.
She did not want anything to happen to the good He had done,
the love and kindness He taught.
She remembered the pleasures of His childhood,
a donkey ride to Egypt, the Passover meals, the joy of His being
a child carpenter making His first table
years before the "love meals." She knew that sometimes
people nursed the sick and dying,
thinking they were helping Him in His suffering.
She said, "It's too late for Him, but do it anyway,
He would like you to feed the sick and hungry—
for the suffering people themselves."
Once a man, twice a child.
Sometimes behind the door or in the street
she heard them call her "Our Lady."
Although the virgin goddess, sister of Apollo, was more beautiful,
what does the moon goddess offer the poor and grieving now.
It was better to be a mother who worked all day.
Sometimes she would bathe, powder her face, put on a blue dress
and sit at the window to hear them talk in the street.

ALLEGORY OF THE LAUGHING PHILOSOPHER

I came to Athens, and no one knew me.
                    —Democritus

1

Not myth, not document or hymn,
but a way of remembering by writing
and rewriting—as it turned out, he wrote
a page about the distance between father
and son, mother and daughter,
as if it were natural law
that they reflect one another. Laughing,
he wrote, "Often they meet like water and sky
that, at a distance, seem to touch . . .
and the moon and sun are like father and son,
each sometimes an eclipse of the other."
Love tore open the oak chest of his memories:
what were names and titles became
figures of speech, slips of the tongue,
the bright day of the soul.
A small child, he remembered his joy before he could read or write,
he wrote the shape of the letter *e*
he knew but could not name.
And so through the years he learned a touch of what was new
that later became something remarkable he could name.
Gray now, in a garden at a stone table
below a trellis of grape leaves he sleeps on his books.

2

The first days of March,
the smell of the newborn in the air
brought his imitations and guffaws
over the miracles and illusions of everyday life:
his birth and death—donkeys
chewing the same grass, breaking the same wind.
Loving donkeys, he was pleased

that in medieval views of the Nativity
the donkey stood for the Synagogue,
the cow the Church of Rome.
Laughing became anapestic giggles,
hee-haws. He wrote a farce
with a chorus of barbers and shoemakers.
Unbalanced, he tripped over his roots
between father and son, mothers and daughters.
He slept with his dogs, laughed
about the seasons passing more quickly,
the worship and praise his god had disregarded.
On the inner surface of a bowl, he wrote scripture,
poured water in, stirred until the writing was dissolved,
then filled his mouth, gargled, swallowed, and grinned.

LULLABY

I hear a *Te Deum* of . . . "Who are you to think . . .
touch religion like a hot stove,
hide bad news and the dead . . . a fool will light candles,
a fool will bless the children, a fool is ceremonious."
I see my first roadside wildflowers,
the lake—every sunfish nibble is a kiss.
On a summer afternoon
the clouds and I are useless brothers;
Eros carves his bow with a kitchen knife.

I read by the light of fire blazing in their hands:
my father who I thought would die forever,
my mother who I thought would live forever.
I won't forget the child who could not speak his name,
Rossini arias, the condoms on the floor,
the studying, the sweet and sour of moral purpose,
under a frowning etching of Beethoven.
The cuckoo clock was moved from room to room.
Age ten, I flew a red flag for revolution
in my bedroom and yearned for a better world.

I've made my family into an entertainment.
Once I named their symbols: the sewing basket,
fruits and animals, as their attributes.
I could show us as we were at home,
walking across a New York street or at the ocean
each brooding alone in the sand.
There is a lullaby children sing to the old.
The truth is, now in death we hold hands.

CENTAUR SONG

A creature half horse, half human,
my father herded his mares and women together
for song, smell and conversation. He taught me
to love wine, music and English poetry.
Like the Greeks he left the temple's interior
for priests, he observed outside
where he could see the pediment and caryatids.
If he saw a beauty out walking, or on a journey,
the proper centaur offered to carry her
over ice, or across a river—he'd bolt
to the edge of a wood, a place of sunlight.
He slid her gently down his back,
held her to him with a hoof.
Hooves cut. How could he touch with tenderness?
I feel his loneliness when I am just with horses,
or just with humans. There was a time
when he was tied to a tree,
so he could not go to one or the other.
Now his city crushed deep in the ground
has disappeared in darkness
—which is a theme for music.
He licked the blood from a trembling foal,
he galloped back to his books.
Today the North Wind fathers,
which is why it is said mares
often turn their hindquarters to the wind
and breed foals without the aid of stallions.

A VISIT TO THE ISLAND OF JAMAICA

I

Foggy weather.
The most aloof birds
come closer to the earth,
confused by the apparent
lowering of the clouds and sky.
I walk in these descended clouds,
set birds off in terror.
The fish don't care.
I surf cast a silver spoon
into the clouds
in the direction of the sea.

II

Last summer in Long Island
I saw a pair of white egrets
standing at the shoreline.
Now in Jamaica I see hundreds of them
swooping above me,
more delicate than gulls—
beyond Fern Gully
where the road leads into fields of sugar cane,
the old slave plantations.
The flights of white birds
remind me of alarmed swallows.
Then I see what they are doing:
hundreds of birds are driving
a single buzzard out of the valley.
I am afraid of what I see.
They are diving again and again
to protect their nests.
In just a few days
I have become accustomed
to seeing egrets perch on cattle

or standing silently beside
motionless.
Now I see them fighting for life,
summoning whatever violence they have ,
unable to be graceless.
One by one, not as a flock,
the birds dive, pursue,
but do not touch.
Off the Caribbean,
a fresh afternoon wind
lifts the egrets higher
and gives the red-throated scavenger,
who must also feed its young,
a momentary passage
down into the tall, moist grass.

IN FRONT OF A POSTER OF GARIBALDI

1

When my Italian son
admired a poster of Garibaldi
in the piazzetta of Venice,
a national father in a red shirt,
gold chain, Moroccan fez and fancy beard,
I wished the boy knew the Lincoln
who read after a day's work,
the commoner, his honesty.
My knees hurt from my life and playing soccer—
not that I see Lincoln splashing with his kids
in the Potomac. Lord knows where his dead son led him.

2

My son tells me Fortuna could have put
Lincoln and Garibaldi in Venice—
Garibaldi in red silk, Lincoln
in a stovepipe hat black as a gondola.
My son mimics Garibaldi:
"Lincoln, you may be the only man in the piazza
to log down the Mississippi
and walk back the 1,500 miles to Illinois
but you are still a man who calls all pasta macaroni.
How do you know where you are going?
Your shoes are straights, no lasts,
no right or left, no fashion, white socks.
How can the President of the United States
make such a *brutta figura?*"

3

I can't speak for Lincoln,
any more than I can sing for Caruso
—toward the end when Caruso sang,
his mouth filled with blood.
Not every poet bites into his own jugular:

some hunger, some observe the intelligence of clouds.
I was surprised to see a heart come out
of the torn throat of a snake. I know a poet
whose father blew his brains out
before his son was born, who still leads his son
into the unknown, the unknowable.

4

My son tells me I must not forget
Garibaldi fought for liberty in six countries
including Uruguay, refused the command
of a corps that Lincoln offered. He asked
to be head of the Union armies and for
an immediate declaration against slavery,
he was the "King's flag," defeated
the papal armies in 1866,
which gave the Jews equality in Italy.

5

I've always had a preference
for politics you could sing
on the stage of the Scala.
I give my son Lincoln and Garibaldi
as guardian angels.
May he join a party and a temple
that offer a chair to the starving and unrespectable.
We come from stock that on the day of atonement
asks forgiveness for theft, murder, lies, betrayal,
for all the sins and crimes of the congregation.
May he take his girls and bride to Venice,
may the blessings come like pigeons.
Lincoln waves from his gondola and whispers,
"I don't know what the soul is,
but whatever it is, I know it can humble itself."

A GAMBLER'S STORY

There was a risk, a dividing of waters,
there was an Irish Jew whose father arrived
in Belfast from Kovno, heard English,
got off the boat and was in Ireland three years
before he discovered he wasn't in England.
His face was something like a distant sky,
his eyes were so restless one looked like the moon,
the other a sunset. Unlucky, he lost the money
for a rainy day, their daily bread, did time, then vanished.
His daughter waited all her life for the miracle
of his return, offered comfort to those beyond reason
who hoped for riches of all sorts. Years passed,
he played roulette in Monte Carlo,
won 100,000 pounds on red 3,
gave it to his wife and children, disappeared
in Provence, where he studied mystical
philosophy, the universe still on a roll,
the greatest of all crap shoots, he wrote poems,
the earth winning the familiar waters, the stars
taking the heavens, and darkness was the big winner.

TO MY SON'S WIFE ON HER WEDDING DAY

First I embrace you. I come prepared with this,
a wedding song, a love song beneath your balcony
because the world is different now,
there is a little more hope, a wild flower of hope.
It is for you to name it.
If marriage were a canoe—a foolish idea,
most will say, marriage may be a canoe in Montana
but not in Tuscany. They are wrong. Be Iroquois.
In a canoe both paddle, see how beautiful the lake is,
in every fiery sunrise the clouds of remembrance.
Waterlilies are wild flowers. Listen to the loons
surrounded by wilderness. Stay far from fashion.
If you ever put on war paint, jump in the lake
as soon as you can. Remember
when your brave husband caught his first fish, he wept
because he thought I would not let him throw it back.
To live together forever in one tent
you will have to learn to make fire by rubbing
two sticks together. Every Iroquois prays
that a great spirit will turn the hearts of the fathers
to the children and the hearts of the children to the fathers,
lest thunder and lightning strike the earth with a curse.

STATIONS

to Federico Zeri

1

I pass a half-naked child
asleep on a marble slab in Grand Central Station.
I remember a painting: the Infant Christ
asleep on a red marble slab,
and another: the man, Christ Dead,
on the same red marble stone of unction.
The great iron clocks
in the railroad stations of Christendom
witness nothing,
they are simply above with their everydayness,
in natural, artificial and supernatural light.
I turn my head away from the faceless
puddles of drying urine
in the marble passageways
between nowhere and the street above.
I turn away from time's terrible sufficiency
that is, like God, in need of nothing whatsoever.
I am not pitchman enough to speak
for the poor of the world so hungry
God only appears to them as bread.

2

Last June under the horologe of the Italian sky,
my mind full of timetables and illusions,
I went back to Siena after forty years,
faithful to something, the city scolded
by San Bernardino of the flaming heart
for loving the Madonna so much it had forgotten Jesus.
Before a painting of the kneeling Archangel
announcing to Mary a child will be born to her:
I noted she wears two delicate, looped earrings,
from which hang two little gold crosses,
signs of the Crucifixion that has not yet occurred.

Time is nothing—an echo;
night and day are only a foreshadowing.
I have not yet disappeared.

ALLEGORY OF SMELL

His smile says he has had the smell of it,
he flies a rooster tail in his hat.
In a torn army jacket
the old soldier pounds the tavern table.
They bring him an onion, garlic and a rose.
He discards the rose. He says, "To hell and back
a man stinks of what he is." He laughs:
"I myself am a sack of piss—thanks to brandy,
mine smells like an apple orchard."
He remembers the gardens of women:
summer women, when they pass, enter
a man's soul through the nostrils, the consolation
the good Lord provides old soldiers.
A smell can be as naked as a breast.
His red eyes shine with tears from the onion he eats.

ALLEGORY OF EVIL IN ITALY

You, a goiter on my neck, lick my ear with lies.
Generously, you mother and father a stolen boy.
The Visconti put you on their flag, a snake
devouring a child, or are you throwing up a man
feet first? Some snakes hunt frogs, some freedom of will.
A man can count years on your snakeskin,
yet I must listen, smile, and kiss your cheek,
or you may swallow the child completely. In Milan
there is a Bramante, the throned Virgin in glory.
On the marble floor below her, two figures:
a human-size dead frog on its back,
and a dead naked man. There's hope!
My eyes look into the top of my head
at the wreath of snakes that sometimes crowns me.

LOST DAUGHTER

I have protected the flame of a match
I lit and then discarded
more than I cared for you.
I had little to go on:
a postcard that came for no reason,
forty years ago,
that told me of your birth and name,
but not who was your father.
I would never give
my child your name.
In the woods and ditches of my life you
are less than a wildflower.
If you have a garden I
am less than melted snow.
I never held your hand
and this is the only bedtime story
I will ever tell you.
No love, no prayer, no flame.

SHOES

Home, I bang the sand out of my shoes.
I haven't the craft to make a goat's-belly bagpipe
from a shoe or the art to play it,
but I can see my cold wet shoes
as unwept-for bodies without a poet.
I speak for the leather ghosts of children.
I hold one up: a newborn infant without breath.
I cannot smack it into life. I face
mountains of shoes, endless lines of children
holding their parents' hands. I hold a shoe to my ear
like a seashell—hear a child's voice: "God is the old woman
who lived in a shoe, she had so many children . . ."
I hear the cries of cattle
begging for mercy in a slaughterhouse,
I smell the stink of the tannery.
I am a shoemaker, not a poet.

SONG FOR STANLEY KUNITZ

Creature to creature,
two years before we met
I remember I passed his table
at the Cedar Tavern.
He who never knew his father
seemed to view all strangers
as his father's good ghost,
any passing horse as capable
of being Pegasus, or pissing
in the street.
I who knew my father
was wary of any tame raccoon
with claws and real teeth.

At our first meeting forty years ago,
before the age of discovery,
I argued through the night
against the tragic sense of life;
I must have thought God wrote in spit.

I keep a petrified clam, his gift, on my desk.
These gray rings and layers of stone,
shape of a whale's eye, are old as any desert.
Measured against it, the morning, the Hudson River
outside my window are modern and brash,
the star of David, the cross, the hand of Fatima,
are man-made weathervanes.
My clamstone has weight and lightness.
It is my sweet reminder that flesh,
perhaps love, can remain in the natural world
long as poetry, tides, phases of the moon.
Tomorrow I shall wear it in my right eye,
a monocle for my talk on the relationship
between paleontology and anthropology.

Bless Celia, the cat of his middle years,
with her ribbons and hats, her pagan smile.
Bless the bobcat that was his in boyhood,
that killed a police dog in battle
on Main Street, Worcester, lost a foot for it
and had to be shot. A child with a leaf in his head,
he walked through devil's bit scabious,
marsh ragwort, vernal grass
until the meadows wept. Bless his first garden,
his bird feeder still there after eighty-one years.
Did any of his long-forgotten kindnesses
alter history a little?

What a *luftmensch* he might have been,
his feet barely touching Commercial Street,
dancing home at three in the morning
with an ocean of money!
But how could he face the moon or the land
beside his house without a garden? Unthinkable.
I think what is written
in roses, iris and trumpet vine
is read by the Lord God.
Such a place of wild and ordered beauty
is like a heart that takes on the sorrows
of the world . . . He translates into all tongues.

IN DEFENSE OF A FRIEND

They say my old friend is "a good man with a worm in him."
An old revolutionary, he denies his least good fortune.
Owning his home makes him uncomfortable,
and it's true he slept in a fruit crate with his sisters,
outside their window on a brick wall he told me:
"Jesus Saves, Free Tom Mooney, Fuck You."
He believes the working class sees a different sunset.
No one will deny his life of wild love
has left him caring, with a sweet intimacy
few others have. When I took him fishing,
he wouldn't put a worm on his hook.

LOWELL

He needed to be held, so his country
held him in jail awhile, nonviolent,
manic New Englander. In conversation
his hands moved across sentences, a music
of almost indiscernible Latin consonants
and Tennessee cakewalking vowels.
What was sight but a God to fool the eye?
Although he looked at you he stared away,
his eyes moved across some distant lawn
like the eyes on a peacock's tail.
Now his life of love, books and nightmares
seems 19th-century American allegory,
without the lofty language.
Could he imagine the lives of those who read
without the slightest attention to form,
the lives of readers of newspapers, books
of passing interest, or nothing at all—
their deaths a slip of the tongue?
A generation that might kill itself
gathered in him as if he were a public place:
to pray, agitate and riot. The man and flame he was
waved back and forth in the wind,
became all tongue. Falling off his ladder
in Ireland his last morning, "Whack. Huroo.
Take your partners," caught without time
to tell what happened, locked in a museum,
he tried to break through the glass door.
That evening in Manhattan he fell silent
on the floor of a taxi, the meter running.
Gluck said of early opera, "It stinks of music."
Cal, your life stank of poetry . . . "Buzz, buzz," he said,
"a few bring real honey to the hive."

KRILL

The red fisherman
stands in the waters of the Sound,
then whirls toward an outer reef.
The krill and kelp spread out,
it is the sea anemone that displays the of,
the into, the within.
He throws the net about himself
as the sea breaks over him.
The krill in the net and out of it
follow him. He is almost awash
in silver and gold.
How much time has passed.
He believes the undulation of krill
leads to a world of less grief,
that the dorsal of your smelt,
your sardine, your whitebait, humped
against the ocean's spine, cheers it
in its purpose.
The krill break loose, plunge down
like a great city of lights. He is left
with the sea that he hears
with its *if* and *then*, *if* and *then*, *if* and *then*.

THE BATTLE

When Yahweh spoke to me, when I saw His name
spelled out in blood, the pounding in my heart
separated blood from ink and ink from blood,
and Yahweh said to me, "Know your soul's name
is blood and ink is the name of your spirit.
Your father and mother longed with all their hearts
to hear my Name and title given to every generation."
When I heard the clear difference between my spirit
and my soul, I was filled with great joy,
then I knew my soul took the hillside
under its own colors, in the mirror red as blood,
and that my spirit stood its ground in the mirror
that is black as ink, and that there raged
a ferocious war in my heart between blood and ink.
The blood was of the air and the ink of the earth
and the ink defeated the blood, and the Sabbath
overcame all the days of the week.

YOU AND I

You are Jehovah, and I am a wanderer.
Who should have mercy on a wanderer
if not Jehovah? You create and I decay.
Who should have mercy on the decayed
if not the creator? You are the Judge
and I the guilty. Who should have mercy
on the guilty if not the Judge? You are All
and I am a particle. Who should have mercy
on a particle if not the All?
You are the Living One and I am dead.
Who should have mercy on the dead if not
the Living One? You are the Painter and Potter
and I am clay. Who should have mercy on clay
if not the Painter and Potter? You are the Fire
and I am straw. Who should have mercy on straw
if not the Fire? You are the Listener
and I am the reader. Who should have mercy
on the reader if not the Listener? You
are the Beginning and I am what follows.
Who should have mercy on what follows
if not the Beginning? You are the End and I am
what follows. Who should have mercy
on what follows if not the End?

SONG OF INTRODUCTION

Ancient of Days,
I hear the sound and silence, the *lumière*
of molds, disease and insects, I believe poetry
like kindness changes the world, a little.
It reaches the ear of lion and lamb, it enters
the nest of birds, the course of fish, it is water
in the cupped hands of Arab and Jew.
Reader, in writing this I become you, I must awake
in your darkness and mine and sleep with your sleep
and mine. As a stone I will not stone the innocent
or guilty, my Arabs and Jews will do
what my imagination wishes: make peace.
If you bring the flood, I will dam you up
as a river, though I do it on lined paper,
with an awkward hand. I believe something is thundering
in the mold, churning the hives of insects,
that the breath of every living creature mixes
in a kiss of life, that the killer's breath may taste of honey,
that when the forms of music change,
the walls of the city tremble.

Gisèle Celan Lestrange

MON PÈRE, ELEGY FOR PAUL CELAN

1

After his death, her blood was glass
that shattered within her, my mother could not bleed
or heal. Once in the moonlit snows of France
she offered his dark soul her breast.
Now for her night meal, she stares
at a little fish and vegetables
ladled out of being,
as if they were a family crucifix.
Her work: etchings she holds up
(the whorls of her fingertips stained by acid),
small, detailed views of mountains,
coastlines, complex clouds.
Sometimes you simply have to repeat
a little of the design of the creator—
nothing whatsoever made by man.

2

My father could turn the word being
into begging, into bed, into please,
his son twists his legs around his own neck,
man of rope, no farther from my father
than where a tree may root;
I hang by my teeth
from a rope fixed to the roof,
while the 19th-century French band below
plays "Art Is the True Religion."
I bite a stranger's leather tongue.

---

* The poet Paul Celan threw himself into the Seine April 21, 1970
(the first night of Passover). His son is an aerialist and juggler.

3

Juggler as poet, not the fire-eater,
not the fat man, like father, like son:
my chilly eyes and two hands keep three, four, ten,
twenty clubs or white plates going in air,
like after likes, the sins of the fathers,
red silk balls, kept up in the air.
I throw up household effects: his Hebrew Bible,
a yellowing toothbrush, shoes and ties,
his murdered family, his thanks
that it happened to them, not to him.
I fling up against the crowd
my father's head, red silk balls, white plates
of the unthinkable, a way of mourning,
Jerusalem remembered, synagogue as circus.
Prophecy has fallen to sleight of hand,
better to learn magic, better to change
two blue eggs in a lacquer box
into three fluttering white doves.

4

Hanging on by a hair,
on that night different
from all other nights,
he could not pull himself out
by a breath.
He was something like hair
with feeling only at its roots.
Coming from a musical family,
he could not bear to hear music,
he could not stop
his constant, endless bleeding
in private, in public,
on the bread he ate,
on my mother's face.
Drowning

sent his life and blood off
in water like smoke.
His fingers were dactyls again.

A fisherman found him
decomposing black below
Notre Dame Cathedral,
where in the Chapel of Virtues
the Virgin wept for her son
surrounded by images
of women without lives:
Temperance, Fortitude, Justice,
and Prudence with her three eyes
to see past, present and future.

Once his garments were warmed
when Jehovah quieted the earth
with the south wind.

The language of the psalms
has a different word
for why asked in the past
and why asked in the future.
Why lose the rest of spring, mon père?

THE ALTAR

One by one I lit the candles of nothingness,
a candle for each nostril, the eyes and ears,
a candle for the mouth, penis and anus.
Under the clouds of nothingness,
below the flaming particles of the universe,
I stood beside the nothing tree,
I ate my fill.

To God I swore nothing.
In the blood and fires of without
nothing was written. I heard the sermons of nothing
and I knew nothing had come, and would come again,
and nothing was betrayed.

I called prayer
the practice of attention. Nothing was
the balance of things contrary.
Disobedient, I did not make
the sacrifice of the lamb or the child.

My candelabrum was ablaze.

LINES FOR A STAMMERING TURKISH POET

to Edouard Roditi

1

When he was a child, he thought of sea birds as Muslim,
fidgety land birds as Christians and Jews;
in his village, when a man approached, the women
squatted down in the roadside and turned away,
the branches of pomegranate and orange trees
heavy with fruit, lowered to the ground . . . .
In the sky-blue copybook of his school days
he was compelled by revolution to change
from an Arabic alphabet, with its gardens and forests,
to twenty-nine Roman letters bare as sticks.
Now he is older, the birds have no religion.
He walks the industrial gutters that cross the silk routes,
faithful to January, two-faced god of beginnings.
He speaks for, stammers for—mothers, mothers
and mothers, he gets tangled in four thousand years
of apron strings of the Hittite, Greek, Roman,
Christian mother Goddesses and ordinary
women who do most of the work.

He has come to a bridge, the tongue of a balance
that crosses the Bosphorus between Europe
and Asia. He says: "Although it seems for commerce
not wisdom, a br-br-br-br-bridge
across the meandering Bosphorus is a Goddess.
They fa-fa-fa-found her statue near Ephesus."
Her face had a beauty exceptional
even for a God—lady of wild things,
sister of Apollo, from her neck she wore
a wreath of eighteen bull's balls to show
the fear and love the Greeks had for her,
the kind of sacrifice she commanded.

419

2

In the agora of rusty girders and broken concrete
sheep graze among burning automobile tires.
At dawn, when Gods roll over in our human beds
and the sea mends the torn robes of the mother Goddess,
in mosques that were churches in Byzantium,
beneath the giant calligraphy of sacred names,
men without shoes, standing,
cup their hands behind their ears at the beginning
of prayer to better hear a voice before they touch
their foreheads to the ground, prostrate themselves.
Strengthened by years of his hatred, and hatred of hatred,
he says, stammering, "They are all covered with dust,
a kind of bone meal of those they have prayed to kill,
hoping to follow the green bird that leads to paradise."

3

He offers two souls, East and West, over coffee
like honey cakes to Muslims, Christians and Jews.
He writes his love poems in a fifteen-syllable
Greek line. Sweet-faced, bearded, sometimes jailed,
lonely Ottoman of extra syllables,
he sees downhill, above the dark river
long accustomed to slaughter,
the marble fragments of ancient tombstones,
the Jewish cemetery, an avalanche of broken writing.
Of course chaos is not separate from form,
above Istanbul exploding stars
may be an embroidered slipper
on the bare foot of the Asian night.
With only his tongue to know, he stammers,
"A word is a sacrificial goat
and the goat sent into the wilderness.
Sometimes my semen turns to blood."

DAYDREAM

In bear country, in a daydream,
near the lake in Canada, to save my dogs,
I fired a shotgun at a bear's head,
turning its face and eyes into bleeding peach pits.
Mama bear gasped something less than a syllable,
made for the forest like a shot,
stood up for a moment at the brambles
like my small son standing in bed asking "Why? Why?"
What can she teach her two cubs now? They are still hungry.
Not the lesson of acorns, not the song of grubs in damp stumps—
that mice are sweet. Once she nursed her cubs while she slept,
two heartbeats per minute, under branches and fresh snow.
Now they tongue the blood from her face—
then they die in my cruel song.

THE PUBLIC GARDENS OF MUNICH

The park benches, of course, are ex-Nazis.
They supported the ass of the SS
without questioning; the old stamp *Juden Verboten*
has been painted out.
The only signs of World War II, photographs,
displayed at the classical Greek museum,
show its roof bombed, now handsomely repaired,
although the sculpture itself has been overcleaned
by a very rough hand.

But the flowers are the children of other flowers,
the hypocrite roses and the lying begonias,
part of gardens so sentimental, so ordered,
they have nothing to say about freedom and beauty,
nothing to say about the burning bush.
They should see the flowers on the hills of Judea,
pushing between limestone and gypsum, ordinary
beautiful flowers with useful Hebrew and Arabic names,
useful to children, old people, everyone,
their colors and grace, the poetry of them,
page after page.

A man can hide under his shirt
flowers made by metal and fire, stems cut,
neck wounds, missing bone, history
of generations, new branches grafted
onto old stumps.
The saying goes in the streets of Munich:
"Wear a good overcoat." Everyone knows,
you can put a dead body under a handkerchief.
Every handkerchief's a grave,
that's why so many gentlemen wear clean handkerchiefs
in their breast pockets. For the ladies, lace gloves
serve the same purpose—blue handkerchiefs, pink gloves,

green, lavender *und so weiter* are symbolic—
but you have to really know—white for Jew,
blue for Jew, green for Polack, pink for—
you'd better watch out, a little joke.

This year in the Spanish garden during Carnival
someone decapitated a donkey,
Renaissance symbol of the Old Testament,
or perhaps the meaning is, as the TV
commentary said: the donkey
stands for a fifteenth-century Jew,
or was it just *Kinderspiele,*
a game like this hee-haw.

Later in Italy, at the Hotel Stendhal, Parma, I discovered
my friend from Munich can sleep through anything,
a lesson he learned for life during the Allied bombings,
while I sleep four hours on, four hours off,
a lesson I learned in the U.S. Navy.
We still sleep at war. Awake, we embrace.

THE MISCARRIAGE

1

You had almost no time, you were something
not quite penciled in, you were more than darkness
that is shaped by its being and its distance from light.
(To give birth in Spanish is to give to light.)
There was the poetry of it:
a word, a letter changed perhaps
or missing and you were gone.
Every word is changed when spoken.
The beauty is you were mine and hers,
not like a house, a bed, a book, or a dog,
unsellable, unreadable, not love, but of love,
an of—with a certain roundness and a speck
that might have become an eye, might have
seen something, anything: light,
Tuscany, Montana, read Homer in Greek—
unnamed of, saved from light and darkness.

2

I was not told of you until long after,
I would not have handed down that suitcase
to her through the train window in Florence
had I known. I might have suggested tea
instead of Strega, might have fanned the air.
Fathers can do something. I didn't ask the right questions.
I did not offer any sacrifice.
I just walked around in my usual fog looking
at pictures of the Virgin impregnated by words.

What if the Virgin Mother had miscarried? What if
the Magi arrived with all that myrrh and frankincense
like dinner guests on the wrong evening?
Our Lady embarrassed, straightening up,

Joseph offering them chairs he made and a little wine,
sinners stoned in the street
while John who would have been called the Baptist
wept in his mother's belly.

THE INHERITANCE

In Canada, on a dark afternoon,
from a cabin beside Lake Purgatory
I saw your two clenched fists in a tree—
your most recent rage—until I came to my senses,
and saw two small lighted glass lamps reflected
through a window onto the maple leaves.
Was it simply that I had stolen away
in the wilderness to go fishing on your birthday,
twelve years after your death, and you
less than your rusty pliers in my fishing box?

It is late August in the moral North.
To answer your first question,
I obey the fish and game laws
of New York State, Ontario and Quebec.
The odd branch has already turned red.
As for me I have turned inside out,
I cry for revolution against myself—
no longer red, I'm parlor pink and gray,
you, less than a thumbprint on a page.

Matters still outstanding: you will not remember—
a boy, I cut school, sneaked out
to the 42nd Street library to read among readers
like a stray lion cub taken into a great pride.
I have kept your Greek grammar,
your 78 revolutions per minute
recording of Rossini's *Barber*
you played to stop me from crying,
almost my first memory.
Your "valuable papers," now valuable
only to me, I fed to a fire years ago.
Frankly I am tired of receiving letters from the dead
every day, and carrying you on my back,

out of the burning city,
in and out of the bathroom and bedroom,
you less than the smoke you wanted for a shroud.

Let us dance with Sarah behind the curtain
where God in his divine humor
tells Abraham Sarah will at ninety bear a son,
and she asks, laughing within herself, "Will I have pleasure?"
Take one foot, then the other . . . Imitate a departure
if you make it not, and each going
will lend a kind of easiness to the next.
Father, you poisoned my father.
I am standing alone, telling the truth
as you commanded. (Without too many
of the unseemly details, like the sounds of you in bed
sucking, I thought, on fruit I later would not eat.)
You, less than a seed of a wild grape.

Today, in the last moments of light
I heard a fish, a "Musky," your nickname, break water.
As I sing my song of how you
will be remembered, if I could
out of *misericordia*, I'd tie you to the mast
and stuff your ears with wax. I regret
some parts of the body forgive, some don't. Father,
do not forget your 18-inch Board of Education ruler
on which I measured my penis, marking its progress.

You kept it on your desk before you till your old age.
One reason, perhaps, for the archaic Greek smile
I wore on my face through boyhood.
I never thought I'd dig your grave with laughter.

NEW MOON

Full of the city and accounting, I stepped out of my car
into the mist and sand near the Atlantic,
to see a bright haze within a cloud,
a wordless passage from an older testament.
I had forgotten in the unreadable night
that once like a child learning to speak I tried to write,
on a dark night of my life, something lunar,
to be my own Ordinary of secrets and rebirth.

In my prayer book I find, after the blessings
called "The Giving Thanks for Trees Blossoming"
and "The Giving Thanks for Fragrance,"
Prayers for the New Moon in large type,
night prayers for unconscious sins and new beginnings,
to be read outside in moonlight or at an open window.
I speak of prayer, it is not prayer.
I count syllables like minutes before sunset.
I have nothing to show the new moon
but a few lines about the present,
the lesser time under the sun.
Old enough, I have learned to be my own child.
To get even, have I lived my life to make adults cry?
Tonight the child runs to and from me,
already full of memory and cruel history,
talking a blue streak about injustices.
The child falls asleep. I'm up late with the moon.
It is not revelation but the mystery itself I praise.

LETTER TO NOAH

Greetings, I hope you will not be disappointed I survived
the flood riding the back of a giant turtle. Adrift
in the waters of chaos, above the ice-covered mountain ranges
that had become part of the deep,
I saw the sun and moon embrace in terror.
I kept my senses counting the days that had no name,
I heard all manner of newborn things
crying for their mothers—nearly the last living sounds.
We swam through islands of angry faces, an ocean of rodents
devouring each other, great serpents of children knotted
together in whirlpools. I saw the beauty of jungle birds
that in mid-afternoon filled the horizon like a sunset.
Once I saw your vainglorious ark, three stories of lights,
your windows filled with riches,
a woman on the deck, her wet blouse
clinging to her breasts—I was that close.
If you had heard my call, saw me alive,
would you have reached down to save me?
It wouldn't have been the end of the world.
But you of course were following orders, a tune as old
as Adam's song to Eve before the serpent.
Then after all the days of nights
I heard my turtle gasp, "Hallelujah."
I turned and saw the rainbow, the raven and the dove,
in sunlight the waters that reflected nothing, receding,
Noah, I think I am as grateful for the rainbow as you.
I have survived, corrupt and unclean.

THE POOR OF VENICE

The poor of Venice know the gold mosaic
of hunger, the grand architecture of lice,
that poverty is a heavier brocade
than any doge would shoulder. To the winter galas
the poor still wear the red silk gloves of frostbite,
the flowing cape of chilblains.

The winged lion has his piazza, lame dogs
and pigeons with broken wings have theirs.
Let the pigeons perform for dry corn
their commedia dell'arte in the palms of tourists.
The rich and poor don't share a plate of beans.

There used to be songs about squid and sardines
in love the poor could make some money from.
A boy in bed with his family asks for a violin,
his father leaps up,
"Violin, violin, I'll buy you a shovel!"
Moored in the dark canals of Venice,
gondolas for prisoners, for the sick,
gondolas for the dying, the hungry,
tied to poles by inescapable knots
looped by Titian.

Salute an old Venetian after his work.
Eating his polenta without quail, he sits
on a slab in the freezing mist, looking back
at the lagoon and his marble city:
years of illusion, backache, sewerage and clouds.

THE HAWK, THE SERPENTS AND THE CLOUD

In writing, he moved from the word *I*,
the word once a serpent curled between the rocks,
to *he*, the word once a hawk drifting above the reeds,
back to *we*: a nest of serpents.
Of course the hawk attacked the serpents.
She became a cloud, nursed us, mothered us,
scrubbed us with rain. *I*, once a serpent, know the Chinese
character for *he* is a standing figure,
the sign for *she* is a kneeling figure,
the word *cloud* is formed by two horizontal waves
above a plain, and that in writing Chinese
you must show feeling for different parts of the word.
Writing contains painting and painting writing.
Each is bird and sky to the other, soil and flower.

THE LACE MAKERS

Their last pages are transparent: The lace makers
choose to see a world behind the words,
not the words, tatting, not stitching, an open page
of knots, never a closed fabric stitched by needles.
They see from the apples and pears on their plates
out to the orchard, from their tatting
to a bird with a piece of straw in his beak.
From combings transferred onto a running thread,
they make a row of rings resembling a reef,
a chain of knots, hammocks, fishnets,
things found in the hands of sailors.
Without looms, with their fingers,
they make bridal objects, knotted hairnets
seen in certain Roman bronze female portraits,
the twisted threads and knotted fringes of dusty
Egyptian wrappings, something for the cuff,
the lapel, the drawing room, nothing to wear in the cold.
They care about scrolls and variations,
a handkerchief, a design on a pillow,
a completed leaf, four ovals with connecting chains
becoming four peacocks, part of a second leaf,
as if they were promised the world would not
be destroyed, with or without paradise.

Noting the French for tatting is *frivolité*,
they make false chains, things obsolete, improper,
in search of new forms. They carry a thread
to a distant point, eight measured peacocks
of equal size with an additional thread
and the ends cut off. It has the heartless advantage
of being decorative in itself.
They sit and work in the aging light
like Achilles hiding from his pursuers
in a dress, tatting among the women,

discovered by Odysseus who offered a trap of gifts:
the women picked hammered gold leaves and bracelets,
deserted by his Gods, Achilles chose a sword.
In any fabric there are constant beginnings
and endings with cut threads
to be finished off and cut out of sight.
The lace makers read their yellow lace,
washing and ironing it is a fine art
—beautiful a straw basket filled with laundry
and language. But shall we call gossip prophecy?
Who will turn the hearts of the fathers to the children
and the hearts of the children to their fathers?
They are unworthy of undoing the laces of their own shoes.

THE GEOGRAPHER

Before the geography of flowers and fruit,
he learned warmth, breast, wetness.
He came late to mapmaking, the arches and vaults
of the compass, a real and unimagined world
of prevailing winds, coastlines and mountains,
large bodies of water, rifts and faults,
altitudes and depth. Under the stars
he studied what he learned as a child:
that geography determined history,
that weather defined places, principal products.
He would simply walk out of doors to find
the Jews of the wind arguing with the Jews of the dust:
who shall be placed among the writings,
who among the prophets, what is legend
and what is visionary dream.

He studied the deserts, the once dry Mediterranean,
the colossal sculpture of Egypt and Assyria,
art that outweathered its gods.
Under *History* his notes linked the Armada—
the entry: "parched Castile had nothing,
had to conquer the world"—to Napoleon leading his armies
into the Russian winter—like a carload of sheep
each marked for slaughter with a splash of red paint.
They too seemed to have a leader.
He believed the molecular connection of all living stuff
since the beginning of life made him less lonely—
no message, but a *cri de coeur.*

He had a small globe of the earth he kept
inside another blue and silver globe of stars.
He learned and relearned touch, flesh and place,
the simple "where is," the colors of nearness,
the light and dark of naked bodies in repose.

He learned countries and cities as if
they were verbs, meaning beyond subject:
the word poetry came from the Greek "to make,"
the Chinese character for poetry is "to keep."
A fine day does not forget lightning and thunder. Facts:
it was not the fifty-degrees-below-zero cold in winter,
or the ten-degrees-below-zero cold in summer,
that caused one percent of the population to die each day
in the coal and blood-black snows of the Soviet arctic.
Memory makes any place part illusion.
Weather remembers, has a long memory of itself,
oceans and landscape, nothing human.

He came to a certain calm in his studies:
the healing and destroying power of water,
the chaos of forest fires, followed by new unheard-of growth.
He noted bougainvillea and oleander
crossing continents like vacationing lovers—
he sketched the universe as an animal belly
full of exploding gases.
He had to make it all human as a bad joke.

He had cause to be frightened,
to turn his head to the beauty of it.
Under the fruit trees of this world, he wrote:
there's a murder for every apple, every peach, every pear,
beneath the oak a starving child for every acorn,
among the evergreens a lie for every pine needle.
These are the forbidden fruit.

THE DEBT

1

I owe a debt to the night,
I must pay it back, darkness for darkness
plus interest.
I must make something out of almost nothing,
I can't pay back by just not sleeping
night after night. I hear them screaming
in the streets of New York, "What? What? What?"

I can't write a check to the night,
or a promissory note: "I'll write songs."
Only the nightmare is legal tender.
I bribe owls, I appeal
to creatures of the night: "Help me
raccoons, catfish, snakes!"
I put my head in the tunnel of a raccoon,
pick up a fish spine in my mouth.
Perhaps the night will accept this?
Dying is my only asset.

These days driving along I turn up my brights.
I love and am grateful for anything that lights
the darkness: matches, fireworks, fireflies.
My friend who's been to Antarctica
tells me when the sun is high against the ice
you see the shadow of the earth.
The night after all is just a shadow . . .
The debt keeps mounting.
I try to repay something by remembering
my Dante, the old five and ten thousand lira notes
had Dante's face etched on the front.
(I bought that cheap.) Hard cash to the night
is finding out what I do not want to know
about myself, no facts acceptable,

a passage through darkness,
where the one I stop to ask, "Why? What?"
is always myself I cannot recognize.

2

If only I could coin nightmares:
a barnyard in Asia,
the last dog and cat betrayed, are no more.
A small herd of three-legged blind cows
still gives milk.
A pig with a missing snout, its face like a moon,
wades in a brook.
A horse, its mane burnt to cinders,
a rear hip socket shot off, tries to get up,
thrusting its muzzle into the dark grass.
A rooster pecks without a beak or a coxcomb.
A rabbit that eats stones, sips without a tongue,
runs without feet.
A ditch of goats, sheep and oxen
locked in some kind of embrace.
All move their faces away,
refuse the charity of man
the warrior, the domesticator.
I see a whale with eyes yards apart
swimming out of the horizon,
surfacing as if it were going to die,
with a last disassociated vision,
one eye at peace
peers down into the valleys and mountains
of the ocean, the other eye floats,
tries to talk with its lids to the multitude.
While in the great head
what is happening and what happened mingle,
for neither has to be.
I pray for some of my eyes to open and some to close.
It is the night itself that provides
a forgiveness.

FOR MARGARET

My mother near her death
is white as a downy feather.
I used to think her death was as distant
as a tropical bird, a giant macaw, whatever that is—
a thing I have as little to do with
as the distant poor.
I find a single feather of her suffering,
I blow it gently as she blew
into my neck and ear.

A single downy feather is on the scales,
opposed by things of weight, not spirit.
I remember the smell of burning feathers.
I wish we could sit upon the grass
and talk about grandchildren
and great-grandchildren.
A worm directs us into the ground.
We look alike.

I sing a lullaby to her about her children
who are safe and their children.
I place a Venetian lace tablecloth
of the whitest linen on the grass.
The wind comes with its song
about things given that are taken away
and given again in another form.

Why are the poor cawing, hooting,
screaming in the woods?
I wish death were a whip-poor-will
the first bird I could name.
Why is everything so heavy?
I did not think

she was still helping me to carry
the weight of my life.
Now the world's poor are before me.
How can I lift them one by one in my arms?

RUSE

A gift of a Greek horse to my enemy,
my body is a ruse so I can sack a city,
my navel, guts, penis and anus—a snake
a goddess dropped upon me. I carry within
a man whose wife was raped, a murdered friend.
Through the eyes of the horse I see death and the sun
I cannot look at steadily.
Behind me—the oceanic snail and floating mollusks
that pass their lives on the open seas.
Eros, perhaps tomorrow I shall envy them.

THE DECADENT POETS OF KYOTO

Their poetry is remembered for a detailed calligraphy
hard to decipher, less factual than fireflies in the night:
the picture-letters, the characters, the stuff
their words were made from were part of the meaning.
A word like "summer" included a branch of plum blossoms,
writing about "summer in a city street"
carried the weight of the blossoming branch,
while "a walk on a summer afternoon"
carried the same beautiful purple shade.

They dealt with such matters distractedly,
as though "as though" were enough, as though
the little Japanese woman with the broom
returning to her husband's grave to keep it tidy
was less loving than the handsome woman in the café
off the lobby of the Imperial Hotel
who kissed the inside of her lover's wrist.
In their flower arrangements, especially distinct
were the lord flower and emissary roses—

public representations now shadows.
Their generals and admirals took musicians
with them to war, certain their codes
would not be deciphered, in an age when hats
and rings were signs of authority and style.
They thought their secrets were impenetrable,
they thought they had the power to speak and write
and not be understood, they could hide the facts
behind a gold-leaf screen of weather reports.

It was Buddha who had an ear for facts:
coins dropping into the ancient cedar box,
hands clapping, the sound of temple bells and drums.
Codes were broken, ships sank, men screamed
under the giant waves, and a small hat
remained afloat longer than a battleship.

FOLLOWING THE SAINTS

From the rock of my heart a horse rose,
that I should ride to follow them,
the night they left by taxi
from the Damascus gate, and fled toward Bombay.
My heart threw me off.
If only I had robes white enough,
But my robes were full of ashes and dust.
The rouge, lipstick, and eyeshadows
you left on my flesh, I washed off before prayer.
My heart was gone, it looked back at me
from a distance, its reins bitten through.

Skull of Adam
(1979)

&

The Wrong Angel
(1966)

ON SEEING AN X-RAY OF MY HEAD

This face without race or religion
I have in common with humanity—
mouth without lips, jaws without tongue,
this face does not sleep when I sleep,
gives no hint of love or pleasure,
my most recent portrait smells of fixative
and rancid vinegar, does not appear
male or female.
I don't look as if I work for a living.

I will ask for fire. I can not risk
lovers, walking in a wood, turn up this face,
see such putrefaction they question
why they've come to lie on the grass,
picnic, fish or read to one another.
I will not have them find me staring
after their lovemaking—
under the leaves and branches of summer,
a reminder of mortality.

I prefer the good life, in real death
a useful skull to house small fish
or strawberries, a little company.
I must remember death is not always
a humiliation, life everlasting
is to be loved at the moment of death.
I hold my lantern head before me,
peer into one eye, see darkness, darkness
in the other, great funerals of darkness
that never meet.

GOD POEM

Especially he loves
his space and the parochial darkness.
They are his family, from them grow his kind:
idols with many arms and suns that fathered
the earth, among his many mirrors, and some
that do not break:
rain kept sacred by faithful summer grasses,
fat Buddha and lean Christ, bull and ram,
horns thrusting up his temple and cathedral—
mirrors, but he is beyond such vanities.
Easy to outlive
the moment's death having him on your knees—
grunting and warm he prefers wild positions:
he mouths the moon and sun, brings his body
into insects that receive him beneath stone,
into fish that leap as he chases,
or silent stones that receive his silence.
Chivalrous and polite, the dead take
his caress, and the sea rolling under him
takes his fish as payment and his heaps of shells.

2

As he will,
he throws the wind arch-backed on the highway,
lures the cat into moonlit alleys,
mountains and fields with wild strawberries.
He is animal,
his tail drags uncomfortably, he trifles
with the suck of bees and lovers, so simple
with commonplace tongues—his eyes ripple
melancholy iron and carefree tin,
his thighs are raw from rubbing,
cruel as pine, he can wing an eagle off a hare's spine,

crouch with the Sphinx, push bishops down
in chilly chapels, a wafer in their mouths,
old men cry out his passage through their bowels.

3

No, no.
No word, none of these, no name, "Red Worm! Snake!"
What name makes him leave his hiding place?
Out of the null and void,
no name and no meaning: God, Yahweh, the Lord,
not to be spoken to, he never said a word
or took the power of death: the inconspicuous
plunge from air into sea he gave to us,
winds that wear away our towns . . . Who breathes
comes to nothing: absence, a world.

ELEGY FOR MYSELF

The ashes and dust are laughing, swaddled,
perfumed and powdered, laughing at the flowers,
the mirrors they brought to check his breath,
and he no longer singular.
Who will carry his dust home in merriment?
These things need a pillow, a wife,
a dog, a friend. Plural now he is all the mourners
of his father's house, and all the nights and mornings too.
Place him with "they love" and "they wrote,"
not "he loves" and "he writes." It took so much pain
for those S's to fly off. It took so much trouble
to need a new part of speech. Now he is
something like a good small company of actors;
the text, not scripture, begins, "Who's there?"

SAILING FROM THE UNITED STATES

In this country I planted not one seed,
Moved from address to address, did not plead
For justice in its courts, fell in love and out,
Thrust my arm into the sea and could not pull it out;
I did not see the summer lose its balance,
Or organize the lonely in a gang, by chance
I did not build a city or a ship, or burn
The leaves that fell last autumn, in my turn
Built by the numb city-building noise,
I learned the morning and the night are decoys
To catch a life and heap the profits of the grave.

I have lost a country, its hills and heroes;
In a country that taught me talk, confined
To the city of myself, I oppose
The marketplace and thoroughfares, my mind
Shaping this history, my mouth to a zero.
The wind in my house is not a wind through olive trees,
I hear no music in the janitor's keys,
I fashion no reed, no pipe, have not the wind for it,
My summer and winter prove counterfeit.
Through the villages of New England and the free country,
I will my unconditional mutiny,
I leave this crockery heaped on a shelf
For an old regime, to work myself
As a mine, subject to explosions and cave-in.

AND NOW THERE IS NO PLACE TO LOOK

And now there is no place to look,
there are no risks. Now we are familiar
with ourselves as unfamiliar things.

My mind spills, my hand wipes it away.
Beyond my reach the sea's gigantic snake
feeds upon itself, repeats the mind's play.

The fields grow dark with darkness that seems to be.
Our plans like burning matches in the wind.
Neither darkness nor light pass through me.

Through Italian cliffs, I have seen great caves,
where water enters for a thousand years,
makes one curve on rough stone—a pretty grave.

The wind has caught my shirt but who will steer?
Another night's debris floats the waves;
I hear the echo and what the echo hears.

THE GIFT

She gave me the gift of my own desire;
hollowed by fire as a tree
I have betrayed love for desire.

Gladly I would betray desire
but I cannot, until once more
love burns me through.

NICKY

She danced into the moonless winter,
a black dog.
In the morning when I found her
I couldn't get her tongue back in her mouth.
She lies between a Japanese maple
and the cellar door, at no one's feet,
without a master.

THE PEDDLER

Can I disentangle
a loose thread pulled out of death?
I tried like the soldiers to disrobe Christ,
to make God sing "Glory Hallelujah."
God did not jig for me. I hawk
a prayer shawl, it is hardly warm.
I save a black hat worn in the temple
to proclaim no matter how full the table
man is not sure of his roof.
I know that at sunrise I can tell
a white thread from a black, at sunset
darkness makes all threads one.
Time feels heavy like gold brocade. I choose
light yarns for my coat of mortality,
I stuff salvation in my pockets like money,
it's too heavy.
I go through death's laundry, anything
that covers a wound—rags, silk handkerchiefs,
blankets, bandages, sailcloth, flags.
I die naked but for words. I sell old clothes.

TRAVELS, BARCELONA

1

Once I took a yellow cab up Jew mountain
to a Golgotha of telephone poles,
I saw a horizon of lovers
suffering a hundred different deaths.
I saw time as a mother in the lap of her mother,
kiss, give suck as women do in the beginning.
Their hands made the wetness they touched.
I had them both and a Magdalene.
Three Marys, oh what confusion!
I went into time and women like entering a cathedral
—they kept telling me what to do.
Above me, higher than the darkness,
stained glass windows told another story:
the speaking of the flesh, the *parlando*, the *hablar*.

I waded across a river, a book in my belt,
a child on my shoulder.
What have women taught me, my beautiful teachers,
after all that lovemaking, that bathing?
how to read, dress and keep clean. Sweet one,
it is time to take on the inconveniences,
time to make and repair,
ways of kindness and deception,
ways to go to funerals and weddings
—*toujours la tendresse.*

2

It's a spring day near the Atlantic—
the sky as blue as her eyes,
time undresses before me,
moves like a girl
lifting her dress over her head.

Now the quarrel really begins:
I tell her I have no complaints so far,
I'm not really speaking for myself
—that I don't want her to go.
I've seen the suffering she caused her lovers,
their utter humiliation.
Yes, old men and young boys,
old women and young girls.

Naked, she takes a mouthful of wine
—smiling her wicked rose-petal smile,
her eyes an endless intelligent blue,
she leans over me and from above
pushes the wine into my mouth
—then puts her hand to my lips
as if to tell me
I was saying the wrong thing.

CLOUD SONG

Working class clouds are living together
above the potato fields, tall white beauties
humping above the trees, burying their faces
in each other, clouds with darker thighs,
rolling across the Atlantic. West,
a foolish cumulus hides near the ocean
afraid of hurricanos.
Zeus came to the bed
of naked Io as a cloud,
passed over her and into her as a cloud,
all cloud but part of his face
and a heavy paw, half cloud, half cat
that held her down.
I take clouds to bed that hold me
like snow and rain, gentle ladies,
wet and ready, smelling of lilac hedges.
I swear to follow them like geese,
through factory smoke,
beyond the shipping lanes and jet routes.
They pretend nothing—opening, drifting, naked.
I pretend to be a mountain
because I think clouds like that.
A cloudy night
proclaims a condition of joy.
Perhaps I remember a certain cloud,
perhaps I bear a certain allegiance
to a certain cloud.

APOCRYPHA

You lie in my arms,
sunlight fills the abandoned quarries.

I planted five Lombard poplars,
two apple trees died of my error,
three others should be doing better.
I prepared the soil,
I painted over the diseased apple tree,
I buried the available dead around it:
thirty trout that died in the pond
when I tried to kill the algae, a run-over raccoon,
a hive of maggots in every hole.
This year the tree flowered, bears fruit.
Are my cures temporary?

I chose abortion in place of a son,
because of considerations.

I look for the abandoned dead,
the victims, I shall wash them,
trim their fingernails and toenails.
I learn to say Kaddish,
to speak its Hebrew correctly,
a language I do not know,
should I be called upon.
I abandon flesh of my flesh
for a life of my choosing.

I take my life from Apocrypha.
Warning of the destruction of the city,
I send away the angel Raphael
and my son. Not knowing if I am right
or wrong, I fall asleep in the garden,

I am blinded by the droppings
of a hummingbird or crow.
Will my son wash my eyes with fish gall
restoring my sight?

You lie in my arms,
I wrestle with the angel.

NIGHT IN THE COUNTRY

In the homelessness of the country
The towns surround the plains with light,
Desolate windows now hunt me.
Love passes through me as light through a window,
Where the old poems as the winter moth
Lift their pale wings to hide, to feed on cold.

Midnight is carved as ivory in this room;
My mind moves through the empty field,
My eye skips like a rabbit, my listening
Glides past the moon like a snake.
Dare I lead your love here to sleep,
To oversleep, the awakening of the world?

NEW YORK SONG

On the way to visit a friend, a physician,
who would soon suddenly die,
I saw pigeons on a heap of rubble
standing more like gulls,
others in wild flight
searching the wreckage
of two Times Square theaters
razed to build a hotel.
They were looking for their roof,
their nest, their young,
in the hollows of broken concrete,
in the pink and white dust,
they fluttered around the wrecking ball
that still worked the façade,
the cornice of cement Venetian masks.

No such birds are without sorrow.
The creatures coo, but cannot sing, are brazen, half-wild.
I'll be no messenger for pigeons.
I saw their sooty feathers, splashes of lavender
on some throats, yellow, red, and blue dots,
the same intention that speckled the trout and butterfly,
a meaning that is joyous. Be brazen and wild,
capable of being each other's messenger.
Were not the twins Helen and Clytemnestra,
born of a single egg, mortal mother and a swan?
A throatless cry of metal tearing away from metal
above a red "exit" sign, the roof settled for a moment,
a giant bird of tarpaper, a cloud of itself,
took its last breaths on the broken stage.
There are no tragic pigeons.
I mourn my sweet friend fallen among the young,
unable to sustain flight, part of the terrible flock,
the endless migration of the unjustly dead.

SHIT

I've been taught my daily lesson,
that man shall squat alone in secret,
I've been taken off my high horse,
I've bent down,
interrupted my day to humble myself,
no need to fall on my knees.
With a genuflection of the gut,
I hunt where my bones stink.

Out of the pain of this world
a kindness, a shape each of us
learns by heart: moon crescent,
jewelweed, forget-me-not,
hot lava. Christ, is this
the ghost in everything,
what I can and cannot,
I will and will not,
I have and have not,
what I must and must not,
what I did and did not?
An infant gasps in ecstasy,
tears of shit drip from a man
who cannot cry.

Most men near death cannot withhold,
they shit on themselves
when what they are
is all out of them:
wind, kindness, cruelty
all done, left behind,
when they must be changed
and cannot remember
who chose to soil us,
who makes us clean.

VOMIT

The stomach and the heart can be torn
out through the mouth if you get the right hook.
Because puking I was held up to this world,
because I have lived, burped in my mother's arms,
it comes out now:
what I thought I had swallowed, matters settled,
understood, kept out of mind—our father,
who keeps us in the speeding car,
who will not stop, let me puke in the grass
where it will hardly be noticed,
among the weeds and roadside flowers.

I throw up on myself the half-digested
meat and salad of what I devoured
in pleasure, the perfectly seasoned
explanation of love and social forces
that made me feel slightly superior.

I put my finger down my throat
so I can become part of this world,
I refuse to hear voices that speak to me
in rage without sense,
because my body and soul are locked
in secret battle, because the soul is voiceless
while the body can speak, gasp, sing, whisper,
utter what it pleases, because the body
becomes what it consumes and the soul
refuses such fires;
because the devil says
vomit is the speech of the soul.

I give the devil his due,
because the soul's speech is so rare,
to hear it

I must listen out of earshot,
I must give myself like a lover
and take like a lover, resisting and giving
till the heart is hooked and pulled out.

SNOT

I cannot forget the little swamp
that grows in my head,
cousin of the tear,
snot, my lowly, not worthy of sorrow,
the body's only
completely unsexual secretion.
No one my dears is hot for snot
or its institutions: catarrh,
asthma, the common cold, although
I've heard "snot-nose" used to mean "darling"
or "my son." There's beauty in it,
familiar as the face of any friend.
Dogs eat it, no one gets rich on it.

AN EXCHANGE OF HATS

I will my collection of hats,
straw the Yucatan, fez Algiers 1935,
Russian beaver, Irish fisherman's knit,
collapsible silk opera, a Borsalino,
to a dead man,
the Portuguese poet, my dear Fernando,
who, without common loyalty,
wrote under seven different names
in seven different styles.
He was a man of many cafés,
a smoker and nonsmoker.
His poets came to live in Lisbon,
had different sexual preferences,
histories and regional accents.

Still their poems had a common smell
and loneliness that was Fernando's.
His own character
was to him like ink to a squid,
something to hide behind.
What did it matter, writing in Portuguese
after the First World War? The center was Paris,
the languages French and English.

In Lisbon, workers on the street corner were arguing
over what was elegance, the anarchist manifesto,
the trial of Captain Artur Carlos de Barros
found guilty of "advocating circumcision"
and teaching Marranos no longer to enter church
saying, "When I enter I adore neither wood nor stone
but only the Ancient of Days who rules all."
The Portuguese say
they have the "illusion" to do something,

meaning they very much want to do it.
He could not just sit in the same café
wearing his own last hat, drinking port
and smoking *Ideals* forever.

FROG

I hold this living coldness,
this gland with eyes, mouth, feet,
shattered mirror of all creatures,
pulsing smile of fish, serpent and man,
feet and hands come out of a head
that is also a tail,
just as I caught him most of my life ago
in the sawdust of the icehouse.
I could not believe in him if he were not here.
He rests my spirit
and is beautiful as waterlilies.
The sound of his call is too large for his body:
"irrelevant, irrelevant, irrelevant."
Once in the dry countries he was a god.

PROPHECY II

You know nothing, not your mother or father.
The world is two snakes copulating,
watch long enough you will become male and female,
no longer know your mother or father.
First in your mother's belly you had a snake's heart,
then chamber by chamber you grew a human heart.
Concealed at night, you do not see the body
but the heat around the body—the subjunctive heat
after wish and desire. In the garden at night
you cannot tell snake from human.
The theater is dark, the play is a comedy:
someone before death is begging for ten last syllables.

ALONG THE TIBER: A COMMENTARY ON *ANTONY AND CLEOPATRA*

RETURN TO ROME

Today in Rome, heading down
Michelangelo's Spanish Steps,
under an unchanging moon,
I held on to the balustrade,
grateful for his giving me a hand.
All for love, I stumbled over the past
as if it were my own feet. In my twenties,
I was lost in love and poetry. Along the Tiber,
I played my Cubist Shakespearean games.
(Even in those days, in writing,
I cannot say it was popular to have "subjects"
any more than painters used sitters. But I did.)
I played with an ignorant mirror for an audience:
my self, embroiled with personae
from *Antony and Cleopatra*. Delusions of grandeur!
They were for a time my foul-weather friends—
as once I played with soldiers
on the mountainous countryside of a purple blanket.

2002

ANTONY WITH CLEOPATRA

Certainly our fields were planted
With lilac and poppies
When there was need of cotton and wheat.
So toward the end of summer
We began our walks on the outskirts of the city
To watch for the coming of strangers.

We were not young—but excellent.
What a long way from Italy,
The Nile never seemed so deep;
It was the very brim of summer,
Still the best time of the year for love,
Roman soldiers dived arch-backed into the sea.

Across the Mediterranean came Caesar and ships,
His spikes and axes multiplying the sun,
His sails full silver;
Our sheets still warm and wrinkled,
Cleopatra pretending to sleep,
Antony still naked beneath his armor.

1956

ENOBARBUS PLANS FOR CLEOPATRA

I'll fatten her on steamy mutton cooked in peasant wine
Of the Chianti hills, no alabaster Eros
Born with unnatural perfections will be our God,
But clay household Gods that break in a season,
Found easily as trees in an orchard, that bend
With the wind and bear a fruit luscious and similar.
I'll make her a common soldier's wife with work
In front of the house; I'll couch her on a hard bed,
Let her make mystery with straw under her back.
Naked Cleopatra cries. Let there be no more vanities.
I offer water in a pail for a mirror, my promise
To guard in the night against thieves and barbarians.
I am a soldier, will not give up my sword to mystery.
But penny honest, when Antony touches her shoulder
I feel useless flesh about my face, a failure
My body separates from itself, like a beaten army
Whose privates hardly follow my hoarse commands;
My hands are smeared with cold and freckles.
I who took girls to Rome, virgins to the sea,
Know this was not soldiery, but a boy's pluck,
I cannot go to battle hoping Cleopatra watches,
If she looks past me I have no retreats or parries.
Great Eros, I wait beside her
To hand her a glass if she will drink.

CHARMIAN TO ENOBARBARUS

I have watched my queen's tricks and when the feasts are over
I eat from plate to plate and have my fill
Of chicken and melon kings and princes did not touch,
Sword buckling and unbuckling in her chamber.
Once Caesar in his prime arrived unexpected,
Cleopatra off on a journey, his hottest lust
Fresh from fighting his death he gave to me.
Love's music is the trumpet not the harp.
Notice she moves her hand like the Nile: a trick.
You think that majesty is closeness to the Gods?
Cleopatra learns from tides and they from her.
Heavy Enobarbus, I like your weight,
I'll hold your head in my lap as she holds Antony's,
No closer can you come to her. Sail here,
I'll wash the honey from our sheets in the Nile.

FULVIA TO CLEOPATRA:
A FIRST WIFE'S COMPLAINT

I fixed my house grandest on the Aventine,
Detailed with flowers, choice rugs and gold lamps;
Love's filament that held for twenty years
Snapped in Egypt's darkness.
Queen of whores,
A rhinoceros horn thrust between your thighs
Would wear to dust in a single evening
Before the rising cocks crow your credits,
And morning drives you to pasture.

Great Rome in need of heroes
Eyed its triumphant soldiers,
Its wharfs for sailors,
Found Mark Antony swaggering along the Tiber.
He came to me
Through the triumphant arched legs of pansies.
They wooed him to the Forum, kissed him
Into war, took advantage of the lonely field.
He gained rank, by turning flank.
Those were his whistling days,
Under the arches, flowers and washlines.
I arranged our meetings near the Temple of Mars,
Boasted my father's lands and ships sacked
At Carthage, begot his proposal
Which I read in my garden on a marble chair
Carved with a single lion, in lovely, lonely May.
We married in the temple: my wedding guests roared
To the baths of Caesar following my groom.
He came to me almost useless, a colt
With a soft bottom, wanting to be mounted.
I just took him to the fields,
Let him idle swordless in the sun,

Watching the hawks attack.
That night Antony conquered all my towns.
My walls are leveled, my roofs are charred.
O Cleopatra, think what he shall do to your kingdom.

ANOTHER REPLY FOR POMPEY

MENAS: *These three world-sharers, these competitors,*
                           Are in thy vessell. Let me cut the cable.
                           And when we are put off, fall to their throats.
                           All there is thine.

POMPEY: *Ah, this thou should'st have done*
                           And not spoken on't! In me, 'tis villainy;
                           In thee had been good service.

Cut the cable! But not their throats. Caesar
Antony and Lepidus are in my sack.
Below common skies, ordinary winds
Sail my miraculous cargo past the Gods.

The world, my world, wherever an eye can see,
Notices no change. Rome, Neptune, Venus,
Keep divinity, I mortality,
The rudder doesn't budge, my oars chained to kings
Rise and fall as Gods, break their locks.
My galley-slave brain holds fast, O Gods let me
Pace beyond my nature, for I am not natural,
On my oar's chain and on my deck I carve
I am not Caesar's.

Caesar snores, Antony sleeps, Lepidus dreams.
The tides and populations follow these moons.
Had I been born to this as Caesar, my dreams
Would be natural; these calm sleepers slept,
Could wake the people, as wolf bitches wake
Their blind young. Cut their imperial throats!
Let the wind pipe through Caesar back to Rome.
Cut their throats! Invited guests,
Given such brief hospitality,
Such poor fare on my ship, as on the earth;
Romans, even the Gods murder all their guests

BACKSTAGE

I am like a book fallen from your lap.
I can tell a tale of base and divine crevices,
of wordless places, unreachable ledges,
high waterfalls, clouds,
dropping down to swamplands.
I lingered on the footpaths in gardens
of lemon trees and oleander,
but my flesh was torn and I tore flesh.
Solo I dangled, whimpered, wept, begged.
I have fathered and mothered.
I offered fruit I would never eat.
I slipped into the furthest valley,
places without ornament.
I am Goliath,
a child has flung a stone into my head.
Actor in a dark theater,
I am *enconado*. In repertory,
I forget who I am playing tonight.

CLOWN

1

He lived in flight from an apartment,
desolate as Beethoven's jaw. On the go
he could put his own life aside as an actor,
he drank till his feet turned purple
or into goat hooves. He could play the serpent,
Eve, Adam, the apple before or after it was bit.
He wandered beside himself, a figure far from himself
as orange rind: he could turn from David into Saul weeping—
to Absalom, his hair caught in a tree. He could play his own fool,
his own column of cloud, the presence of God.
He could throw himself out into the garbage,
or, like a child's top on a string,
turn red and blue then whirl into a single color.
He played a Buddhist priest reading from his Book
into the ear of a corpse who hears
the reader's voice telling him all these visions
are his own unrealized, undiscovered forms,
the horrible furies and the calm
he must come to understand are his.

2

"Far below the salt cliffs," he wrote in his Book of Hymns,
"the river's tongue has emptied into the sea."
Only the man-bird flies from the Dead Sea to the Himalayas,
from the ancient dead shrouded in poetry
to the never-ending ice so thick, the dead
are ritually butchered and fed to vultures that,
surrounded by haloes of the sun, rise like doves
out of the jeweled snow. In the glacial silence
a man's leg-bone makes a sweeter whistle than your ram's horn.

To bathe at birth, marriage and death, "a rule in Tibet,"
was not enough for him. "No one has ever slid down
the Himalayas so fast," he said in a coarse aside.
Unteachable, he learned, he fell
more like Richard II than Adam.
In a farce he came closest to the stinking breath
of his own mortality, trying to lift a snapping turtle off a busy road,
it bit into his shoe, he fell back out of the blue—
broke his ankle and elbow.

What did he know that no one knew?
The care he wanted to give, that no one else would give.
He had lived to sing to his dying mother
from her bedside. Now memory is his mother,
she keeps his life from burning off like a morning mist.
One black tear painted at the corner of his right eye,
a red tear at the left,
he wept over a glass of spilled milk. He pretended
to play Mozart on a violin without lessons.
He bought himself a fiddle and a bow
strung with circus-horse hair, an earthly bow, not a rainbow.
Who was he to know so many tunes?
He just played his everyday music—
he would never wrap the letters of the holy name
around his fingers. He wrote a song that began:
"I fall back from making love
to the kind of day it is. . . ."

LOST POEM

Time has appetite
for milk and meat. Man is good eating,
smeared with sex that he himself has fed upon
like the sow the slop of the trough
and the hummingbird its flower.
The light stunned and entertained.
Love a human being?
Why not lie down with a river or a tree?
I will no longer say that man is meat,
or night and day are bread for a God.
There is wheat in the fields, a little for the starving.
Because beauty belongs to no one,
you lie in my arms and I am a thief.

WALKING

1

His stride is part delusion.
They laugh at him, "A little water in the boot,
he thinks he walks on water."
At home to get a cup of coffee
he walks across Norway, and his talk—
sometimes he speaks intimately to crowds,
and to one person as to a crowd. On principle
he never eats small potatoes.
Illusion, mirage, hallucination,
he loves a night painting of a fable: a man
is grinning at a boy lighting a candle from an ember,
a monkey on his shoulder chained to heaven—
a reminder that art apes nature.
When they told him "reality is simply what is,"
it was as though he had climbed Sinai,
then walked down to get the laws.
He dreams only of the migrations of peoples
beneath the migrations of birds,
he wakes to new nations, he yawns
riddles of the north and south wind,
whistles his own tune in the Holy Sepulchre.
Some afternoons he stretches out in a field
like an aqueduct. "All we do," he says,
"is carry a bucket or two of God's waters
from place to place."

2

Under a roof, and in the open air,
hangs an amusing tragedy, a kind of satyr play,
where not every fat man dancing by
is wrapped in grape leaves. Facing himself
in a bronze mirror like the one
the ancient Chinese thought cured insanity,
tongue-tied he speaks to his own secret face,

or standing in the sunlight
against the lives of mountains, sky and sea,
he speaks, made-up and masked, the lyrical truth,
the barefaced lie.
Not speaking the language of his fathers,
a hero may die because all flesh is grass
and he forgets the password.

From a lectern, or the top of a hay wagon,
or leaping down,
a few steps away from everyday life,
into something like a kitchen garden,
he unearths in the wordless soil
things sung or said, kinds of meaning:
what is denoted or symbolic,
or understood only by its music,
or caught on to without reason,
the endless twisting of its roots, its clarity.
He points to the old meaning of looking
to the Last Judgment,
while he believes nothing is merely or only.

3

At a garden party he almost said,
"Madame, it is not in the bones of a lover or a dog
to wait long as the bleached mollusk
on the mountain. Time is an ice cube melting
in a bowl, the world is refracted, ridiculous.
In life, you often reach out for a stone
that isn't where you see it in the stream."
But it was summer,
no one would believe time was so cold
on a hot day, so comforting,
when the purple iris was already dry
and the tulips fallen.

MECOX BAY

On a bright winter morning
flights of honking geese
seem a single being
like the sky itself.
When my kind comes into such formation
I watch for firing squads.
I never saw a line of praying figures take flight.
On an Egyptian relief I've seen heads of prisoners
facing the same direction,
tied together by a single rope twisted around each neck
as if they were one prisoner.
Again the honking passes over my roof.
A ridiculous, joyous bird
rises out of my breast, joins the flock,
but I am left on earth with my kind.

I DRIVE A HEARSE

I drive a hearse, a black limousine.
I send a black Valentine.

I drive a hearse for Woodlawn.
Caught in traffic, Death blows my horn.

I drive a hearse for Riverside,
come along just for the ride.

There's a little plot outside the city
that's terribly pretty,

a gorgeous grave for the man of words
who would like sheep to graze over him afterwards.

The green fields yellow, they turn to ash.
I turn black death into a little green cash.

THE HANGMAN'S LOVE SONG

In the house of the hangman
do not talk of rope,
or use death, half death,
little death; the victim
always hangs himself,
trap sprung, tongue ripped
like love in the house.
Despite the world's regalia,
I want a useful funeral.
High, on tiptoe,
swinging back
and forth, the victim,
who cannot speak,
mimics the bell,
such things as bait
for wild game, and love.
Brain hung and heart,
hope swings, sun creaks,
rope in the wind,
and the hangman sings.

DULCIE

I fly the flag of the black dog:
a black dog dripping blood over us all.
My flag barks, licks my face.
My flag says, "I am alive, willing,
part of the natural order of things.
You are a supernatural creature."

I walk across the road to the stream.
In a rush of water—something surfaces
—I hold my dog back.
A snake has caught a trout by the vent,
lifts the fish out of the water. The snake's head
cuts a line through the shaded water
into the sunlight,
crosses the stream to a ledge of gravel and jewelweed.
The trout is held up to late summer,
its brightest colors already begun to fade.
The snake uncoils, begins to devour the fish
head first.

The trees remembering my mother
kiss me, because she told me:
cherish the dog that licks the face and feet
of the bum passed out in the park.
She caught a seed flying over a city street,
put it in her glove, took it home and planted it.
I sprawl with my dog on the floor
of all-night restaurants
because the entire shape of time
is a greater, more ferocious beast
than anything in it.

THE RETURN

It was justice to see her nude haunches
backing toward me again after the years,
familiar as water after long thirst.
Now she is like a stream, and I can lie beside
running my hand over the waters, or sleep;
but the water is colder, the gullies darker,
the rapids that threw me down have shallowed;
I can walk across.

A VALENTINE'S DAY SKETCH OF NEGRO SLAVES, JEWS IN CONCENTRATION CAMPS, AND UNHAPPY LOVERS

The survivors have something in common—
captured by superior forces of violence,
probably in the middle of the night,
dumped into slave ship, boxcar, or bed,
the smell of urine and feces in their nostrils,
the useless are directed by a finger
to the right, the useful to the left,
—examined naked. They cannot worship
their own Gods or the Gods of their masters,
"the old-timers" become like children, they steal,
inform, giggle; learn to seem not there,
not to do anything extraordinary
like whistling or talking. They grow proud
of how smartly they stand at attention;
finally they come to believe the rules
set down from above are desirable,
at least in camp or bed. You who are free,
relax, your stomachs will soon settle.
Isn't it May? Aren't you happy as larks?

TWO FISHERMEN

My father made a synagogue of a boat.
I fish in ghettos, cast toward the lily pads,
strike rock and roil the unworried waters;
I in my father's image: rusty and off hinge,
the fishing box between us like a covenant.
I reel in, the old lure bangs against the boat.
As the sun shines I take his word for everything.
My father snarls his line, spends half an hour
unsnarling mine. Eel, sunfish and bullhead
are not for me. At seven I cut my name for bait.
The worm gnawed toward the mouth of my name.
"Why are the words for temple and school
the same?" I asked, "And why a school of fish?"
My father does not answer. On a bad cast
my fish strikes, breaks water, takes the line.

Into a world of good and evil, I reel
a creature languished in the flood. I tear out
the lure, hooks cold. I catch myself,
two hooks through the hand,
blood on the floor of the synagogue. The wound
is purple, shows a mouth of white birds;
hook and gut dangle like a rosary,
another religion in my hand.
I'm ashamed of this image of crucifixion.
A Jew's image is a reading man.
My father tears out the hooks, returns to his book,
a nineteenth-century history of France.
Our war is over:
death hooks the corner of his lips.
The wrong angel takes over the lesson.

SEPTEMBER EVENING

In late September on a school day
I take my father, failing, now past seventy,
to the rowboat on the reservoir; the waters
since July have gone down two hundred yards
below the shoreline.
The lake stretches before us—a secret,
we do not disturb a drifting branch, a single hawk.
For a moment nothing says, "thou shalt not."
If I could say anything to the sky and trees
I'd say things are best as they are.

It is more difficult for me to think
of my father's death than my own.
He casts half the distance he used to.
I am trying to give him something,
to stuff a hill between his lips.
I try to spoon-feed him nature, but an hour
in the evening on the lake doesn't nourish him,
the walk in the woods that comforts me
as it used to comfort him makes him shiver.
I pretend to be cold.

We walk back along the drying lake bottom,
our shoes sink into the cold mud—
where last spring there was ten feet of water,
where in early June I saw golden carp
coupling on the surface. It's after dark,
although I can barely see
I think I know where the fence is.
My father's hands tremble like the tail of a fish
resting in one place. As for me?
I have already become his ghost.

ROETHKE'S PAJAMAS

I change apartments,
find my dead friend's pajamas.
I remember him in blue linen
crossing the living room,
a half-awakened child going to pee,
except for the varicose.
I kept his old pajamas,
they were my size,
but they were too wise for me to wear,
they would not rhyme with anything,
old washed-out blue—
I wear the famous raccoon skin coat
he gave me—I need the excuse
of snow, below zero weather.
Without thinking, I take his advice
"Write songs!" I begin with—
"She has given me the gift of my own desire."

WINTER IN VERMONT

Where is the green, the revolutionary?
What good can come of snow and slate?
Vermont or father, what's my theme?
I eye the skin of a woodchuck
left hanging on barbed wire.
A stream moves under a foot of ice.
I read the last words of Henry Adams:
"My child keep me alive."

JANE'S GRANDMOTHER

Near her 104th year, light as a sparrow
she sits on a burnished leather Davenport,
the kind you can't slump in.
Her death is almost lost,
a comb keeps her hair in place.
The rivers are older than she is.
In Montana the clouds are younger—
there's not much standing between anything
and the sky—the darkness older,
some trees older, the great withstanders.
Barbed wire runs from U.S. 6
into her fingers and arms.
Her daughters care for her fingernails,
brown shell of box turtle.
Honest homesteader, she still loves a kiss.
Her smile moves to the rings of a tree,
her daughters' faces and their daughters'.

PANDA SONG

I hear the panda's song,
on lonely afternoons
he strips bamboo with a false thumb,
uooh, uooh,
an inefficient contraption, part of his wrist,
while his real thumb is committed,
uooh, uooh,
for evolutionary and historical reasons,
to other work, mostly running and clawing,
uooh.

Neither lover nor patriot, there is a cricket,
err, err,
that left in Puerto Rico
lives out its days,
err,
that dies if moved, *err,*
off its sugarcane island,
to Santo Domingo, Curaçao or Florida.
Err . . . . . . uooh, uooh,
small matters the law does not correct,
uooh, err, err.

POEM BEFORE MARRIAGE

I am part man, part seagull, part turtle.
What remains? I have a few seasons
of vanity and forty years in the muddy lake.
I float on the reservoir in Central Park,
my gull eyes, man flesh, turtle mouth, tear the water
hunting shadows of fish that never appear.
I live on things a great city
puts in a small bowl for emergencies.
I "Caw Caw," wishing the shell on my back
were a musical instrument.
I have already been picked out of the mud
three times and thrown
against apartment house walls, left for dead.

Jane, in my bed you will find feathers
and fragments of shell. When, swallowing darkness,
I have a nightmare in your arms, my eyes
film over, let me sink to the bottom
of the artificial lake.

Fish for me.

SWEET QUESTIONS

Why does she pick only the smallest wildflowers?
The daisy and daylily aren't gross,
lilacs, peonies and roses
are not base company.
Why are they so small, the wildflowers
she brings me,
the most delicate, purest of color?
What is their purpose
brought by her hand to the hand of her lover?

POTATO SONG

Darkness, sunlight and a little holy spit
don't explain an onion with its rose windows
and presentiment of the sublime,
a green shoot growing out of rock
or the endless farewells of trees.
Wild grasses don't grow just to feed sheep,
hold down the soil or keep stones from rolling;
they're meant to be seen, give joy, break the heart.
But potatoes hardly have a way of knowing.
They sense if it is raining or not,
how much sunlight or darkness they have,
not which wind is blowing or if there are dark clouds
or red-winged blackbirds overhead.
They are not aware if there are soldiers in the field,
or not, moles or underground humpings.
Potatoes do not sleep, but must find pleasure
in their flowering. Sometimes
I hear them call me "mister" from the ditch.
Workers outside my window in Long Island
cut potatoes in pieces, bury them, water them.
Each part is likely to sprout and flower.
No one so lordly as not to envy that.

SIGN ON THE ROAD

1

The Atlantic a mile away is flat.
I rent this summer in Amagansett;
I see bayberries and pines. A one-eyed hound
Visits. Nothing is very far from the ground,
This is potato country, yellow and white
Blossom barely. Above the gravel pit
It is hardly wild. I find a snake skin
Pressed into the asphalt. I use tin
Roofing to scrape it up, and throw deep
Into a field the pearl leather. I keep
The tin to paint my sign MOSS in red,
Lean it on a fence where worms have fed;
I make my own target, throw my stone,
I nail my name down into my bone,
It falls in grass, I pick it up again
Like a sock-apple sweetened in the ditch.
I hope my sign will stand against the pitch
Of summer rain; crash in Atlantic hurricanes,
Drumming my name that creaks and grinds,
above the ditch on a piece of tin colder than the wind.

2

My friends, Moss is on the fence in Long Island,
The sea, a distance away like a grandfather
At a family reunion, says it's all sand.
But Moss is on the fence; it might as well
Be charged with high voltage, or painted blue
For all the good that will come of that.
It is a fact and if I scrape my name off
With a knife, the wood is wet underneath,
Just as sand is moist when you kick it up.
I suppose something like this wetness and the sun
Made the first living thing, the first sub-roach

497

That danced its way from under dead matter.
In the beginning before darkness was there a death?
Of course the wind or a telephone call
Moves the earth a little. Damn little.
The apple falls like an apple, and leaves
Hit the earth in their leafy way, and Moss
Shall be no exception. One fine day
I shall fall down like myself in a prison of anger.
Any day is a good day to be born.
I obey the orders of trees.
Moss is on the fence in Amagansett.

PRAYER FOR ZERO MOSTEL

Señor, already someone else,
O my clown,
the man in your image
was a bestiary,
sweet as sugar,
beautiful as the world,
lizard sitting on a trellis
follows blonde into john,
now he is a butterfly on the edge
of a black-eyed Susan
—rhinoceros
filing down his own horn
for aphrodisiac.
Señor, already someone else,
a band of actors under bombardment
played Shakespeare,
the last days
of the Warsaw ghetto,
a few of the survivors
who crawled through the sewers
heard the SS was giving out visas
for America
at a certain hotel,
went to apply.
If you love life
you simply can't believe
how bad it is.
Señor, someone else,
a Yahweh clown,
rectal thermometer of the world.
Farewell art of illusion,
playing yourself as a crowd.

THE RED FIELDS

Should anyone care, I love those red fields
of poppies growing under the wheat;
imagine ten miles of it—fields, mountains,
valleys, solid red; the Mediterranean to the south,
blue to the end of the world, blue as—
I think of eyes, bookbindings, flags,
I'm lousy on blue, but when I think of red
I know what I'm talking about . . .
Damn fool poppies in Rome one spring,
growing like dandelions; or the loner
near the railroad track in Long Island,
coming out of nowhere—impossible.
Another thing about poppies, to pick one
is to sleep with a woman who doesn't love you;
a poppy gets that look on her face of "you beast
you've done it." And I've seen poppies
turn black at the first sign of the wind,
and twenty miles of poppies in a storm,
an ocean of blood you wouldn't dare cross,
except dragged by a team of white horses.

PLUMAGE

Off Montauk speedway I watch a swan
clam-gray in the remnant marsh, surrounded
by yesterday's swollen bread; jabbed, he attacks
the stick and an old automobile tire,
like great adversaries—moves out of reach,
trumpeting at the stone-throwing rabble.

Those ancient kisses, those first days were best,
my flesh in cloud almost moved the world.
Did I survive that first winter, first deceit?
For fifteen years my mind: a bird that would
not fly south—something like a swan circling
one place, refusing shelter.

I stand in the reeds under faded cloud.
All that plumage, the pomp of generations
in my wings, push back the mob,
the mercenary cold, the perjuring snows.
Lady, this summer when the world beckons,
I shall follow; next winter I go south.

SCARECROW

Honeysuckle grows over the sleeve
Inside out. Once used as a scarecrow
A canvas jacket splashed with red paint
Thrown over a fence
Keeps the shape of someone's body; despite
Summer that burned the field brown by mid-August,
Winter that froze an oak tree's knuckle,
Despite grubs, the mildew, the six-inch nails.

I should be grateful if my poems
Keep some shape, out in the open field,
Year after year, a thing like this canvas
Splashed with mock blood, scaring off nothing.
The harvest is in
Now the field snail lodges in my cuff:
I wink at the sky, all weathers, all creatures,
Telling them to come on.

THE GOOD THINGS

I cannot sanctify. Take heart,
One step and I am over my head;
Holy to me is not the thing surviving,
Rather what I wish had survived. Take heart,
The harvest is in, all the green collected,
We heaped the good things in our car
And carried them off down the country road
Certain of our good fortune.
Christ, the things that could have gone wrong.
Still fast to the vine, a melon kicked open.

THE MEETING

It took me some seconds as I drove toward
the white pillowcase, or was it a towel
blowing across the road, to see what it was.
In Long Island near sanctuaries
where there are still geese and swans,
I thought a swan was hit by an automobile.
I was afraid to hurt it. The beautiful creature
rolled in sensual agony,
then reached out to attack me.
Why do I feel something happened on the road,
a transfiguration, a transgression,
as if I hadn't come to see what was,
but confronted the white body,
tried to lift, help her fly,
or slit its throat.
Why did I need this illusion,
a beauty lying helpless?

CLAMS

Ancient of Days, bless the innocent
who can do nothing but cling,
open or close their stone mouths.
Out of water they live on themselves
and what little seawater they carry with them.
Bless all things unaware that perceive
life and death as comfort or discomfort:
bless their great dumbness.

We die misinformed
with our mouths of shell open.
At the last moment, as our lives fall off,
a gull lifts us, drops us on the rocks, bare
because the tide is out. Flesh sifts the sludge.
At sea bottom, on the rocks below the wharf,
a salt foot, too humble to have a voice,
thumps for representation, joy.

LOT'S DAUGHTER

"Let us make our father drink wine, and we will lie with him that we may preserve seed of our father." —*Genesis*

I

What did I do? What wives do. But no wives
Came to this mountain under the green leaves,
Or husbands. Short breath, he pretended ease,
While Sodom's ashes fruited Eden's trees,
He looked for caves, spoke of building temples
He could not build—he wished to set example.
But I led.

By night the boyish angels scattered
The fires of Sodom—he wanted to give advice.
My gathered hair fell to my waist,
He combed hard, braided tight. His hands were ice.
Despite a sheltering tree
Young winds blew through him cleanly.

As if by custom, I poured wine, mountain domes
Above, he said, "Remember mountain domes
When you build your temple." I touched him first,
Felt as if pushed into a crowd, powerless
Against a heavy mob, its yells and rudeness—
I heaved off the old man, bit him to let go,
My thighs wet with languages and populations.

II

Can you weep away a father, a fault?
I remember the honey, the somersaults,
The moral lessons, back there
In the playrooms of Sodom. I am parts.
Loose, lost, tongue of a man

Go lick your brain—what is your plan?
To bring more wineskins out in the sunshine
Or flowers for hope? I should bring you mine,
My hands tremble, I would pick despair.

LOT'S SON

Three in his arms we sleep, Lot lies awake
All night, he does not let me lie awake
Or cut my own meat. All night
Through my ribs, I feel his body's heat.
He will not let me drink from a bright cup
(Unless he wash it), or climb high up.
His game: he points a finger at my eye,
Saying, "You are crying," until I cry,
To make me a man. Rope, he holds me taut,
He knots, undoes the knots, I am caught
Round myself. A knot ties mother to son
Not father to daughter; all rope, but Lot,
Lot who tied us together is undone.

PHOTOGRAPHY ISN'T ART

1

If I gave up the camera
or really made myself into a camera
or into a photograph,
if the sight of that photograph
made me change my life,
if I really held my darkest self
up to the light,
where life cannot be violated
by enlargers, light meters—
what creature would such changes keep alive?

My work changes color because of the work
like the hands of people handling coins.
The pregnant black woman
I saw during the blackout in New York City
carrying a refrigerator on her back
was not only a likeness.
Visions hide more than they reveal.

2

If I could really become a blur,
if I became for the joy of it—say a photograph
taken in a forgiving light
of the guests seated around the table
at Delacroix's dinner party, Paris, 1857,
when he had just made an omelette
so beautiful no one would eat it—
then if they called me to join at table
that company of poets and painters,
I would sweep the skull of Adam off the cloth,
smile for the photographer,
give thanks and suggest
we eat the omelette while it's still hot.

MORNING

Usually I wake
to a dreamlike landscape,
face outside my window—
the Atlantic, a Catskill stream,
or the lake in Central Park.
My breath stares,
my tongue regards,
I whisper in my wife's ear,
"Are you up?"
Some voices can see,
some see for others, change the world.
She has given me the gift of my desire.
All my voice can do is sleep near her ear,
while she chooses to sleep or wake.

RETURN FROM SELLING

I comply with these disorders to give
myself food and lodging, a wanderer's hope
of inn or friendship, return to room
like a starfish out of its element,
not a man back from fields; I wash my hands,
rest my eyes as astronomers at dawn,
lie with no fewer turnings of my head
than men scanning Homer or charts of seas.
I exchange day for a room, the room for night,
and briefest thoughts of people still aloof,
common among these city rooms as sleep.

I look back to Greece and Assyria,
forward to the wall, back to the mind's wall
become a fortress, corrupting its kingdom
with idle craftsmen and shouts of selling at the gate,
walls keeping back neither ooze of Africa
nor the Arctic's superfluous snow,
nor will I be made traitor to love's loyalty
by the empty bed that informs against me;
nor will I forget the angel smiling in the doorknob.

TWO RIDERS

I am death's Sancho Panza.
What is my Lord like, you ask,
"is he kind, is he clean?"
He likes to watch a ship in high seas,
lifted almost out of the water,
and the crash of the ship sounding.
He will not listen to Saint Jude,
patron of lost causes and incurables.
When some men die, their beds,
tables and chairs fly out with them.
I ride a length behind.
I know how to make do.
Even in hell
a hundred years from now,
I'll teach English or sell.
You can always find
a little sanguine drawing
of paradise in hell.

WAR BALLAD

(after Voznesensky)

The piano has crawled into the quarry. Hauled
In last night for firewood, sprawled
With frozen barrels, crates and sticks,
The piano is waiting for the axe.

Legless, a black box, still polished;
It lies on its belly like a lizard,
Droning, heaving, hardly fashioned
For the quarry's primordial art.

Blood red: his frozen fingers cleft,
Two on the right hand, five on the left,
He goes down on his knees to reach the keyboard,
To strike the lizard's chord.

Seven fingers pick out rhymes and rhythm,
The frozen skin, steaming, peels off them,
As from a boiled potato. Their schemes,
Their beauty, ivory and anthracite,
Flicker and flash like the great Northern Lights.

Everything played before is a great lie.
The reflections of flaming chandeliers—
Deceit, the white columns, the grand tiers
In warm concert halls—wild lies.

But the steel of the piano howls in me,
I lie in the quarry and I am deft
As the lizard. I accept the gift.
I'll be a song for Russia, I'll be
an étude, warmth and bread for everybody.

512

WHO ARE YOU?

(after Voznesensky)

There is no physicist no lyricist blood.
What are we? I choose to be Promethean.
Genius is in the planet's blood.
You're either a poet or a Lilliputian.

We are injected with time through a fold
of flesh and veins, as against smallpox.
"What are we?" ties us to this rock:
An exploding engine uncontrolled.

Who are you? Who are you? The vulture's head
sleeps gently on my chest, a sparrow drags
a carcass through the snow. The tortured crags
of Aphrodite's quarry shape her marble head.

And a young girl, a poet shocked by the question,
moons at the North star, working in an office
she files invoices, but her hands are ice.
"What are you?" She half learns the lesson,
she cuts her braids and leaves the rest undone.

And again as though playing hide-and-seek
you run half across Moscow, stop and peek
between theater posters and the wreck
of a snowman. Out of breath you blow
the world away like steam on a window.

After the browsing and the books, who are you?
You look into men's eyes
as if through a toy telescope, and the skies
crack your thin glass of anguish. Where are you?

Under the Promethean stars I wander alive
with you Vera, Vega, I am myself
among avalanches—abominable!
Like the snowman, absolutely elusive.

THE GENTLE THINGS

I have had enough of Gods
And disaster;
The gentle things,
All loved ones survive,
Water survives in water,
Love in love.

I lie! Our dead
Tumble over our dead,
The wolf tears at the world,
Says, *nothing is:*
And the wolf is not the wind,
Is death's fingernail.

Dampness to dampness,
Had I been given
Only life's issue,
Not the song, or the silence
After the singing,
I should be content.

THE GARDEN

1

Since they were morose in August,
a hundred years old,
I thought the junipers not worth saving,
like useless old men.
I paid to have them torn out,
trunk and root. The roots had enough strength
to pull the truck back down so hard
the wheels broke the brick walk.

Heaped in front of my house,
cousins of the tree of mercy,
the dry gray branches,
that did not suffer but had beauty to lose,
a touch of new growth.
Damp roots, what do I know
of the tenderness of earth,
the girlish blond dust?
Wrong, I dragged the junipers to the cliff,
and pushed them into the sea.
Then I put in my garden.

2

Go in darkness is the command.
Executioner,
I cared for the garden
not wanting to speak
of the suffering I have caused.
Sacred and defiled,
my soul is right
to deal with me in secret.

PRAYER

Give me a death like Buddha's. Let me fall
over from eating mushrooms Provençale,
a peasant wine pouring down my shirtfront,
my last request not a cry but a grunt.
Kicking my heels to heaven, may I succumb
tumbling into a rosebush after a love
half my age. Though I'm deposed, my tomb
shall not be empty; may my belly show above
my coffin like a distant hill, my mourners come
as if to pass an hour in the country,
to see the green, that old anarchy.

CELIA, A DITTY

Most of my life Celia has made me laugh.
When I was a boy at school, I made the teacher
stop teaching with my laughter.
"Why are you laughing?" she said.
"Celia made me laugh."
She turned on the girl sitting near me,
cracked her hard right in the face.
"Why are you laughing now?"
"She's the wrong Celia."

ON THE OCCASION OF STANLEY KAUFFMANN'S FIFTIETH BIRTHDAY

How lucky we are to have Stanleys,
Kauffmann and Kunitz and me,
like three wines at dinner,
one's heavy, two thinner,
two saints and one sinner,
one loser, two winners.
How lucky we are to have Stanleys,
Kauffmann and Kunitz and me.

Friends, lift your glasses,
the lower and upper classes,
a name betters or worsens
when worn by three persons.
I sing the praise
of two Stanley K's,
a name that houses,
one suit with three pairs of trousers.

LOVE'S EDGE

It is summer in my apartment, like last summer,
I have only to touch the thermostat,
the air cools and fans.
What was that? A light turns on and off
at a distance, as if someone crossed
between me and fire, or was signaling.
Possibly the wind bent a branch across
a lighted window, or an automobile
turned away.
Her passion was almost unnoticeable,
—like the statue of Saint Teresa in ecstasy,
looking to heaven, a single toe crooked sharply,
her mouth barely open, showing the edge
of a marble tongue. How was I to know?
Flesh is a ghost, inarticulate.

FOR UNCLE LEM

I have a Baroque painting—a martyr, Saint Simon,
is being sawed in half by two soldiers.
The saw cuts Simon down the middle,
does not bend around bone obstructions.
The painting troubled my uncle, a physician.
"Why glorify death?" he asked. "Isn't there enough
death in the world?" I answered lamely,
"But it is a beautiful painting."
I've been told—before I can remember
I cut my tongue mysteriously in two.
My uncle would not stitch it up.
He let my tongue dangle, bleed disgustingly.
He saved my speech.

SCROLL

Long after dark
In my throat and thought
My mother wrote
A scroll of dangers:
Salt is poison,
And white bread;
If you wrong someone
Only he
Can pardon you,
—Not God. Your knee
Cut while playing
Is still infected,
So if you must,
Pray standing.

KANGAROO

My soul climbs up my legs,
buries its face in blood and veins,
locks its jaws on the nipple that is me.
I jump my way into the desert.
What does my soul, safe in its pocket, care
what I say to desert flowers?
Like a kangaroo
I pray and mock prayer.

I never took a vow of darkness.
I sit beside a boulder writing
on yellow lined paper. Once I thought
I'll pull my soul out of my mouth,
a lion will sleep at my feet,
I'll spend forty days in the desert,
I'll find something remarkable, a sign:
strains of desert grass
send the root of a single blade
down thirty feet.
I remember flakes of dry blood,
the incredible rescue of the man by the soul.

Under the aching knuckles of the wind,
move down in your pocket
away from remorse and money.
Learn discomfort from the frog,
the worm, the gliding crow,
they all hunt in repose, like men in prayer.
I can hardly distinguish myself from darkness.
I am not what I am. I demand the heart
answer for what is given. I jump into the desert,
a big Jew, the law under my arm like bread.

OLD

The turtles are out,
loners on the road listening for mud,
old people looking for money.
Father, too old for hope,
when trees are burned black with cold,
what belongs to man, and what to nature?

With a penknife you used to make
ashtrays of turtles,
scraped out the living flesh—
gifts for friends,
now mine to take home if I want to.
A shell of your old self,
I want to whisper to you
the prayers and psalms you never taught me.
I never learned a healthy disrespect.
On my table I keep a bronze turtle—
a handle torn from an African sword,
a symbol of destroyed power.

The turtles move under the snow
in the dead of winter, under the loam,
chewing and scratching into frozen sand,
deeper than moles or grubs,
far from the loneliness of sunlight and weather.
I offer my hand, a strange other element.

THE LESSON OF THE BIRDS

The *Birds* of Aristophanes taught me
before there was sky or earth or air,
before there was mystery or the unknown,
darkness simply entered from darkness and departed
into darkness: it moved back and forth as the sea does,
all shells, grottos and shorelines that were to be
were darkness.

Time weathered such things,
had a secret heavy underwing;
an urge toward a warm continuum,
its odor of nests made a kind of light.
Before there was pine, oak or mud, seasons revolved,
a whirlwind abducted darkness, gave birth,
gave light to an egg. Out of the egg of darkness
sprang love the entrancing, the brilliant.
Love hatched us commingling, raised us
as the firstlings of love. There was never
a race of Gods at all until love
stirred the universe into being.

THE VALLEY

Once I was jealous of lovers.
Now I am jealous of things that outlast us—
the road between Route 28 and our house,
the bridge over the river,
a valley of second-growth trees.
Under the birches, vines
the color of wolves survive a winter ten below,
while the unpicked apples turn black
and the picked fruit is red in the basket.
I am not sure that the hand of God
and the hand of man ever touch,
even by chance.

FOR JAMES WRIGHT

Hell's asleep now.
On the sign above your bed
nothing by mouth, I read *abandon hope.*
You sleep with your fist clenched,
your tongue and throat swollen by cancer,
make the sound of a deaf child
trying to speak, the smell
from the tube in your belly
is medicinal peppermint.

You wake speechless.
On a yellow pad your last writing
has double letters—two Zs and Ys in "crazy,"
you put your hand on your heart
and throw it out to me.
A few pages earlier you wrote,
"I don't feel defeated."

In your room without weather,
your wife brings you more days,
sunlight and darkness, another summer,
another winter, then spring rain.
When Verdi came to his hotel in Milan
the city put straw on the street
below his window
so the sound of the carriages
wouldn't disturb him. If I could,
I'd bring you the love of America.

I kiss your hand and head, then I walk out on you,
past the fields of the sick and dying,
like a tourist in Monet's garden.

LENIN, GORKY AND I

1.

That winter when Lenin, Gorky and I
took the ferry from Naples to Capri,
nobody looked twice
at the three men having a lemon ice
in Russian wool suits hard as boards.
Behind us, a forgetful green sea,
and the Russian snows storming the winter palace.
We descended, three men a bit odd,
insisting on carrying our own suitcases
heavy with books: Marx, Hegel, Spinoza.
We took the funicular
up the cliffs of oleander and mimosa,
yet through the fumes of our cheap cigars
we observed how many travelers had come
to Capri with a beauty. Lenin to Gorky:
"In Moscow they'd kill on the streets for the girl
who showed me my room."
Within an hour of our arrival
we were sitting in the piazza drinking fizz,
longing for the girls strolling by:
a mother, a sister, a daughter.
You could smell an ageless lilac in their hair.
Lenin warned, raising our level from low to high,
"Love should be like drinking a glass of water . . .
You can tell how good a Bolshevik she is
by how clean she keeps her underwear."

2.

It was then I split with the Communist Party.
Gorky welcomed the arrival of an old flame
from Cracow. Lenin bought white linen trousers
but would not risk the Russian Revolution
for what he called "a little Italian marmalade."

It was I who became the ridiculous figure,
hung up in the piazza like a pot of geraniums,
not able to do without the touch, taste and smell
of women from those islands in the harbor of Naples.

SONG FOR CONCERTINA

Here in Naples if you starve, fight,
Cry, it's like a bride and bridegroom;
I teach my son to piss down the street
And make rainbows.
Our ice cream's filled with blessings:
Oranges from Sicily, grapes from Tuscany;
I've traveled, know the great capitals.
Take it from me, stop worrying;
Even if the rent's not paid,
And Russo wants the money back,
Our saints get the most favors,
Our harbor is on the calendars of the world.

COMMUNIQUÉ FROM AN ARMY DESERTER, PROBABLY ITALIAN

Now it's so quiet I can hear a dog
Driving his sheep through the dry valley
Out of sight. I look ahead and back,
There's nothing on the road. I obey
The order of trees.
Look how the sea deserted, pulled out,
Left snails and fish spines on mountains.
I'd like to be a shepherd guarding his sheep
with a dog doing most of the work.
I salute the snail. But the senators
And generals won't let me. They talk of war:
The end of the world, as if it were theirs.
The thieves! The liars!

When I was a child I made a chariot
Of a rusty spoon. Now on a cloudless day
I've deserted the battle to sack
For soft madonnas and extravagance;
Where once Charles the Fifth
Conquered the Roman,
In peacock satin and Castilian lace,
His red-plumed troops covering the fields down there,
And his cavalry sprawled in the hay.
They've already crippled the fields. Let the living
And the dead beware any government
Or church headed by sexless men—just one
Can pull us all into his rancid sheets.

I call for deserters.

OFF TO THE FAIR

Barbed wire and ground glass,
I take to the main event, cutlass
And shield axe and gun I pack
With knife and razor strapped to my back,

An acid bottle with a zig-zag edge,
An eight-inch pipe, a trusted sledge,
Drill, ice pick and tiger fang,
Gunpowder and boomerang,

Six cobras, and two great Danes,
Surgical scissors and iron chains.
My bright armor now complete,
Crashes to my lady's feet.

AN ENGLISH DEFEAT

On artichoke and wine she chose to sup,
I followed her course by course, her every step,
I would not have my breath buttered
While hers was vinaigrette.
Had any royal hunt such royal game,
Such a fawn, such a fox? American
To the end I wanted to know
The facts. Was she contralto or soprano?
My rival had a beard combed in reverse,
A wife and three books of brilliantined verse;
She knew by heart her dumpty dumpty,
My book stayed closed, the sofa,—empty.
I must find an exit, an airport . . . Sir,
They say the English woman's a kipper
Beside the dames of France. Never take a chance
On English women of middle circumstance.

FACT SONG

1

Ancient Hebrew judges
listed the crimes
for which the penalty of death
might be given, but added
woe be unto any judge
who had given the sentence
more than once in seven years,
any court in which the death penalty
had been pronounced
should be known from then on
as the court of the assassins.

2

Benjamin Franklin, late in his 84th year,
his last year,
on a voyage across the Atlantic,
kept throwing a bottle out on a string,
pulled it up, then threw it out again.
He arrived in New York,
tossed his hat from ship to shore,
having just charted
the warm Gulf Stream.

3

Obscure orders of monks and nuns
make the Seder, observing
most Christians base their holiest sacrament
on something Christ said when he celebrated
the Passover meal
"This is my body, this is my blood,"
the promise of everlasting life,
—ignoring the other lesson
that he was himself spending the evening

celebrating the escape of the Jews from Egypt,
drinking to the everlasting life of a people
as a people.

4

It is good to keep the future holy,
I know more of what isn't than what is.
The Talmud says if working in your garden,
they run to you saying the Messiah is coming,
first plant another tree
then go meet the Messiah.

VOICE

My voice has been imprisoned
in the voice of a crowd in a stadium,
before grandstands empty
leaving behind my voice among the stragglers,
in idle conversation, in the odd shout.
I wanted to have a river to work with,
a voice that thirsts and drinks,
swimming and diving among the nude bathers,
surrounding the body it chooses.
I did not want my voice to be only a difference
of shadow as a black pine is in the night.
I wanted my voice to be a different, moon-like thing
that those on foot can see by.
I wanted my voice to reappear
suddenly in the night,
to last after touch, taste, sight, hearing.
I whisper in my wife's ear, "Are you up?"
All my voice can do is sleep near her ear,
while she chooses to sleep or be awake.

CHE GUEVARA

Anyone can see suffering
made him look like Christ,
tied on a donkey,
fainting like a girl,
an icon on the front page
of the *New York Times*,
somebody's dead lover.

TWO MINUTES EARLY

I'm two minutes early.
You say I read clocks like a Roman
reading chicken guts for omens.
Something sacred may happen.
Waiting, I can tell time.
The woodpile is a clock,
dead hours and weeks
cut and stacked,
left to dry out and weather,
till the last green minute
burns without hissing.
At the crotch of a tree,
a beehive is a clock,
minutes and seconds swarming
over each other,
till a fat second stings me.
The sweetest honey
isn't made of clover
but of wild thyme
and its blue flower.

BEFORE THE FIRE

My face leans to touch
things fallen through blades of grass,
things too small to pick up between my fingers:
fleck of stem, edge of husk,
fragments of petal and old grass
—my brothers and sisters of no consequence.
Autumn, under the loneliness of smoke,
I cross out such lines as
". . . no wind can turn the fire
from dry grass,
from king maple or scrub oak,"
—because any wind can turn fire a little.
Beside the non-existing,
every grub is an elephant
with arms of sunlight and prayer,
every leaf a civil servant
accountable to an ancient dynasty.
A branch of white pine two yards long,
still green with sap and privilege,
represents the last joy in the October fire.

THE BRANCH

I know the story of a tree:
of Adam's skull at the foot of Jesus crucified,
of the cross made of timbers nailed together
that Roman soldiers saved from the destroyed temple,
that King Solomon built from a great tree
that rooted and flourished
from a branch of the tree of mercy
planted in dead Adam's mouth,
that the branch was given
to Adam's third son Seth by an angel
that stopped him outside the wall
when he returned to the garden,
that the angel warned him
that he could not save his father
who was old and ill
with oil or tears or prayers.
Go in darkness, mouth to mouth
is the command.
I kiss the book,
not wanting to speak
of the suffering I have caused.
Sacred and defiled,
my soul is right
to deal with me in secret.

CASTELLO SERMONETA

I

You could only be in Italy;
Beyond the windows cornered with marble roses
A villager carved for a Borgia Pope,
Above the tower thrust up to a stone sky,
An old falcon the colors of the walls,
Whose race adapts most easily to castles,
Half blind and alone, chases
An imaginary field mouse across Latina.

II

Nothing that was saved remains:
A dog in the courtyard too old to bark,
An iron bridge shadows the roots of olive trees,
Betrayed a cat in the moat licks itself.
Chains that rotted heretic and slave bone,
Gossip now of archangels and martyrs,
A headless angel
Sings with collars of bees about his throat,
Three kingless donkeys stray on the hill.
Every man's back breaks.
Old guests and old hosts in hell and paradise.

III

Down a tower passage
I follow a Gregorian summer,
Savior of insects, to a Christ scraped on a wall
By a boot nail,
Flies humming about in search of a carcass.
Scraped on a wall in Middle Italian
I see His suffering:
"21 *Enero 1531*
Hanno tolto i catene dai miei piedi."*

* 21st January 1531 / They took the irons off my feet..

540

A DEAD NUN'S COMPLAINT AFTER THE DANCE

As a protest against conscription, anarchists took nuns from their graves and danced
with them in the streets of Barcelona, July 1909.

Where is the Bridegroom?
Whose music turns the loom?

My embroidery tangles out of sense.
Christ among the saucepans, made me dance

away old days in the village: hot suppers,
obedience thin as Bible paper.

Once Christ chased me and took all I feel,
made death exceptional.

Has the ocean swept into His cathedral,
left Noone on the cross? O make me real.

In my clean, busy cell. Real on my knees,
a donkey, a sparrow, a wind of flies.

In the clear sunlight Christ and Satan rage
over the rights of fallen angels. I see their image.

I tasted salt
in living bread. My mouth is stuffed with salt.

Not ten thousand Colombos would cross death's sea,
nor Saint Francis accept this poverty,
nor Christ keep death's chastity.

DEATH OF A SPANISH CHILD

I

It never snows, but snow is on the mountain top
Above Granada, the almond trees below
Blossom pink and white for miles into the valley.
A child died, his village plants wheat in the snow.
The women weep at home, may not see the grave
Whose sex is too masculine, keep the black fashion
Of a modest death dressed in long sleeves
In a house of oranges and want.
A newborn goat romps bloody in the yard.
Some pray, but in Spain, Jesus is a rain God,
Whose mother is water man or goat may drink.
A pity, a child's body is put to bed for the last time.
The holy ghost of oil
Cooks in the wide pan. From bed, from village,
Death, in a violet haze of poverty, eats.

II

I do not believe in salvation,
Yet I accepted their hospitality,
Their bread-soup under a black cross.
As water spills from a pail, the child died,
Upstairs a room for chickens, below
In its crib, in the cool stable asleep,
The accidental child smothered in a pillow,
A fly buzzing a halo around its head,
Near feed for the donkey and an extra wheel.

III

Walking behind the wagon stuffed with white lace,
Each in his way missing seeks protection,
One brought an umbrella, another weeps the loudest.
A Christ of moving cars ascends the hill.

In a land of bombs and drought,
I know the ocean is under the olive trees,
In the yard and marriage bed, the secure ocean,
And the hysterical land. Where is the child?

The mother of seven stumbles remembering his name,
With the work in the sun, minding Saint John,
Saving dirty water for dry land—a son
Who lies with perverts and virgins in a wild heap.

Along the ill-fed coast the peasants occasionally
Throw puppies into the sea, a young dog
Snaps off the head of a lizard two feet long;
It is January, even by the fire the wind hurts.

IV

They wear his black band,
Whatever the price in the market
For dried fish and wine,
They hold death off
With vegetables;
Sprawling lengthwise
Across the width of the grave,
They keep their word
Clean as Christ's feet.
All differences lie
Naked between any man or woman.

V

I leave them to pray on their anarchist knees,
Furrows must be straightened for water to pass.
Eighteen winds are familiar in these trees,
That do not cross less bloody ground. Eighteen
Names from the bone-white Pyreneees
Can not cover the black that is. March, April—
Through sand a dead child rains flesh on the earth.

THE SCHOLAR

I know the morning thaw scrawled something;
now it is night, winter really sets in,
demanding punishment.
A shawl of snow and rags, an old Jew,
stands in a doorway half in wilderness.
The wind, great swallower, gorges on the world.

Out of the dark hand squandering night,
groundless, the heart's ignorant angels
announce the Magi come, bearing gifts.
No, no, a woman hands him money
he throws off—screaming in scalding snow—
because she took him for a beggar
in a doorway, standing open to all pedestrians.

He tries to run off,
a nail catches the lining of his coat.
He cannot rip himself loose, cannot move.
Scrawled in torn snow, the saying on his shawl:
"He who gives charity in secret
is greater than Moses." I tear his coat

and pull him down. In an instant
he escapes through my hands like a fish.

SQUALL

I have not used my darkness well,
nor the Baroque arm that hangs from my shoulder,
nor the Baroque arm of my chair.
The rain moves out in a dark schedule.
Let the wind marry. I know the Creation
continues through love. The rain's a wife.
I cannot sleep or lie awake. Looking
at the dead I turn back, fling
my hat into their grandstands for relief.
How goes a life? Something like the ocean
building dead coral.

Skipped-Over Early Poems

DEATH IN PARIS

We know only our actions and our sleep
In a country where the children weep
For parents who are dead. To watch we must
Hold a pose, always learn, for we distrust
The weaker stance; we must among the poor
Observe their suffering near ourselves, tour
The galleries of the Louvre, before we stand
Among our buildings with our lives in hand,
Impoverishing the present with our ends,
For no one gives; alone the torturer lends.

As is the risk with love, love extends;
When lovers' needs are one, one love depends,
For quick as burning straw our thoughts succumb
To brief desires the winds in coldness drum
Upon cold trees, and the larger embrace
Becomes the small, and thinking is a place
To go, because the sun will not dry the sea,
And I may love, but you may love to be
In dying gardens where the dying meet,
Though I may be wandering on a street

Where nothing remains but the quick defeat,
Where your eyes darkly seek the stars for heat
In empty mirrors that mark the striking hour
In empty rooms. On highways dogs devour
Pain, stalking hope back to an aimless night
Of buyers and sellers in dancehall light.
We masque with looks of love deceiving,
Our memories grown old, drag the sea weaving
Great shells, amid shrieking gulls, and word
Each object of regret, as screams once heard,

Forgotten in the brass delays. One bird
Separates in a wilderness. A stilled herd
Moves slowly as a hand, and political man,
Unloved, denies, discovers his plan,
Reflects: we are placed as stones, our skin torn
Souls allow the seasons, as man, the first born
Hour in a wasted day, gives love to sell
And works to hide, hides desire where he dwells,
With fears of questions, and the separate room;
Love needs love dying, rejects the tomb.

We live, without a color, as a cold bloom
Breathing, breathing till one blossom and doom
Cast spring upon the ground and open wide
Her thighs from dawn till night, till she can't hide
The moaning of her breasts and lips, still seas forth-
Splash night across her in her arms, till North
Leaves flowers, and dead children can not weep
Their dead lives, and beauty is just sleep.
Love and all we will never see or be,
Rests on this shore, then softly drifts out to sea.

(Nowhere tending the white graves, the clown,
So high upon a mountain you can't see up or down.)
Let me begin, if I could begin, now,
If you or conscience would allow the vow,
I could bring you clear water from the sea
And say I bring you not a part of me,
But the beauty I can in a day observe,
Some useless gift on evening's curve,
These words, all things that disappear in space,
Before tipping the sunlight on your face,
I bring you the things I can't forget,
Though now we kiss, (perhaps we have not met).

Since days become as sounds within the night,
Whatever gives love permanence is right.

What part of reason is left behind?
Does fear clarify necessity and kind?
We've lived in a circle of the missing,
Of physical time, and emotional time, and kissing;
So terror leaves us to calculate,
A segment of our mood, the date,
How history has flung events upon the floor,
What the coroners of time deplore:
Our souls, our labors, the declined roulette
Of buying, selling, murder, and the sign "to let."

    Paris, 1948

GRINDER

The hope of our lives is life to speak;
Oh God and children and all things now unreal,
What does the brightness of the sun conceal?
Beauty lies exhausted and hot skies shriek,
The idiot highways up and down a hill,
Are not so still, as we who live by will.

Our dulled hands must hold roundness to the earth,
And scrape with flat claws at time's decay;
We create mornings and destroy a day,
And sail fast seas and hide the fields in birth
Among the seasons and a frightened day;
The sun breaks, and the winds blow winds away.

I do not want within my life to look,
Nor mark the prisms of my life with light,
How frightened were your kisses in the night,
How gentle was your yearning that I took,
And when you left there was no tolling bell,
There were no secrets left we could not tell.

A violent star may kill but can't compel
A star. We sing to thoughts. We cannot see.
We have seen the dark and know the dark must be
Within the shadows where the sunlight fell.
No one sees frozen lakes begin to melt,
We feel and slowly feeling is not felt.

ON CROSSING THE ATLANTIC

This plain of sighs has known the whole concourse
Of the sun, this second of eternity
Contained here, to unpray a God, arranged
By wisdom, an unlit room to stare within,
And see love scald darling, and work chide death;
What bodies, what commerce of emotions,
Have lain their jaws across this graveless sprawl,
Watering their bones to salt, and their hopes
Pale, paler, till another midnight burns.

Blue sun darkens the sea with frozen leaves
As the fierce dawn storm begins, onto itself
Inflecting its own system and its rage.
And we so weak, see only reflections
Of our lives, seek logical requirement
Of wind worn waves, grasp iron, or rails, or rust,
Unchurch philosophy, whelp after prayer
That it leave us unharmed; we watchman's fears,
Become belief and temperament. O tides,
I have stood a moment near your roaming
To choose my small disasters and my plans.

HOW SUDDENLY EXHAUSTED

How suddenly exhausted, singed and empty as shells broken.
How is where, is nowhere.
Nothing left.
Yet like a fire just out,
We could soar again through forest—
But for a breath of air.

We can get on a train
Leave every face we have known
To go to a hotel register,
Accept the name of the first name in the directory,
Would be called that name. We could be known as anyone,
Shall we do this in a form listening to our words?

How suddenly exhausted, clinging lovers, empty as shells broken.
Peering under rocks and covers, for our lovers;
The atom bomb, the stock exchange and subway shovers,
Kiss them all as you would kiss your darling's breast,
And the rest. We love what we are most with; we are these,
Our myths, filed away in drawers of Dupont and tanks of Shell.
Tell and tell me darling that you love me like a breeze,
That you will give me yesterday and today all I please,
As you please. That we can sing like Mozart arias, in a cell
Among the trees, and sit looking at one another,
Though the gentle may more gently smother,
From time to time we love no other,
So little is left of time's thin cover
Or of rhymes.

We are what we believe, though we make believe
And cannot often grin, we are water falling
In laughter at summer falling after.
So in haste we often sin.

Thinking what is right,
What do I want.
What's on tonight?
We hunt.
Until one day, someplace, anywhere,
As weather,
(Since we care),
We have smoothed a stone,
We live a moment of a poem.

FOR LOVING IS REAL

One thought, you and I are cut as if by broken glass!
Wherever I am, I am not.
Only the sun can lie upon the grass,
Nothing is enough, whatever is, is not.
I lie upon my life and stumble home,
As stars we fall alone; if cold nights pass
Simple, we lead our souls in humble riot;
Since once we were now we cannot become.
You are winter, and the sun is like a slum.

Now spring has gone and we are left instead;
Chance neither made us meet nor separate,
Since illogical love must die in bed,
Since night is old the sun is always late.
I will not speak of places out of sight,
Nor ask for things unknown, nor what is dead,
For loving is real, more real than love or state . . .
O, if the wise and courageous hold the light,
Why don't they lie closer in bed at night?

What frozen, broken, windless, eyeless day,
Has left us to these circles we must solve,
Counting umbrellas in the rain. Now play
No more. Weeds choke the drowners they involve,
And we emerge carelessly as light.
Now to speak of next spring and where it moves,
From season to season though love can't stay,
I am as loving is, pain is my sight;
Where do you wake this morning, where shall I go tonight?

It is nothingness I carve as wood,
(Who dared to make me this, to speak of this?)
Once left no love is understood;
No love is pure, revenge is touch or kiss,

Unless I say, I give you this. We're strange,
(How much can we lose, how much can we miss?)
One death and love's away! I'd love if I could
Though close as laughter I in haste arrange.
I learn to see the sun at night, and change.

ROLLING OUT OF BED

Time take me now, I begin with prisons,
Moon's sleeve of cold dressing me
Death making me naked for play;
Time is escape, I'll take time to my bed.

One man heavily is confined by his life,
Another jump sharply to break the sky,
Each feels the sun's body bone by bone,
Eyes the whole sun, thuds into his grave.

Time take me now into your wheelbarrow,
Into your tomb, across the yard, pack me
With flowers, hay, manure, stone,
And wheel me away from the heap.

Does a wild substance remain? Out of time
At any angle or precipice, is time
Diminished? I roll down the sun-high leap
To practice difficult passages.

Wind, ropes and tackles drag me,
I drop the mumbling roots
All things on earth have warmth within,
And love willing make a comfortable bed.

THE SHIPS GO NOWHERE

Love passes through us as light through a window,
Though we love first in an unknown country,
Run to each other and forget our voyage,
Forget readers can't see the future,
That love is not for desperate people,
Who have in their eyes a terrible blackness.

The ships go nowhere holding helpless people
Who leave loves and hates to make the feared voyage
To what they can not find in another country,
Past dirty rivers, and cities of blackness,
Past hall lights left unlit behind a window;
Even readers have lost the future.

Measuring past time is measuring future.
No history will wait for its lost people,
Nor can lovers look from behind a window
At the silent sea of a lover's voyage,
Where they can find no one in the blackness,
Nothing but themselves in a foreign country.

The cold migrant winds know there is no country,
Where there is more than the past and future.
There is only ourselves in the crowd's blackness,
Nothing to find but our work and our people,
No one to love on the desperate voyage,
Nothing can be seen from an unseen window.

Who will sleep beside the night in the blackness,
Who can watch nothing but the empty window
Casting its shadow on the frightened people;
Only travelers in a dead country,
Where the past comes twice, but only one future,
And sorrow is the compass for the voyage.

We have never returned from our first voyage,
Never met out of the earliest blackness,
We have long forgot that we want the future,
Though we stand quite still and wait at the window,
Though no one stays who can walk in the country,
No one to walk with among the people.

Among the people who took your cold voyage,
In a foreign country, past distant blackness
Behind your window, you are now the future.

THE LONGEST JOURNEY

Born where the hill is fertile, on soiled earth,
Past the flesh's soft valley, we stray from home,
Peer across pale streams, frightened as we rise
On a curve of highway burned with moonlight.
Breathing nothing but sky we stare ahead,
Monotony: where weeds and woods destroy,
Where nothing lives but those who hide from death;
We raise a wooden dish and drink the night.
Railroads are close now emptied of people,
Our wrists, our arms our muscles: without hands;
Clerks without cities, watch ships sail no where,
We are statues left in the marketplace.
At dawn as workmen we wake the coldness,
Explore the salt skeleton of our cells;
Paled, our wills as children are not for sale.
The reefs, the seas, the shores, are laughing now.
Some leopards in the zoo sleep and fold night
Within their eyes, blind the days where suns flow,
Rip the throat of air. In the soft darkness
The impossible sunken soul is god.
Yesterday we kissed the surface of lakes,
To threaten the young peasants and their flocks
Who lie in the cold morning and hot noon
As one. Time became a church though we watched
Its benediction of machines and pain.
Each day, each unknown hour we stray alone;
We race, braid vines and solitude, sing songs
Without names or words, in place of change.
We dare not return. How gently we still kiss,
Exchange our quietest thoughts as gifts. We see
The last day, and love beneath the first sky,
And language is not dead though no one speaks.

VISITING THE EGYPTIAN ROOMS OF THE LOUVRE

Angular Egypt lived for the dead,
its city silent in chains like the Nile,
the monuments stiff, the words eyes;
what could an incestuous pharaoh dream
entering a triangle for eternity?
Was this death round? It fit the human form,
as life went flat and outward, it held the curve.
Despite the hook and whip Osiris arranged
the heavy dead kept shifting into view.
For the dead they broke stone, cut, carved,
—down the ages, baked cake, flayed hides,
burnished mirrors. The fisherman mended his nets,
the sailor stood watch not noticing the sea;
the thumb print in clay became a painted vessel,
and the sarcophagus, the fountain in the square,
till carelessly death the mastercraftsman,
taught his apprentice to finish the work.

BAD DAY, GOOD DAY

A word, I have a life to speak.
From a nearby field a cowbell
is more cathedral than my life real.
The earth's serpent strikes, time shrieks
not I, not I, a hawk in the sky shrieks,
wings: bad day, good day, good day, bad day.
I find death less holy than birth.
I play it small, but large and inclined to leak
I school myself in what is peace on earth;
largely now for my meter's sake,
I sound my cowbell along the way,
I chew my cud, tongue a salt lick—
I'm sick of death. The day lives another day.
The winds blow down Jehovah, Christ and all his men.
Good old God, I shall not see His like again.

A SONG AND DANCE FOR AARON AND ANTONIA

Something early in him
Married something late in her,
Something separate in her
Married something joined in him.
Something free in her
Married something imprisoned in him,
Something warm in her
Whirled around something wintry in him.
Something weeping in her
Married something laughing in him,
His joy leapt over her sorrow,
Her sorrow leapt over his joy.
Something ending in him
Whispered to something beginning in her,
Something beginning in him
Whispered to something ending in her.
Something loving in her
Married something loveless in him,
Something loving in him
Married something loveless in her.
Something singing in her
Married something singing in him,
Something dancing in him
Married something dancing in her.

In democratic Boston
Apollo, unchallenged at music,
Plays at the wedding feast
Eros and Dionysus dance in the vineyard.
The Angel of Separation
Walks alone on the Commons.

PEACE TALK

Peace for this poor earth; this plant, bloom
Of dreaming dogs in swimless swirls of intellect,
Peace in drunken gardens where butterflies swoon

Into a sun, living one day, and dying in puddles
Of that night—wing and blood, a flowered sail wrecked
While God stands for a moment at the window and red bells

Ring. Beside a fountain lovers drink wines
Of the loveless ages formless in each glass, in peace
Praying their lips to kiss, but the future of oceans, times

Of wanton voyages, the sounds of space, their silent sun,
All stale, slain on the beach of no where. O peace
Do not touch my skull, for had I words I'd run

Beneath a sun of fable and fire, romping toward pinwheels
Of things unknown and things beautiful, break
Around the Capes of Good Hope and Horn
While love grows as grapes, naked earth steals

Naked to my arms and the chapels of each morning
Become a harbor where ships of night, dark and Godlike,
float to the playing children on the shore. For death is worn,

And spawning blood sets fire to the wind and trees,
And fishermen lift their nets, hoist death weeping,
Tossing death twinkling as a small coin into the profitless seas.

THE WANTON VOYAGER

I wish I had a room with a bed, a flower pot, and a windowsill.
I could rest my head upon the floor and not strong or weak
Conceive a world that unconceived is happier still;
Bailing sun from the day, taking part in no anyway or anywhere,
To speak of happiness, to hear it purr, cough, reek
The breath of hour after hour, lung and blood bare
To sunlight, time, song to song and silences to wit,
Of sorrow: to scold its wail, crack, ruin it, flare
Against its eyes, give it horns, and I not wanting this will hit
 Its face with a rail of stars, and twirls upon its brows the moon,
And light darkness with wild fires a cold wind lit.
My mood is animal that cannot roughly sleep in candlelight.
Cold seas to ashes, trees and leaves over this, and moon,
At the end coming closer but in this ending no ruin
Of winter or its sky in winter walls beneath the snow,
No corpse of leaf or paper, now weaving dead sunlight
This hand that never weaved, no snow to lie beneath and know.
Name, place, date, particular,
I'm right here, and you are where you are.

LOVE IS CONFINED

Jump into Ophelia's grave if you think
Love is confined
to the smallest gesture,
is always faithful,
alone and grateful,
will live beyond
our death and dreaming
though death is handsome
when beauty falters.

Love has no children,
no tears, no trophies,
when life is spilling
its death is gentle,
already thinking
as worms and beetles
which stone is gayer?
which root is laughter?

TWO HAYSTACKS

To Edward Field

Under the sun,
the haystacks are yours, you did the work,
you knew how to keep them from the rain,
the timothy, dried grasses, and blue weed.
The roof is mine, my roof of loose nails and wire,
boards that don't join the sills or floor.
The haystacks are yours, the lightning rod
mine. I don't know how to direct
lightning into the ground. The cellar is mine,
the drains and gutters. Which pipe leads
to the septic tank, which to the well?
I bow to the screendoors I cannot fix,
the organization of sockets and circuit breakers,
the darkness of closets and crawl space,
and my friend, I bow to your haystacks
that have already lasted two weeks of summer,
and are meant for the deer in winter
when they come down from the mountain.

DESERTION

Now the earth has been still for many days,
Runners are drowned along the roads
Where they sense death
Without understanding.
They open their arms above their heads,
Reach to some mouthless monument,
As though people pass.

In other days, when thought was real,
I saw wildfire's hiding place.
Wild horses running hard on snow,
And then I took my hand,
And cried under the hand's face.

Within one heart a roadside,
I remember lying drunk,
Sipping a potion of yellow sky,
Searching the mind, the earth, the land, for adventure,
In the mornings, beautiful mornings
The trees were pale as wheat in the sun,
And the dancers walked alone upon the streets.

MAN'S WIFE

In spring a woman can run from love,
Or draw her lover closer to her.
She can lie across the hot mountain of morning,
Make life a gentle ceremony,
Pass her lips into forgetfulness.
And the tree upon which she leans,
A tree can be a winged chime, or a clock,
Iron, and wet marble, or her lover's hand.

Her children can be born from darkness,
Or some fierce closet
Where pain beats the sky into the sea,
Or she may add children to some rough farm,
While the stiffened men stare away.

Yet always woman remains the creature first refused,
And when one died, I saw another woman
Take a stone onto her breast, as if it were a grave;
Then even the earth was forgotten,
And the church was a great forest.

LADY OF TURQUOISE

Lady of turquoise I believe
in the land where men are never wrong,
flowers do not bloom in spring.
I look for strangers, I listen for birdsong.
I need winter, summer, fall and spring.
I believe the right way to grieve
for the dead is to rejoice for the living.

I've jumped into the Atlantic and Pacific,
but I do not know how they jumped from hieroglyphic
to consonants and vowels, from polytheistic
to monotheistic. Blinded by sandstorm,
they found their way from cuneiform.
Moses did his trick
with a snake and walking stick.
Long before there was a fishnet,
there was forgiveness and an alphabet.

INDEX OF TITLES AND FIRST LINES

B

C

D

G

H

I

J

N

O

P

R

S

587

T

U

V

W

SEVEN STORIES PRESS is an independent book publisher based in New York City. We publish works of the imagination by such writers as Nelson Algren, Russell Banks, Octavia E. Butler, Ani DiFranco, Assia Djebar, Ariel Dorfman, Coco Fusco, Barry Gifford, Martha Long, Luis Negrón, Hwang Sok-yong, Lee Stringer, and Kurt Vonnegut, to name a few, together with political titles by voices of conscience, including Subhankar Banerjee, the Boston Women's Health Collective, Noam Chomsky, Angela Y. Davis, Human Rights Watch, Derrick Jensen, Ralph Nader, Loretta Napoleoni, Gary Null, Greg Palast, Project Censored, Barbara Seaman, Alice Walker, Gary Webb, and Howard Zinn, among many others. Seven Stories Press believes publishers have a special responsibility to defend free speech and human rights, and to celebrate the gifts of the human imagination, wherever we can. In 2012 we launched Triangle Square books for young readers with strong social justice and narrative components, telling personal stories of courage and commitment. For additional information, visit www.sevenstories.com.